1991

COMPUTER ALGORITHMS:
KEY SEARCH STRATEGIES

IEEE Computer Society Technology Series

Computer Algorithms:

Key Search Strategies

Edited by Jun-ichi Aoe

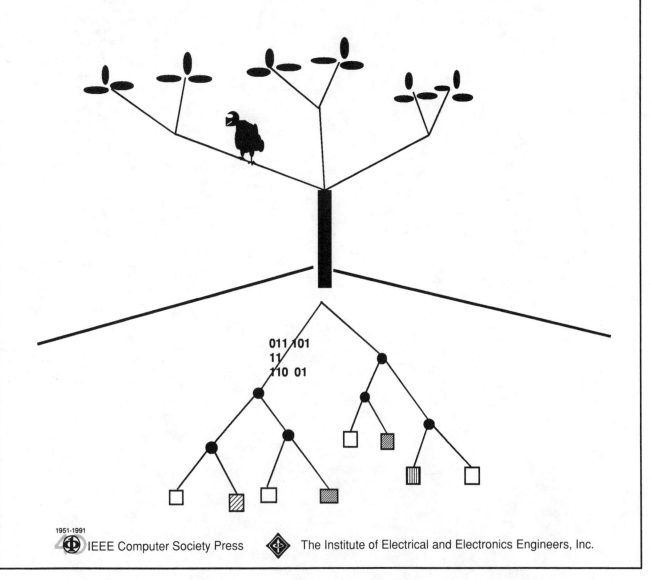

1951-1991
IEEE Computer Society Press   The Institute of Electrical and Electronics Engineers, Inc.

COMPUTER ALGORITHMS:
KEY SEARCH STRATEGIES

Edited by

Jun-ichi Aoe

1951-1991

IEEE Computer Society Press
Los Alamitos, California

Washington • Brussels • Tokyo

Computer algorithms: key search strategies / edited by Jun-ichi Aoe.
    p.   cm.
    Includes bibliographical references.
    ISBN 0-8186-6123-2. -- ISBN 0-8186-2123-0 (pbk.)
    1. Computer algorithms.   2. Data base searching. I. Aoe, Jun
-ichi, 1951-
QA76.9.A43C66   1991
005.1--dc20   90-27443
                                                                  CIP

Published by

IEEE Computer Society Press
10662 Los Vaqueros Circle
P.O. Box 3014
Los Alamitos, CA 90720-1264

Robert Werner, Production Editor

Cover design by Wally Hutchins

Printed by Technical Communication Services, North Kansas City, Missouri

IEEE Computer Society Press Order Number 2123
Library of Congress Number 90-27443
IEEE Catalog Number EH0330-1
ISBN 0-8186-2123-0 (paper)
ISBN 0-8186-6123-2 (microfiche)
ISBN 0-8186-9123-9 (case)
SAN 264-620X

Additional copies can be ordered from:

| IEEE Computer Society Press Customer Service Center 10662 Los Vaqueros Circle P.O. Box 3014 Los Alamitos, CA 90720-1264 | IEEE Computer Society 13, Avenue de l'Aquilon B-1200 Brussels BELGIUM | IEEE Computer Society Ooshima Building 2-19-1 Minami-Aoyama, Minato-Ku Tokyo 107, JAPAN | IEEE Service Center 445 Hoes Lane P.O. Box 1331 Piscataway, NJ 08855-1331 |

 The Institute of Electrical and Electronics Engineers, Inc.

PREFACE

Storing and retrieving information efficiently is an important challenge in computer science because data retrieval is the most time-consuming part of many programs, and the use of a good search method rather than a bad one often leads to a substantial increase in processing speed. A key search strategy that finds which record has a special field as its key is widely used in database management, compiler construction, natural language processing, and many other applications. This volume introduces the basic concepts and characteristics of key search strategies, and provides references, classified by consideration of their problems, for further reading.

CLASSIFICATION OF KEY SEARCH STRATEGIES

Key search strategies can be classified as follows:

   1) The addressing vs. tree method
   2) The internal vs. external method
   3) The static vs. dynamic method
   4) The digital vs. nondigital method
   5) The actual vs. attribute method

Addressing methods calculate immediately the address of an identified record on the basis of its key. Hashing is a well-known addressing technique with effectively constant retrieval time, but it generally has no order-preserving property that makes sequential access to the records easy. Tree methods, on the other hand, utilize a hierarchical series of key-related comparisons in a process that eventually locates the record. Tree methods also have order-preserving properties. Tree method strategies include binary search trees and B-trees. Tree methods exhibit logarithmic behavior upon search, but hashing methods are generally faster. The extendible variants of hashing seem less elegant than tree methods. Moreover, there are hybrid techniques that do not fit neatly into either category.

Internal methods keep the records in the computer's high-speed random-access memory; and, external methods, when there are more records than can be held in main memory, use secondary memory. A main problem with external methods is to reduce to secondary storage the number of accesses (probes) required for retrieval of a record.

Static vs. dynamic methods depend on whether or not a set of keys is essentially unchanging. When using the static method, we can concentrate our efforts on the construction of a fast and compact retrieval table without regard for the time required to set up the retrieval table, but, when using the dynamic method, extra space and/or redundant searching time must be taken into consideration in order to update the items quickly.

Digital methods can make use of keys as a sequence of digits or alphabetic characters, instead of basing a search, or nondigital, method on comparisons between keys. "Trie," derived from retrieval, is a well-known digital search technique originally introduced by Fredkin [1960] and belongs to a type of search tree. Tries enable us to retrieve variable-length strings.

A problem with actual methods is that records are located according to the value of a single key attribute. However, a file can have several attributes that can be used to retrieve records, so attribute methods that use multiple keys can provide fast answers to exact-match and improve partial-match query performance. Attribute methods are called multikey, or multidimensional methods.

ORGANIZATION OF BIBLIOGRAPHY

The organization of this volume's bibliography is essentially a combination of the classifications mentioned above.

Primary References

Most of the key search techniques are treated in great detail in the works cited, with mathematical analyses and suggestions for practical applications. Papers by Faloutos [3], Price [7], and Severange [9], respectively, are good surveys for general key search techniques.

Hashing

In hashing methods, a hash function that mathematically converts a key into a storage address is used, but one needs to choose a suitable hash function in the applications to avoid the collisions that two or more different keys can map into an identical integer. The paper by Maurer [13] is a useful introduction to classic hashing methods. A survey of hashing functions is given by Knott [18] and Lum [19],[20]. Note that the hashing approach by Amble [26] has order-preserving properties. The two general classes of collision resolution schemes are open addressing and chaining: open addressing uses various offset rules to find empty cells within the table; and chaining places all synonyms together in a linked list that is allocated outside of the table.

A perfect hashing function, which maps each key to a unique table location, has two main advantages: first, it can determine in exactly one probe the location of the record with the search key or the fact that the record is not present, and second, it needs no collision resolution. A perfect hashing function is considered minimal if no empty table locations exist. Minimal perfect hashing functions are perfect hashing functions with no unused locations. There are two systematic schemes—quotient reduction and remainder reduction—for generating perfect hashing functions [115], but their application is limited to small sets of keys. Composite perfect hashing, or segmentation, extends perfect hashing to large sets by partitioning the set into smaller sets [111] and finding perfect hashing functions for each set.

Binary Search Trees

The important property of a binary search tree is that all keys stored in the left subtree of any node x are all less than the key stored at x, and all keys stored in the right subtree of x are greater than the key stored at x. The binary tree search can support the search, insertion, and deletion operations, taking $O(\log n)$ steps per operation on average for a set of n keys. By static vs. dynamic methods, binary search trees might be classified into optimal binary search trees and balanced binary search trees [128]. In the static case, suppose that we know the access probabilities or frequencies for all records. One is primarily interested in efficient algorithms for constructing optimal binary search trees that minimize (exactly or approximately) the average search time. Now suppose that a binary search tree is used under conditions involving insertions and deletions of keys, as well as searches. Over time, the shape of the tree might change. We assume that each key in the tree is equally likely to be used in a search. We know that the average search time can be minimized by keeping the tree completely balanced (so leaves appear on, at most, two adjacent levels). This idea lies behind a range of techniques such as weight-balanced, height-balanced, and bounded-balanced binary trees, where weight is related to the access frequencies of keys and height is to the maximum level of any of its nodes [10]. A tree is said to be a height-balanced k-tree, or HB[k] tree, if the respective heights of the left and right subtrees of the root differ by at most k. An HB[1] tree is called an AVL tree, after Adel'son-Vel'skii and Landis [164], who first defined them. If insertion and subsequent searches are only operations of interest, then pure AVL trees are found to have the best performance. An empirical study of height-balanced trees is shown by Baer [165] and Karlton [179].

Multiway Search Trees

By increasing the branching factor m of a tree, and using a multiway search tree, instead of a binary tree, this worst case (and, indeed the average cases, too) can be improved to the order of $\log_m n$ comparisons. A better way to handle searching in a dynamic situation is to use balanced trees. In order to reduce the number of (relatively expensive) disk accesses, it is reasonable to allow a large number of keys per node so that the nodes have a large branching factor. Such multiway trees were named B-trees by Bayer [253]. As with most file organizations, variations of B-trees abound. Actually, Knuth [5] defines a B*-tree to be a B-tree where each node is at least two-thirds full instead of just half full. In B$^+$-trees implemented by Knuth [5] and termed by Comer [251], all keys reside in the leaves. The upper levels, which are organized as a B-tree, consist only of an index, a roadmap enabling rapid location of the index, and key parts. The B$^+$-tree implementation retains the logarithmic cost properties for operations by key, but gains the advantage of requiring at most one access to satisfy a next operation. Moreover, during the sequential processing of a file, no node will be accessed more than once, so space for only one node needs to be available in main memory. Thus, B$^+$-trees are well suited to applications that entail both random and sequential processing. Prefix B$^+$-trees by Bayer [255] save space for nodes using separators based on prefixes of keys. Another version, binary B-tree, makes B-trees suitable for a one-level store [251]. Essentially, a binary B-tree is a B-tree of order 1; each node has 1 or 2 keys and 2 or 3 pointers. To avoid wasting space for nodes that are only half full, a linked representation is used. A symmetric binary B-tree by Bayer [254] is an extension of the binary B-tree, which allows for both left and right links to point to sibling nodes, and exhibits symmetry lacking in binary B-trees. A 2-3 tree is a B-tree of order 1. The small node size makes 2-3 trees impractical for external storage, but quite appropriate for an internal data structure. Miller [295] and Rosenberg [303] consider the problem of constructing optimal 2-3 trees for a given set of keys.

Tries belong to multiway trees [5],[10]. Each node of the trie on level h represents that set of keys that begin with a certain sequence of h characters; the node specifies branches, depending on the (h+1)st character. These properties include fast retrieval time, quick unsuccessful search determination, and finding the longest match to a given key. The main drawback is the space requirement. Al-Suwaiyel [311] reviews tries and presents the compaction technique.

Dynamic Hashing

Several dynamic hashing schemes for external files have been developed over the last few years. This approach is a hybrid method of hashing and tree methods, and allows the file size to grow and shrink gracefully according to the number of records actually stored in the file. Fagin [337] introduced extendible hashing, an access technique guaranteed to use no more than two page faults to locate a record having a given key. Extendible hashing uses tries that are well balanced and provides an attractive alternative to balanced-tree methods. Larson [340] introduced dynamic hashing, a file-organization technique that permits space to be increased and decreased without reorganizing the file. The expected storage utilization is 69 percent at all times, an idea based on a forest of binary trees with no overflow records. Linear hashing, another scheme for handling overflow, exemplifies an external file-hashing scheme adapted to internal hash tables. The hash table is a dynamic array of pointers and each table entry (bucket) is a pointer to a linked list (chain) of all records hashing to that address. When the average chain length exceeds a threshold, the table is expanded in a predetermined order by one bucket.

Multikey Searching

This problem is important within itself (having applications in such areas as database systems, statistics, and design automation) and, in addition, serves as a representative of the entire class of multikey searching problems. There are a number of search methods for multikey searching. Each search method is specified by a data structure for storing the data and algorithms for building and searching the structure. For the number of k attributes, a k-dimensional binary search tree, the k-d tree is a well-known data structure of multikey searching, which is a natural generalization of the standard one-dimensional binary search tree. The quad tree described by Funkel [358] is also a well-known structure of multikey searching. It is a generation of the standard binary search tree in which every node has 2^k sons. The other structures are sequential scan, projection, cells, k-ranges, and range trees. The differences and comparison of these structures are investigated in survey: cf. Bentley [359]. Haung [386] describes data structures based on extendible hashing.

Overflow Handling

For access methods such as B-trees and dynamic hashing, all data records are stored at the bucket, or the page. File organization, or overflow handling, schemes allow the file size to grow and shrink gracefully according to the number of records actually stored in the file. Note that many papers concerning these techniques appear in references to B-trees and dynamic hashing. For any page overflow associated with dynamic hashing, Enbody [333] reviews splitting schemes, and full and partial expansion techniques.

ON THE PAPERS SELECTED

Serious efforts have been made to select comprehensive papers for each subtopic. For an introduction to hashing methods, the paper by Lewis [12] was selected. It provides a comprehensive tutorial for a variety of hash strategies, including hash functions, collision resolutions by open addressing and chaining, extendible and linear hashing for dynamic keys, and perfect and minimum perfect hashing for static keys. Cercone [98] is useful for practical applications because it reviews in detail perfect and minimal perfect hashing, and shows the empirical results for three kinds of lexicons: small—500 entries or less; medium — 5000 entries; and large—10,000 entries or more. Papers by Nievergelt [128] and Comer [251] were selected to survey the basic concepts of binary and B-tree techniques, and their variants. Nievergelt's paper describes the properties of optimal trees, weight-balanced trees, and height-balanced trees associated with binary search trees. Comer's paper reviews balancing, insertion and deletion of the basic B-trees, and discusses the major variants of the B-trees, especially B*-trees, B$^+$-trees, and prefix B-trees, contrasting the relative merits and costs of each implementation. Jonge [320] proposes two access methods, binary digital search trees and separator trees. With both methods the index is represented so compactly that it usually will fit in main memory, which means that records usually can be retrieved in one disk access. The author [310] proposes a fast digital search algorithm using a new data structure, a double-array, compressing tries, and shows that the method presented is well suited for the search of natural language dictionaries. Bentley [358] describes the basic concept of multikey methods based on binary search trees and discusses their variants. Kelley [359] introduces multikey implementation techniques using extensible hashing. Bentley and Kelley also include an introduction to binary search trees and extendible hashing methods, respectively. Baeza-Yates [432] presents a B^+-tree based on partial expansions and compares it with the traditional variants of B-trees by using a variety of numerical results. The idea is simply to increase the size of an overflowing bucket instead of splitting it. It is found that an overall storage utilization of 81 percent can be achieved in practice.

TABLE OF CONTENTS

Hashing Methods

Hashing for Dynamic and Static Internal Tables

Ted G. Lewis and Curtis R. Cook

Oregon State University

Reprinted from *IEEE Computer*, October 1988, pages 45-56.
Copyright © 1988 by The Institute of Electrical and Electronics
Engineers, Inc. All rights reserved.

A classic problem in computer science is how to store information so that it can be searched and retrieved efficiently. That is, given a set of records—each partitioned into a unique identifier called the *key* (K_i) and a "data part" containing all other desired information (D_i)—we want to retrieve arbitrary records from the set in the shortest possible time. The unique key in each record is needed to implement operations such as lookup, insert, delete, and update, as well as maintenance operations such as overflow. The data part of each record contains one or more fields of arbitrary type, such as numbers, text, and dates. In a computer program, the set is typically implemented as an internal list, table, or file on an external storage device.

Minimizing retrieval time can conflict with other goals such as minimizing storage space or program size, or can introduce undesirable side-effects on other data manipulation algorithms, such as deletion algorithms. For example, a sorted list is relatively easy to search quickly, but insertion and deletion of new keys can become difficult because all records must be kept in order. Therefore, selection of an appropriate storage organization and retrieval algorithm can involve trade-offs.

Retrieval speed and memory efficiency differ according to the type of storage structure, the storage device, and the search algorithm. For files stored on external disk drives we usually want to minimize disk accesses, even if it leads to more key

Hashing offers one of the best answers to one of computing's oldest problems: how to find and retrieve keyed information in the least amount of time.

comparisons. For internal lists or tables stored in computer memory, we want to minimize key comparisons, memory use, and overall processing time of the search algorithm. We restrict this survey to internal lists. Internal lists are important in their own right because they are used in symbol tables (compilers and interpreters), operating systems tables, and database tables. Fast access to a symbol table can significantly improve compiler performance.

Hashing, a technique that mathematically converts a key into a storage address, offers one of the best methods of finding

and retrieving information associated with a unique identifying key. In this article we survey the classical hashing function approach to information retrieval and show how general hashing techniques exchange speed for memory space and flexibility in data manipulation operations such as insert, delete, and overflow. We also discuss more recent developments in perfect hashing and minimal perfect hashing that provide speed and memory compactness when the keys are known in advance.

The calendar problem

The calendar problem contains most of the problems encountered when designing a hash function retrieval program. Suppose R is a list containing three-letter abbreviations for the months of the year and their number of days:

$$R = \{(JAN, 31), (FEB, 28), (MAR, 31), (APR, 30), (MAY, 31), (JUN, 30), (JUL, 31), (AUG, 31), (SEP, 30), (OCT, 31), (NOV, 30), (DEC, 31)\}$$

Obviously, the three-letter abbreviations are the unique keys and the number of days the data part. Given a key K, a typical operation involves finding the number of days in month K. To find how many days are in August, R must be searched for matching key $K = AUG$; the

Table 1. Hashing function pattern for the calendar problem.

Index i	KEY	h(KEY)	No. compares
0	MAY	12	2
1	NOV	1	1
2	APR	2	1
3	JUN	3	1
4	JUL	3	2
5	OCT	3	3
6			
7	AUG	7	1
8	DEC	7	2
9	JAN	9	1
10	FEB	9	2
11	SEP	9	3
12	MAR	12	1

corresponding data value 31 tells how many days are in August. The problem, then, is to find ways to store R such that retrieval of the number of days in a specific month is fast and storage efficient. We restrict our attention to internal memory storage structures and try to minimize the comparisons needed to find a given record.

Solutions to the calendar problem. We can solve the calendar problem in a number of ways. First, we can store R in an array that is searched sequentially from top-to-bottom using a linear search algorithm. An average search would require $(12 + 1)/2 = 6.5$ comparisons to find an arbitrary month. This solution is memory efficient, but the search time grows linearly with the size of R—doubling the list size also doubles the average time to locate an item. In many applications, linear growth in search time with an increase in list size is not acceptable.

A second way to solve the calendar problem is to sort the list of months and use a binary search algorithm. Binary search requires an average of $37/12 = 3.08$ comparisons to locate a record. While the binary search algorithm is a dramatic improvement over the linear search algorithm, it has three major drawbacks. First, the set R must be sorted, which is generally time-consuming even if done only once when R is entered into computer memory. Second, the cost of maintaining order in the list for fast retrieval makes the insert, delete, and update operations more costly. Finally, even though the average lookup time grows more slowly than does linear search, search time remains a function of the size of R.

A third way to solve the calendar problem involves hashing. The records in R are stored in an array indexed from zero to some upper limit, and a mathematical function, called a *hashing function*, is used to convert each key into a unique array index. When searching the array for a certain month, the function transforms the search key into the corresponding array index, so the desired month and day are retrieved in one comparison. Success depends on finding the hashing function that maps each key to a unique array index. Many hashing functions can solve the calendar problem. One such function is

$$h(KEY) = (First\_letter(KEY) + Second\_letter(KEY)) \bmod 13$$

This hashing function maps each key of R into a corresponding number between zero and 12 by summing the ASCII code equivalent of the first and second letters in each key. The remainder of the sum is used to scale the index value to a number between zero and 12—corresponding to the index of each array element. Assuming the keys arrive in chronological order, the following mapping is obtained for all 12 months in R.

To insert JAN in Table 1,

$$h(JAN) = (ASCII(J) + ASCII(A)) \bmod 13$$
$$= (74 + 65) \bmod 13$$
$$= (139) \bmod 13 = 9$$

Thus, the record with a unique key equal to JAN is inserted in location 9. Conversely, when retrieving the record containing key JAN, the hashing function is

calculated a second time, again yielding $i = 9$. Probing location 9 reveals the record (we call comparisons "probes").

Consider what happens when we insert FEB.

$$h(FEB) = (ASCII(F) + ASCII(E)) \bmod 13 = 9$$

Its hashing function value is also 9. In this table FEB is placed in the next available empty position. This unfortunate event destroys the unique correspondence between key and table index. The final column of Table 1 reveals many keys that require more than one probe to insert a record—thus, this particular mathematical function does not guarantee uniqueness. This occurs because converting alphanumeric strings to relatively small integers often results in a collision where two or more different keys map into an identical integer. Keys that collide in this manner are called synonyms. For example, synonym sets (JUN, JUL, OCT), (AUG, DEC), (JAN, FEB, SEP), and (MAR, MAY) contain keys that collide in the hash table shown in Table 1. In some situations, such as a static table where the entries are known ahead of time, we can find a hashing function with no collisions. Later, we will consider a class of hashing functions called *perfect hashing functions* because every key maps to a unique position and requires only one probe for retrieval.

Collision resolution. Various rules have been proposed to correct the collision problem. The simplest rule, called *linear offset*, finds unique index correspondences using a forward linear search. We used this rule to resolve the collisions in Table 1. For example, when FEB collides with JAN, the next cell in ascending order—cell 10—is probed, and the first empty cell is used to satisfy the insert operation.

Each forward search increases the comparisons needed to map a key to its index. Also, imperfect mapping reduces the speed of subsequent searches. The comparison column in Table 1 gives the number of comparisons to locate each key in the hash table. The average number of comparisons is 1.67—an improvement over either linear or binary search. Furthermore, this number is a function of hashing-function quality and table density (the ratio of filled cells to total cells) instead of list length. This important feature lets us trade memory space for speed, or speed for memory space.

Hashing functions belong to a general class of key-to-address transformations that map one set of values into another. If the set of keys changes through a series of insertions and deletions, we call the hash table *dynamic*; otherwise it is *static*. We can classify hashing functions by a variety of characteristics:

- mathematical function used in the key-to-address transformation;
- key set (dynamic versus static);
- collision resolution scheme;
- insertion, deletion, and lookup algorithm; and
- overflow algorithm.

Measures of a function's "goodness" include memory efficiency and the average and worst-case time needed to perform lookups, insertions, and deletions.

Dynamic tables

Hashing a dynamic key set into a table belongs to a class of techniques for implementing rapid associative searches of random- or direct-access memory. Although the term "hashing" first appeared in the mid-1960s in reference to a class of rapid table-search techniques for compiler construction, hashing techniques have actually been used by programmers since the early days of the direct-access disk drive (circa 1957).[1-3]

Hashing poses several problems. First, we must find a suitable hashing function that uniformly distributes the keys. If the hashing function permits collisions, we must devise an acceptable collision resolution method. In addition, when the keys are dynamic, we must decide how to select initial table size, how to handle problems such as overflow when R exceeds initial table size, and how to handle difficulties associated with deleting records.

Hashing functions. Mapping a key to a table index is done in two stages when keys are alphanumeric strings instead of integers. We must first convert the alphanumeric key to an integer, and then map this integer to a table index. In some instances, such as when the key is short, the alphanumeric key can be directly interpreted as an integer. However, if the string is relatively long, this straightforward conversion would result in numerical overflow. Thus, we must use one of several compression algorithms to convert from string to integer.

Folding is a popular method of converting a long alphanumeric key to an integer. Two common folding schemes are XOR and radix K. The XOR scheme adds, shifts, and exclusive-ORs the characters in the key. Radix K converts the key to a base K number by treating each character in the key as a digit in a base K number, where K is the number of possible distinct characters, and then reducing this number modulo a large prime.

Ramakrishna[4] found fewer collisions occurred with the radix K folding scheme. Figure 1 shows this algorithm and its application to the calendar problem for radix 26 (the number of distinct characters in uppercase English) and key FEB. Regardless of the number of characters in the string key, the value of TabIndex is controlled in this algorithm so that it does not overflow the computer's registers. In Figure 1, this is done by computing mod N on intermediate results.

Extensive tests have shown that, once the key is converted to an integer, functions based on multiplication and division work well.[5] For example, the division scheme, $h(\text{numeric\_key}) = \text{numeric\_key}$ mod N, produces an integer in the range $[0, (N-1)]$ corresponding to array subscripts in the range $[0, (N-1)]$. The radix K string-compression function does this division as a by-product of compression, making radix K folding effective for key-to-address transformation. Later, we address an added benefit of making the table size N a prime number, such as 13 in the calendar problem.

Collision resolution. The large number of possible key sets makes collisions inevitable. A good hashing function minimizes collisions but does not eliminate them altogether. Thus, we need some scheme for resolving collisions. The two general classes of collision resolution schemes are *chaining* and *open addressing*. Chaining places all synonyms together in a linked list that is allocated outside of the table. Open addressing uses various offset rules to find empty cells within the table.

Chaining. Instead of storing a key in each cell of the table, chaining stores the head of a linked list containing all records with keys that map to that table location. This method provides an additional benefit because the table never overflows; instead, the chains get longer. However, synonyms are stored in the same chain and must be searched linearly along the chain, so this method degrades in performance as

Algorithm:

Str : = "Alphanumeric key"
Blank : = "ASCII space"
K : = "Radix, e.g. 26 for English"
N : = "Length of table"
TabIndex : = 0
For i : = 1 to Length(Str) Do
    TabIndex : = (K * TabIndex + Char(Str[i]) − Blank) mod N

Example:

Str : = 'FEB'; Blank : = 32
TabIndex : = (0 + 70 − 32) mod 13
        = 12
    : = (26 * 12 + 69 − 32) mod 13
        = 11
    : = (26 * 11 + 66 − 32) mod 13
        = 8

Figure 1. Radix K string compression.

the chains increase in length. We can significantly improve speed for a small increase in insertion time by keeping chains in ascending order (using an exchange-insert sort to insert new synonyms in the chain). When the chain is ordered, lookups can be abandoned as soon as a key greater than the search key is found. A variety of other schemes have also been proposed to improve chaining.[5]

To illustrate chaining, let h be the hash function for the calendar problem. Using chaining, we recompute the mapping in Table 1, with the exception that synonyms are placed in a linked list rooted in the hash table. Figure 2 shows the resulting chained hash table. The average number of comparisons to find a key is 1.67. Note the obvious space-time trade-off: the larger the table, the smaller the average chain size. Hence, fewer comparisons are needed to find a key.

In another chaining technique, called *coalesced hashing*, the synonym-chain pointers point to locations in the table itself.[6] For the calendar problem, we find the next available location for colliding keys by working back up the table, starting at location 12. The coalesced table in

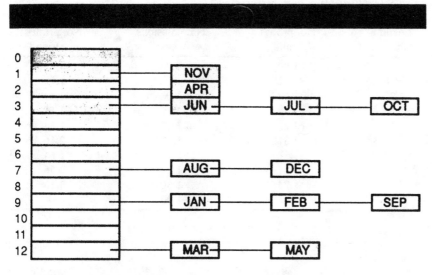

Figure 2. Chaining method.

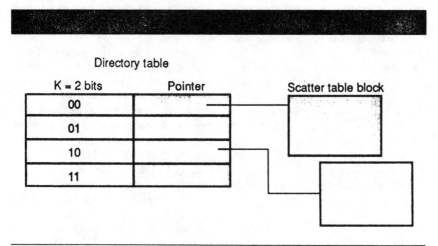

Directory table

Figure 3. Data structure for extendible hashing function.

Table 2. Coalesced chaining.

Location	KEY	Pointer
0		
1	NOV	
2	APR	
3	JUN	8
4	DEC	
5	OCT	
6	SEP	
7	AUG	4
8	JUL	5
9	JAN	12
10	MAY	6
11	MAR	10
12	FEB	11

- an empty location is found (failure), or
- the complete table is searched without success (failure).

For example, we can use a simple linear-offset search pattern to search forward from a collision point until we attain one of the termination conditions above. The mapping in Table 1 illustrates open addressing. The offset rule is given by

$$location(KEY) = (h(KEY) + i) \bmod 13$$

where i equals the probe number.

This collision resolution function is called a linear offset function because it scans the array linearly, looking for an empty element. For example, $h(SEP) = 9$, but this table location is already filled, so the function examines locations 10 and 11 before finding an empty location.

Linear offset is 'not recommended because it tends to cause primary clustering around "popular" cells. A variety of solutions to clustering have been proposed.[1,2,7] One approach is called quadratic search: the offset is i^2 for the ith probe. However, this has the undesirable side-effect of secondary clustering, where all synonyms form a cluster along the same pattern of probes. The best known offset pattern is known as double-hashing, rehashing, or quotient-offset hashing. This pattern eliminates both forms of clustering by computing different offsets for each synonym. A simple rule for double-hashing is

$$h(key) = key \bmod N$$

which gives the "home" address (remainder), and

Table 2 illustrates this. Note that $h(MAR) = 12$, but since FEB collided with JAN and was placed at location 12, MAR is placed in location 11 (the next available location when working back up the table from 12). Two comparisons are needed on average for the coalesced table.

A variation of coalesced hashing involves setting aside the upper part of the table, called a *cellar*, for handling collisions. Keys hash to the noncellar part of the table, called the *address region*. If a collision occurs, the key maps to the next available location in the cellar. This scheme restricts the range of the hash function to the address region, but seems to improve search time slightly. However, we do not know the percentage of the hash table that should be allocated to the cellar

for optimal performance. Empirical studies indicate that 14 percent works well.[6]

Storing the chain in a fixed-size table in this way limits the options for handling overflow. What can we do when the table becomes full? When separate chaining is used as in Figure 2, overflow becomes a problem only when physical memory is exceeded.

Open addressing. In this method of collision resolution, part or all of the table is searched for an empty cell. The search pattern is specified by an offset rule that generates the sequence of table locations to be searched until

- the record containing the key is found (success),

$$q(\text{key}) = 1 + \text{key} \bmod (N - 2)$$

which gives the offset.

Because the offset depends on the key, the quotient-offset function spreads the keys across the table by searching out different sequences of elements, even though colliding keys are synonyms. The table length should be a prime number so that the offset will cause consideration of every possible table position.

As the number of records increases, the length of a path through the table can grow, decreasing performance. Various techniques can reduce lookup time, but only by sacrificing performance of other operations. For example, when inserting a new key, the chain of synonyms can be split into two shorter chains. This increases insertion time but reduces lookup time.

While we can obtain some performance improvements by these means, performance of open addressing schemes is largely governed by table density, not list size. To illustrate this and show the speed of a typical quotient-offset function, we randomly sampled keys from 1 through 32,767 and hashed them into a table of size $N = 11$. We obtained each result by averaging more than 25 experimental cases at each table density as measured by its loading factor (loading factor equals the number of entries in the table divided by N). Table 3 shows the results of this simulation.

The number of probes in the second column tallies the average number of comparisons made when the key was found—including collisions and the final probe that matched the search key. The third column tallies the average number of collisions during a successful search. The last column tallies the average number of probes in the worst case (when no key was found). Note that lookup performance is independent of list size.

Overflow. One of the most damaging limitations of dynamic hashing into fixed-size scatter storage tables is the problem of predicting the best array size. Except for the chaining method, hashing performance largely depends on density of the storage array. (When using chaining, each new key is allocated memory space as needed, so overflow only occurs when no more memory exists.)

For performance reasons, we recommend that hash tables not exceed a density of 80 percent. Thus, overflow occurs whenever insertion of the next key would

Table 3. Quotient-offset hash performance.

Loading factor	No. probes found	No. collisions found	No. probes not found
.09	1.00	1.00	1.04
.18	1.02	1.02	1.28
.27	1.08	1.08	1.12
.36	1.22	1.19	1.56
.45	1.22	1.18	1.84
.55	1.31	1.22	2.16
.64	1.37	1.23	2.64
.73	1.51	1.29	2.56
.82	1.74	1.30	3.16
.91	2.08	1.40	------

exceed this threshold. In any case, what happens when the hash table overflows?

We can accommodate overflow by (1) allocating a larger array, and moving the contents of the old array into the new array by rehashing all records, or (2) incrementally extending the old array to accommodate growth.

In the first solution, a larger array is allocated when overflow occurs and each entry is rehashed into the larger storage. The old array is deallocated and discarded. This method is awkward and slow, but it has the advantage of being simple and straightforward. The second solution rehashes only part of the table. Incremental schemes differ in the frequency and the portion of the table rehashed.

Extendible hashing. Extendible hashing[8] is a hashing function and scatter table data structure for accommodating table growth. It divides the storage array into fixed-length blocks and allocates one block at a time as needed. The blocks are managed by a directory table containing pointers to each block and a number K telling how many bits of each key to examine during a lookup (see Figure 3). The low-order K bits of a key determine which block to examine. These low-order bits usually map the key directly into a location in the directory block containing a pointer to a scatter table block. The pointer is followed, and the whole key hashes into a location in the scatter table block.

When a scatter table block becomes too full (by exceeding either the acceptable loading factor or the block size), it splits into two blocks of the same size. The number of low-order K bits increments by one to reflect the split, and the keys in the old block rehash into either of the two new

blocks. Using $(K + 1)$ lower bits, each key can hash into either the 0 or 1 block, depending on the value of the $(K + 1)$st bit in each key. We might need to double the size of the directory table because a pointer to the new (split) block is added to the directory.

The extendible hashing technique limits rehashing overhead by keeping the blocks relatively small. Thus, the time to rehash all keys in a split block is much less than the time to rehash an entire list. Nevertheless, this method requires two or more probes (one into the directory and at least one into the block) per lookup.

Suppose the calendar information is stored in an extendible hash table. Each block is five elements long, and overflow occurs whenever block density = 3/5 is exceeded. This means a maximum of three of the five elements of each block are occupied.

Initially, the directory table contains two elements and $K = 1$, indicating that one least-significant bit decides which of the two blocks to search. The first block contains all keys ending in a 0 bit, and the second block contains all keys ending in a binary 1. We use the quotient offset hashing function to place each key in its appropriate block.

When an overflow condition arises and a new block is allocated to accommodate the overflow,

- the directory table doubles in size, and K is incremented (K bumps up to 2);
- a new block is allocated to hold the overflow from one of the existing blocks, and the directory pointer points to it; and
- the overflowed block is "split"; that is, all keys with the same least-

significant bits are placed in the same block (the two least-significant bits determine the block).

The extendible hash scheme preserves a measure of performance while using a relatively simple extension technique to overcome the limitation of the fixed-length array structure. Performance studies suggest that this method is competitive with other methods of storing and retrieving records from disk files.

Linear hashing. Linear hashing,[9] another scheme for handling overflow, exemplifies an external file-hashing scheme adapted to internal hash tables. The hash table is a dynamic array of pointers, and each table entry (bucket) is a pointer to a linked list (chain) of all records hashing to that address. When the average chain length exceeds a threshold, the table is expanded in a predetermined order by one bucket.

For example, suppose the hashing function is $h(KEY)$ mod 5 and the hash table consists of five buckets: 0, 1, 2, 3, and 4. All keys with $h(KEY)$ ending in 0 or 5 are in bucket 0, all ending in 1 or 6 are in bucket 1, and so forth. If the average chain length exceeds the threshold, bucket 5 will be added to the hash table, and bucket 0 will be split. All records with $h(KEY)$ mod 10 = 5 are moved from bucket 0 to the new bucket 5. All records with $h(KEY)$ mod 10 = 0 remain in bucket 0.

The next time the average chain length exceeds the threshold, bucket 6 will be added to the hash table and the records in bucket 1 with $h(KEY)$ mod 10 = 6 will be moved to bucket 6. The hash function is modified slightly. If $h(KEY)$ mod 5 maps to a bucket that has been split, then the hash function $h(KEY)$ mod 10 is applied to determine the bucket containing the record. Otherwise, $h(KEY)$ mod 5 gives the bucket containing the record.

Other methods of handling overflow establish an area to hold keys that spill over from the primary table. While these approaches are simple, performance can suffer as more and more keys are placed in the overflow area.

Deletion. A final problem must be overcome—deletion. For hash tables using chaining to resolve collisions, deletion is straightforward. However, for open addressing, collision resolution schemes are complicated by the fact that a deleted record leaves a gap in the probe sequence. This gap can cause failure in subsequent lookups because a search prematurely

Table 4. Perfect hashing of calendar.

w	E2 + E3	h(w)
JAN	49,621	5
FEB	50,626	6
MAR	49,625	0
APR	55,257	7
MAY	49,640	11
JUN	58,581	2
JUL	58,579	10
AUG	58,567	4
SEP	50,647	3
OCT	50,147	1
NOV	55,013	9
DEC	50,627	8

terminates as soon as it encounters an empty cell. If the cell previously held a colliding key, the search path leading to the correct key is destroyed by removing the colliding key.

If we simply leave deleted records in the table and treat them as empty cells, they increase the effective loading factor, which increases the number of probes during a lookup operation. In fact, the appearance of a "table full" condition can arise during lookup, even when most of the array contains deleted elements.

A simple solution involves adding an additional field to each record. This new field can take on one of three values: empty, occupied, or deleted. Then, when searching for a particular key, we can treat deleted records the same as occupied ones. When inserting a record, we treat deleted records the same as empty ones.

We can overcome the artificial loading of a table with deleted records by moving keys to fill the gap created by a deletion. This approach reduces performance but removes the gap problem. One straightforward algorithm searches a path of synonyms, moving each one following a deletion up in the table. Each record can be marked as either full or empty.

Deletion in an extendible table performs an inverse operation. Two "buddies" (blocks containing keys that differ only in the Kth bit) coalesce when depleted to a level where their combined loading factors are less than the maximum load factor. That is, the keys hash into a single block, and the directory pointers are updated. The unused block is deallocated and returned to the memory manager. Similarly, deletion in a linear hashing scheme

is the inverse of expanding the table by a bucket.

These solutions to the deletion problem are not exceptional and point to the need for more research into deletion techniques. We might not be unduly concerned about the high cost of deletion if a storage table is used predominantly for lookups, but we should consider other techniques if insertions and deletions are the predominate operations on the structure.

Static tables

The internal table for many applications is static. That is, its entries and size are known ahead of time and no insertions or deletions will occur. Examples include compiler keyword tables, assembler operation codes, and dictionaries. For these applications, the extra effort to find a perfect hashing function that maps each key to a unique table location pays dividends.

We can also apply perfect hashing to large external files stored on disks, where it is common practice to store 10 to 50 records on each disk page. The number of disk page accesses (probes) largely determines the speed of an external file search because the access operation is so slow. A perfect external hashing function locates the page containing the desired record in a single probe.

Perfect hashing. A perfect hashing function, which maps each key to a unique table location, has two main advantages. First, it can determine the location of the record with the search key, or the fact that the record is not present, in exactly one probe. Second, it needs no collision resolution, deletion, or overflow scheme. Some perfect hashing schemes create auxiliary tables that are accessed in determining a record's location. Several schemes coalesce these auxiliary tables with the hash table, requiring two or three probes.

Perfect hashing functions are rare. Knuth[5] showed that in the set of all possible mappings of a 31-record set to a table with 41 locations, only about one mapping in 10 million is perfect.

Sprugnoli[10] developed two systematic schemes—quotient reduction and remainder reduction—for generating perfect hashing functions. Assuming the key has been converted to an integer w, the quotient reduction scheme finds integers s and N so that

$$h(w) = (w + s)/N$$

is perfect, while the remainder reduction scheme finds integers d, q, M, and N so that

$$h(w) = \lfloor ((d + qw) \bmod M)/N \rfloor$$

is perfect. For example, the function $h(w) = ((3w + 4) \bmod 23)/2$ can perfectly hash the calendar problem. The character string has been converted to an integer by the transformation $w = E2(KEY) + E3(KEY)$, where $E2(KEY) + E3(KEY)$ is the numeric equivalent of the EBCDIC codings of the second and third letters in the key. Table 4 shows that this function places each of the 12 months in unique locations using only 12 storage cells.

Unfortunately, Sprugnoli's schemes are not practical for sets with more than 15 elements. Quotient reduction has exponential runtime and can produce an extremely sparse table. Although remainder reduction is much faster, it is not guaranteed to work for all key sets. Furthermore, Sprugnoli does not give a systematic method of converting character keys to unique keys.

Composite perfect hashing[4] extends perfect hashing to larger sets by partitioning the set into smaller sets called *buckets* and finding perfect hashing functions for each bucket. Such a scheme must store information about the partition and perfect hashing functions for each bucket.

For larger sets, Sprugnoli suggested a two-stage composite hashing scheme called *segmentation*, which applies the first-stage hash function to the entire set R to hash all records into buckets. Each bucket contains all records with the same hash value. In the second stage, a different perfect hashing function for each bucket maps the keys in the bucket to unique locations in the table segment allocated for that bucket.

By adjusting the first hashing function, we can make the bucket size small enough to reduce the difficulty of finding a perfect hashing function for each bucket. Table 5 illustrates this two-stage process for the calendar set. The FIRST(KEY) function is simply the ASCII coding of the first letter of the KEY mod 2, and the function A2(KEY) + A3(KEY) is the sum of the ASCII codings of the second and third letters.

Segmentation requires two probes—one to determine the bucket and obtain the information for the second hashing function for that bucket, and a second to access the table location containing the key. Perfect hashing usually requires knowing the records in R in advance, but we can modify the segmentation scheme to handle updates (insertions and deletions) in a reasonable amount of time.

The next two composite schemes require a family of perfect hashing functions and several levels of accessing. In the segmentation scheme proposed by Fredman, Komlos, and Szemeredi,[11] the family of perfect hashing functions for the buckets are of the form

$$h(KEY) = (k * KEY \bmod p) \bmod m$$

where p is a prime number greater than the largest key, k is a constant, and m equals the square of the number of keys in the bucket. For a given bucket, the family of hashing functions is obtained by varying k. Fredman, Komlos, and Szemeredi showed that for a set with r keys, there always exists a perfect hashing function of the above form where $m = r^2$. Since r is known in advance, the value of k is found by trial-and-error.

Tables 6 and 7 illustrate this scheme. Table 6 shows the values for KEY and $h(KEY)$ for the three-letter month abbreviations. Each w is the sum of the ASCII coding of the three letters in the key. For key SEP, $w = 83 + 69 + 80 = 232$. The values for $h(KEY)$ are computed using a hash function of the form above with $k = 1$, $p = 251$, and $m = 7$. We arbitrarily selected k, and we did not need a perfect h.

The initial segment in Table 7 contains the header entries for the buckets. Each header entry is an index for the hash table

segment containing the bucket. In Table 7, the header entries are in locations 0 through 6. They indicate that the table segment for bucket 0 begins at index 7, bucket 1 begins at index 18, and so forth. Each segment contains the information needed to compute the particular perfect hashing function (k and the square root of the bucket size are the first two entries in the segment) and the hashed bucket entries.

To locate the record containing KEY, we first apply the header-table hashing function to KEY to obtain the index in the hash table. This number gives the starting location of the bucket's hash table segment. Using the segment's first two entries (encoded size and k), we can locate KEY's

Table 5. Segmented perfect hashing of the calendar.

KEY	FIRST(KEY)	(A2(KEY) + A3(KEY)) mod 12
JAN	0	11
FEB	0	3
JUN	0	7
JUL	0	5
NOV	0	9
DEC	0	4

KEY	FIRST(KEY)	12 + (A2(KEY) + A3(KEY)) mod 10
MAR	1	19
APR	1	14
MAY	1	16
AUG	1	18
SEP	1	21
OCT	1	13

Table 6. Header table hash function.

KEY	w	$h(w)$
JAN	217	0
FEB	205	2
MAR	224	0
APR	227	3
MAY	231	0
JUN	237	6
JUL	235	4
AUG	221	4
SEP	232	1
OCT	230	6
NOV	243	5
DEC	204	1

8

position in the segment. For example, to locate SEP in the hash table, we first find the index of its header table entry.

$$h(SEP) = h(232)$$
$$= (1 * 232 \bmod 251) \bmod 7 = 1$$

Hash table [1] = 18, so the segment for the bucket containing SEP starts at hash table location 18. To locate SEP, we find the

Table 7. Hash table.

Location		
0	7	
1	18	
2	24	
3	27	Header table
4	30	
5	36	
6	39	
7	3	
8	1	
9		
10	JAN	
11		
12		Bucket 0
13		
14		
15	MAY	
16		
17	MAR	
18	2	
19	6	
20	DEC	
21	SEPT	Bucket 1
22		
23		
24	1	
25	1	Bucket 2
26	FEB	
27	1	
28	1	Bucket 3
29	APR	
30	2	
31	1	
32		Bucket 4
33	AUG	
34		
35	JUL	
36	1	
37	1	Bucket 5
38	NOV	
39	2	
40	1	
41		Bucket 6
42	JUN	
43		
44	OCT	

values of m and k for the perfect hashing function for the bucket. Hash table [18] = 2, which is the square root of the number of bucket entries ($m = 2^2 = 4$), and hash table [19] = 6 = k. The actual bucket entries start at hash table location 20. Thus, $h(SEP) = h(232) = (6 * 232 \bmod 251) \bmod 4 = 1$, which means SEP is in hash table [20 + 1].

Major problems with this segmentation scheme include the impracticality of finding the family of perfect hashing functions, the fact that retrieving a key requires several probes, and the large number of unused hash table locations. These problems suggest that increasing the header table size, thereby decreasing bucket size, might improve storage utilization. A similar scheme by Cormack, Horspool, and Kaiserswerth[12] uses less storage and allows insertions and deletions.

The composite perfect hashing scheme given by Du et al.[13] is based on rehashing and segmentation. A hash indicator table (HIT) is constructed from a set of hashing functions $h_1, h_2, \ldots, h_s$ as follows.

Each key that h_1 hashes to a unique value is placed in that hash table location, and its HIT entry is set to 1. That is, if $h_1(KEY) = j$ and h_1 hashes no other key to j, then HIT[j] = 1 and KEY is inserted in location j of the hash table. The second hashing function h_2 is then applied to all keys. All keys not in the hash table and that are hashed by h_2 to a unique unoccupied location are inserted in the hash table. The HIT entries for these keys are set to two. This process continues until all keys are inserted in the hash table or all s hash functions have been applied. Note that the HIT value indicates which hash function mapped the key to the hash table.

To find $h(KEY)$ apply the hashing functions $h_1, h_2, \ldots, h_s$ to KEY until HIT[$h_i(KEY)$] = i. If the search fails, $h(KEY)$ is undefined. Tables 8 and 9 illustrate this scheme. Table 8 gives the hash values for the four hashing functions for the calendar data. Table 9 gives the HIT and hash table entries.

To find $h(JUN)$, we see that $h_1(JUN)$ = 13, but HIT[13] ≠ 1 since $h_1(MAR)$ = 13; $h_2(JUN)$ = 14, but HIT[14] ≠ 2 because location 14 in the hash table was filled by JUL ($h_1(JUL)$ = 14); $h_3(JUN)$ = 3 and HIT[3] = 3, so $h(JUN)$ = 3.

The problems with this scheme are that

- selecting the set of hash functions h_1, $h_2, \ldots h_s$ is difficult;

- retrieving a key can require up to s accesses to the HIT;
- the hashing function is not guaranteed to work (in this example, MAY was not mapped to the hash table); and
- when only a few keys remain unhashed, the probability that the remaining hashing functions will map these keys to unique and unoccupied hash table locations is small.

Du et al.[13] report improved performance when the hash table locations are partitioned into segments with separate HITs and different sets of hashing functions.

Minimal perfect hashing. Recall that a hashing function is minimal if no empty table locations exist. The hashing function in Table 4 is both minimal and perfect. Minimal perfect hashing functions are perfect hash functions with no unused locations.

There has been a recent flurry of theoretical and heuristic algorithms for minimal perfect hashing functions. Jaeschke's[14] reciprocal hashing scheme is an example of a theoretical algorithm. The hash function for key w in R (a set of distinct positive integers) is

$$h(w) = (C/(Dw + E)) \bmod N$$

where C, D, and E are integer constants computed by special algorithms and N is the size of R.

Although the existence of the function h is guaranteed, there are several practical problems with this scheme. First, it assumes that R is a set of distinct positive integers. Second, the reciprocal hashing algorithm performs an exhaustive search, resulting in exponential time complexity and making it impractical for sets with more than 20 elements. Finally, the constant C can become very large.

Chang[15] developed a similar theoretical scheme based on the Chinese remainder theorem. His hashing function is of the form $h(w) = C \bmod p(w)$, where C is an integer constant computed by his algorithm and $p(w)$ is a prime number function; that is, $p(w)$ is a different prime for each integer w. Unfortunately, the number of bits to represent C is proportional to $m(\log 2m)$ where m is the size of R. Chang gives no general method of finding the prime number function.

Cichelli[16] presents a simple heuristic hashing function for small static sets. His hash function for a word w is

$$h(w) = \text{Value(First\_Letter}(w)) + \text{Value(Last\_Letter}(w)) + \text{Length}(w)$$

Table 10 gives the letter values and resulting hash table for

$R = \{$JANUARY, FEBRUARY, MARCH, APRIL, MAY, JUNE, JULY, AUGUST, SEPTEMBER, OCTOBER, NOVEMBER, DECEMBER$\}$

Building the hash table in Table 10 involves finding the Value function that makes $h(w)$ a perfect minimal hash function; that is, finding a set of character values that map each word in the set to a unique table address such that the table contains no internal blank slots. To find the character value assignments, Cichelli also provides an algorithm that uses an intelligent, exhaustive search with backtracking that considers one key at a time.

Cook and Oldehoeft[17] improve Cichelli's backtracking algorithm by developing a letter-oriented algorithm that considers groups of key words rather than a single word in finding letter-value assignments. Also, when the letter-value assignment algorithm reaches an impasse, Cichelli's algorithm backtracks one word at a time, while the Cook and Oldehoeft algorithm immediately backs up to the letter-value assignment that caused the impasse.

Cichelli's hashing function is simple, fast, and machine-independent. The last property is especially important because once a hash function (assignment of character values) has been found for a word set, we can used it for the word set on any computer.

However, Cichelli's algorithm has several shortcomings. Because the letter-value assignment process uses an exhaustive search with backtracking, its time complexity is exponential. Hence, the algorithm is only practical for small static sets with fewer than 45 words. In addition, the algorithm is not guaranteed to work for all sets. For example, it cannot work for sets with conflicting word pairs, that is, two words with the same length and same pair of characters at their ends (such as JAN and JUN, or TYPE and EXIT). This is why Table 10 uses the full names for months rather than abbreviations.

Conflicting word pairs are common in moderate-sized sets of English words, as shown by a Monte Carlo study[18] that generated random word sets with English-language probabilities of first letters, last letters, and word length. About half of the sets with 30 words contained conflicting letter pairs. Choosing other letter positions is not a solution; for example, every letter pair conflicts in the seven-word set $R = \{$CASE, ELSE, PAGE, READ, REAL, TRUE, TYPE$\}$.[19] Jaeschke and Osterburg[20] point out many other cases for which Cichelli's heuristic does not work.

Extensions to Cichelli's hash function. Cichelli's hash function is attractive because of its simplicity and machine-independence. Several attempts have been made to extend his function while preserving its attractiveness. Some of these extensions handle large static sets with up to several thousand words, overcoming Cichelli's word-pairs conflict problem. The extensions are significant because they extend minimal perfect hashing to practical applications in electronic dictionaries, natural language processing, and textual database processing.

The first of two general extension schemes modifies Cichelli's hashing function by adding more terms, changing the character evaluation function, and considering different character positions in a word. The second scheme segments or partitions the large set into buckets and finds minimal perfect hashing functions for each bucket.

Modification. Many modifications of Cichelli's hashing function add terms or change the letter positions. For example,

Table 8. Hash values for composite perfect hashing scheme.

KEY	h_1	h_2	h_3	h_4
JAN	3	5	12	7
FEB	9	8	11	6
MAR	13	13	7	1
APR	2	3	8	5
MAY	3	6	11	6
JUN	13	14	3	3
JUL	14	1	5	9
AUG	3	4	9	11
SEP	4	12	7	6
OCT	6	3	6	2
NOV	2	7	13	9
DEC	12	3	12	1

Table 9. HIT and hash table entries.

Location	HIT	Hash table
1	0	
2	0	
3	3	JUN
4	1	SEP
5	2	JAN
6	1	OCT
7	2	NOV
8	3	APR
9	1	FEB
10	0	
11	4	AUG
12	1	DEC
13	2	MAR
14	1	JUL
15	0	

Table 10. Letter value and resulting hash table based on Cichelli's heuristic hashing function.

Letter	VALUE(LETTER)	KEY	h(KEY)
A	0	JANUARY	7
D	-7	FEBRUARY	2
E	5	MARCH	10
F	-6	APRIL	11
H	5	MAY	3
J	0	JUNE	9
L	6	JULY	4
M	0	AUGUST	12
N	-3	SEPTEMBER	8
O	-1	OCTOBER	6
R	0	NOVEMBER	5
S	-1	DECEMBER	1
T	6		
Y	0		

Table 11. Hashing function for the full-word calendar set.

Letter	d(Letter)	C(Letter)	p(Letter)
-			
A	0	119	
B			5
C	3	1	7
E	4		
G			11
L			13
N			2
O	7	1	
P	8	1	17
R			3
T			19
U	9	211	
V			23
Y			29

KEY	Letter pair	h(KEY)
JANUARY	(A,N)	1
FEBRUARY	(E,B)	5
MARCH	(A,R)	2
APRIL	(P,R)	9
MAY	(A,Y)	3
JUNE	(U,N)	10
JULY	(U,L)	12
AUGUST	(U,G)	11
SEPTEMBER	(E,P)	7
OCTOBER	(C,T)	4
NOVEMBER	(E,V)	8
DECEMBER	(E,C)	6

Ada's 63 reserved words contain three pairs of conflicting words (EXIT-TYPE, RAISE-RANGE, and PRIVATE-PACKAGE), and Modula-2's 40 reserved words contain one conflicting pair (TYPE-EXIT). Sebesta and Taylor[21] found a minimal perfect hash function for the Modula-2 words by adding the term

> alphabetic position of second to last character in word

to Cichelli's hashing function, and found a minimal perfect hashing function for the Ada reserved words by adding the same term twice.

Chang and Lee[22] developed a letter-oriented minimal perfect hashing algorithm based on ideas from Chang's previous algorithm and Cichelli's algorithm. The hashing function for a set of words is

$$h(L_i, L_j) = d(L_i) + C(L_i) \bmod p(L_j)$$

where L_i and L_j are the ith and jth letters in the key; d and C are integer-valued functions, and p is a prime number function. Chang and Lee give algorithms for finding the functions d, C, and p. Table 11 gives the hashing function for the full-word calendar set. We selected second and third letters for the letter pairs because they are all unique.

Thus, $h(\text{SEPTEMBER}) = d(\text{E}) + (C(\text{E}) \bmod p(\text{P})) = 4 + (156 \bmod 17) = 7$. However, Chang and Lee do not give a method for selecting the pair of letter positions or the general prime number function.

Cercone, Boates, and Krause[23] developed an interactive system that allows the user to specify the set of character positions and whether or not to include the key length in the hashing function. Their algorithm uses a nonbacktracking, intelligent, enumerative search to find the character value assignments. If the user's selection of character positions results in a conflict, the system invites the user to make another selection. The user can also specify the hash table loading factor (1 for a minimal perfect hash, and less than 1 for a nonminimal perfect hash). Their algorithm found minimal perfect hashing functions for sets with up to 64 elements and almost-minimal solutions for sets with up to 500 elements.

Haggard and Karplus[19] generalized Cichelli's hashing function by considering every character position in a key. They search for functions of the form

$$h(w) = \text{length}(w) + g_1(\text{first\_char}(w)) + g_2(\text{second\_char}(w)) + \ldots + g_k(\text{last\_char}(w))$$

where the g_is are called selector functions. Their algorithm finds a set of selector functions that uniquely identify each word, and then uses backtracking heuristics to find the character value assignments for each selector function. They found minimal perfect hashing functions for sets with up to 181 words and nonminimal perfect hashing functions for sets with up to 667 words.

Sager[24] developed a hashing function of the form

$$h(w) = (h_0(w) + g(h_1(w)) + g(h_2(w))) \bmod N$$

where h_0, h_1, and h_2 are pseudorandom functions, g is the function found by Sager's mincycle algorithm, and N is the size of the word set. Cichelli's hashing function is a special case of Sager's hashing function where $h_0(w)$ is the length of w, $h_1(w)$ is the first character in w, $h_2(w)$ is the last character in w, and g is the character-value assignment. Sager gives several pseudorandom functions that "seem to work well," but he does not give a general scheme for choosing the pseudorandom functions. He claims his algorithm is practical for sets with 512 or more words.

These modification schemes seem to be aimed primarily at overcoming the problem of conflicting word pairs. Even though they handle larger sets, they do not represent a general solution for very large sets with several thousand words. In addition, many of the schemes generate perfect but not minimal hashing functions. Hence, these schemes seem limited to minimal perfect hashing functions for sets with 500 words at most.

Segmentation. Segmentation seems more promising as an extension scheme for very large sets. It involves finding one hashing function (grouping function) to partition the large set into buckets (all words with the same hash value are in the same bucket), and then finding an individual (minimal) perfect hash function for each bucket. The grouping function partitions the large set into buckets with at most "maxsize" words, where "maxsize" is the practical limit for the minimal perfect hashing function. Buckets are stored in unique segments (consecutive locations) in the hash table. Thus, the hash function is

$$h(w) = b_i + h_i(w)$$

where i is the grouping hash function value for w, b_i is the base address for bucket i in the hash table, and h_i is the perfect hash function words in bucket i.

We developed a minimal perfect extension of Cichelli's hash function based on Ramakrishna's scheme.[4] Ramakrishna was primarily concerned with finding a perfect hash function for large external files. His hash table (hash file) consisted of m pages, each with a capacity of b records. The hash function maps each record onto a page. A hash function is said to be perfect if no page receives more than b records. The family of hash functions that worked well for Ramakrishna was of the form

$$h(w) = ((c * w + d) \bmod p) \bmod m$$

where c and d are integers, p is a prime number greater than the largest key, and m is the size of a page. He successfully hashed files ranging from 3,000 to 24,000 records. Significantly, he showed it was practical to find a perfect hash function from the family by randomly generating (c,d) integer pairs. Depending on the load factor of the tables, only a small number of (c,d) pairs need be generated to find a perfect hash function. For example, for a load factor lower than 70 percent, the probability of a randomly chosen (c,d) pair yielding a perfect hash function is greater than 0.5.

While Ramakrishna was interested in finding a hash function that partitioned the set of records into pages with b records at most, we were interested in finding a hash function that partitions the set of words into small buckets with 40 words at most, such that no bucket contains a conflicting word pair. We chose the same family of hash functions for the grouping function to compute a word's bucket number, where c, d, and p are the same and m is the number of buckets. Hence our minimal perfect hash function is

$$h(w) = offset(i) +$$
$$value(i, first\_char(w)) +$$
$$value(i, last\_char(w)) +$$
$$length(w)$$

where i is the bucket number computed by the grouping function, length (w) is the number of characters in w, value(n,ch) is the value for character ch in bucket n, and offset(n) is where the segment of words in bucket n begins in the hash table. Thus, the algorithm to locate a word or conclude that it is not present is a simple two-step process: first, compute the bucket number and word length; then, perform a table lookup to find the values of the word's first and last characters and the bucket's offset.

Table 12 gives a perfect minimal hash table constructed via the segmentation scheme for the calendar problem (with three-letter abbreviations). Thus, for SEP, the bucket number is 1. So

$$h(SEP) = offset(1) + value(1,S) +$$
$$value(1,P) + length$$
$$= 0 + 3 + 1 + 3 = 7$$

Ramakrishna[4] found his perfect hash function through a trial-and-error process by fixing p and generating random (c,d) pairs. We wanted a more systematic method. We found that selecting c, d, and

Table 12. Perfect minimal hash table.

Bucket 1 = {JAN, MAR, MAY, JUL, SEP, NOV, DEC}
Bucket 2 = {FEB, APR, JUN, AUG, OCT}

Letter	Bucket 1	Bucket 2	KEY	h(KEY)
A		0	JAN	1
B		2	MAR	5
C	0		MAY	4
D	3		JUL	2
F		0	SEP	7
G		-1	NOV	3
J	0	2	DEC	6
L	-1		FEB	12
M	0		APR	8
N	-2	-1	JUN	11
O		0	AUG	9
P	1		OCT	10
R	2	-2		
S	3			
T		0		
V	2			
Y	1			

	Bucket 1	Bucket 2
Offset	0	7

p from different small sets of prime numbers partitioned the word sets into relatively uniformly sized buckets. A (c, d, p) triple is successful if no bucket contains a conflicting word pair.

Our scheme worked successfully for the 447 Forth words, the 288 Forth assembler words, and sets of 500 and 1,000 random words. However, for the 1,000 most-common and 2,000 random English words, the same exhaustive generation scheme was unsuccessful unless we reduced the bucket size to about 10 because of the skewed distribution of the word lengths and the letters at the ends of the words. We did notice that very few buckets contained word pair conflicts. This suggested modifying our scheme to move the second word of a word pair conflict to a special extra bucket. After this process, none of the original buckets contained word pair conflicts, and only the extra bucket needed to be checked for conflicts. Using the extra bucket decreased the effort and increased the bucket sizes for the solutions to the 1,000 most-common and 2,000 random words. The additional cost for this scheme was slight, since the number of words in the extra table is small relative to the size of the set.

This points out the two major problems with the segmentation approach:

(1) It is difficult to find a general segmentation scheme that partitions the words into buckets such that the words have the required properties for a minimal perfect hash function.

(2) There is no systematic and practical scheme for generating minimal perfect hashing functions. We only considered Cichelli's minimal perfect hashing function. Additional research must consider variations of Cichelli's scheme or other types of minimal perfect hash functions for the buckets.

Choosing a good internal hashing technique depends on many factors. The factors for a dynamic table are the distribution, number, and size of keys, the frequency of retrieval versus insertions and deletions, and the likelihood of overflow.

For a static table, perfect or minimal perfect hashing functions depend on prior knowledge of the size and distribution of the keys and the amount of storage overhead that can be tolerated. Comparison of perfect and especially minimal perfect hashing functions is extremely difficult because the articles describing them provide little information about their performance. Bounds for expected runtime or sparseness of the table are rare. Bounds are especially important for schemes that depend on an exhaustive search or trial-and-error process.

Knowing the range of set sizes for which a scheme is practical is important for segmentation schemes. Minimal perfect hashing performance is reported for a few special sets, such as programming language reserved words and common English words. Perfect and minimal perfect hashing schemes have time-space trade-offs. For example, it is easier to find perfect hashing functions for sparse tables than to find minimal perfect hashing functions. Even when found, integer values computed by a perfect hashing scheme can be huge. This points to the need for empirical studies of perfect and minimal perfect hashing functions to discover their performance characteristics and time-space trade-offs.

Selecting the best hashing technique for an application requires detailed knowledge of the data and operations on the data. We hope this article will serve as a guide. □

10. R. Sprugnoli, "Perfect Hashing Functions: A Single Probe Retrieving Method for Static Sets," *Comm. ACM*, Vol. 20, No. 11, Nov. 1977, pp. 841-850.

11. M.L. Fredman, J. Komlos, and E. Szemeredi, "Storing a Sparse Table with O(1) Worst-Case Access Time," *Proc. 23rd Symp. Foundations of Computer Science*, IEEE Computer Society, 1982, pp. 165-168.

12. G.V. Cormack, R.N.S. Horspool, and M. Kaiserswerth, "Practical Perfect Hashing," *Computer J.*, Vol. 28, No. 1, 1985, pp. 54-58.

13. M.W. Du et al., "The Study of New Perfect Hash Scheme," *IEEE Trans. Software Eng.*, Vol. SE-9, May 1983, pp. 305-313.

14. G. Jaeschke, "Reciprocal Hashing: A Method for Generating Minimal Perfect Hashing Functions," *Comm. ACM*, Vol. 24, No. 12, Dec. 1981, pp. 829-833.

15. C.C. Chang "The Study of an Ordered Minimal Perfect Hashing Scheme," *Comm. ACM*, Vol. 27, No. 4, Apr. 1984, pp. 384-387.

16. R. Cichelli, "Minimal Perfect Hash Functions Made Simple," *Comm. ACM*, Vol. 23, No. 1, Jan. 1980, pp. 17-19.

17. C.R. Cook and R. Oldehoeft, "A Letter-Oriented Minimal Perfect Hashing Function," *ACM SIGPlan Notices*, Vol. 17, No.

9, Sept. 1982, pp. 18-27.

18. R.C. Bell and B. Floyd, "A Monte Carlo Study of Cichelli Hash-Function Solvability," *Comm. ACM*, Vol. 26, No. 11, Nov. 1983, pp. 924-925.

19. G. Haggard and K. Karplus, "Finding Minimal Perfect Hash Functions," *ACM SIGCSE Bull.*, Vol. 18, No. 1, Feb. 1986, pp. 191-193.

20. G. Jaeschke and G. Osterburg, "On Cichelli's Minimal Perfect Hash Functions Method," *Comm. ACM*, Vol. 23, No. 12, Dec. 1980, pp. 728-729.

21. R. Sebesta and M. Taylor, "Fast Identification of Ada and Modula-2 Reserved Words," *J. Pascal, Ada, and Modula-2*, Mar./Apr. 1986, pp. 36-39.

22. C.C. Chang and R.C.T. Lee, "A Letter-Oriented Minimal Perfect Hashing Scheme," *Computer J.*, Vol. 29, No. 3, 1986, pp. 277-281.

23. N. Cercone, J. Boates, and M. Krause, "An Interactive System for Finding Perfect Hash Functions," *IEEE Software*, Vol. 2, No. 6, Nov. 1985, pp. 38-53.

24. T. Sager, "A Polynomial Time Generator for Minimal Perfect Hash Functions," *Comm. ACM*, Vol. 28, No. 5, May 1985, pp. 523-532.

References

1. C.E. Price, "Table Lookup Techniques," *Computing Surveys* Vol. 3, No. 2, June 1971, pp. 49-65.

2. W.D. Maurer and T.G. Lewis, "Hash Table Methods," *Computing Surveys*, Vol. 7, No. 1, Mar. 1975, pp. 5-19.

3. V.Y. Lum, P.S.T. Yuen, and M. Dodd, "Key-to-Address Transformation Techniques: A Fundamental Performance Study on Large Existing Formatted Files," *Comm. ACM*, Vol. 14, No. 4, Apr. 1971, pp. 228-239.

4. M.V. Ramakrishna, "Perfect Hashing for External Files," Technical Report CS-86-25, Computer Science Dept., University of Waterloo, June 1986.

5. D.E. Knuth, *The Art of Computer Programming: Vol. 3*, Addison-Wesley, Reading, Mass., 1973.

6. J.S. Vitter and W. Chen, *Design and Analysis of Coalesced Hashing*, Oxford University Press, New York, 1987.

7. R. Morris, "Scatter Storage Techniques," *Comm. ACM*, Vol. 11, No. 1, Jan. 1968, pp. 38-44.

8. R. Fagan et al., "Extendible Hashing—A Fast-Access Method for Dynamic Files," *ACM Trans. Database Systems*, Vol. 4, No. 3, Sept. 1979, pp. 315-344.

9. P. Larson, "Dynamic Hash Tables," *Comm. ACM*, Vol. 31, No. 4, Apr. 1988, pp. 446-457.

Ted G. Lewis is a professor of computer science at Oregon State University, Corvallis, and editor-in-chief of *IEEE Software*. His interests include software engineering, distributed operating systems, and computer organization and architecture.

Lewis received the BS degree in mathematics from Oregon State University in 1966, and the MS and PhD degrees from Washington State University in 1970 and 1971, respectively.

Curtis R. Cook is a professor of computer science at Oregon State University, Corvallis. His research interests include software complexity metrics, human factors in the programming process, graph theory applications in computer science, and minimal perfect hashing.

Cook received the PhD in computer science from the University of Iowa in 1970. He is a member of the Association for Computing Machinery.

Readers can write to the authors at the Computer Science Dept., Oregon State University, Corvallis, OR 97331.

Hashing for Static Keys

Reprinted from *IEEE Software*, November 1985, pages 38-53.

An Interactive System for Finding Perfect Hash Functions

Nick Cercone, John Boates, and Max Krause
Simon Fraser University

The interactive implementation of this hash function algorithm presents several examples of large lexicon design, illustrating how the minimality criterion and execution efficiency can vary when various problem parameters are adjusted.

Many applications, including natural language understanding systems and programming systems such as compilers and interpreters, use a database of a fixed vocabulary of frequently used words. Advantages accrue when direct random access to items in the database is possible. Perfect hash functions will organize the database so that only a single probe is necessary to retrieve any data item.

Perfect hash functions transform each data item, or key, into a unique hash table address.* For example, if each letter was transformed into the numeric value of its place in the alphabet, and each word was represented by the sum of the numeric values, the word *disk* would be 4+9+19+11=43. The word *cats*, however, would also be hashed to 43 (3+1+20+19=43). The given hash function is not a perfect hash function since it results in a collision where different hash keys are transformed into the same hash table address.

Perfect hash functions are difficult to find because it is difficult to find an assignment of integers that does not cause collisions. Knuth[2] estimates that only one in 10 million functions for mapping the 31 most frequently used English words into 41 addresses will locate each key at a unique address, thus making it a perfect hash function.

Criteria for a good hash function include
- The hash address is easily calculated.
- The loading factor (LF) of the hash table is high for a given set of keys. (The LF is the fraction of used or occupied hash table locations in the total number of hash table locations.)
- The hash addresses of a given set of keys are distributed uniformly in the hash table.

A perfect hash function is optimal with respect to the uniform distribution of hash addresses in the hash table. Adding minimality to the perfect hash function also makes it optimal with respect to the LF.

Sprugnoli[3] used algorithmic methods to produce perfect hash functions of the form

$$H(k_i) = \text{floor}\,[(k_i + A)\,/\,B]$$
$$H(k_i)\,\text{floor}[[(A + k_i \bmod B)\bmod C]/\,D]$$

where k_i is the ith key in the set of N keys and A, B, C, and D are constants. Jaeschke[4] devised reciprocal hashing to generate perfect hash functions of the form

$$H(k_i) = \text{floor}(A/B * k_i + C)\bmod D$$

where k_i is the ith key in the set of N keys and A, B, C, and D are constants. Sprugnoli's and Jaeschke's methods will only produce minimal-perfect hash functions for a limited set of keys. Key sets larger than 15 keys must be partitioned into smaller segments with a perfect hash function computed for each. Both Sprugnoli's and Jaeschke's solutions are machine-dependent, since the number-theoretic properties of the machine character code representa-

---

*The utility of hash functions has been known and the search for good hash functions pursued for more than 20 years. For an excellent survey of hash address encoding techniques (sometimes referred to as scatter storage techniques), see Morris.[1]

EH0330-1/91/0000/0016$01.00 © 1985 IEEE

tions of keys are used to guide the search for appropriate values of the hash functions.

Cichelli[5] developed an algorithm for computing machine-independent, minimal-perfect hash functions of the form

hash value =
    hash key length +
    associated value of the key's
      first letter +
    associated value of the key's last letter

Cichelli's hash function is machine-independent because the character code used by a particular machine never enters into the hash calculation. The algorithm incorporates a two-stage ordering procedure for keys. This effectively reduces the size of the search for associated values, but excessive computation is still required to find hash functions for sets of more than 40 keys. Cichelli's method is also limited, since two keys with the same first and last letters and the same length are not permitted.

Cook and Oldehoeft[6] presented a letter-oriented algorithm that improved Cichelli's word-oriented algorithm. They correctly observed that, after partitioning the data set into word groups, each word group had one associated letter (rarely, two) whose value assignment completely determines the placement of all the words in the group. Thus the critical performance issue is the letter order derived from the word order and not the order of words within a particular letter group. Algorithm CBK[7] incorporates a similar strategy. Cook and Oldehoeft also investigated the possible speedup of their algorithm whenever the minimality criterion was relaxed. They recommended that the minimality restriction be removed for data sets of 50 or fewer keys.

The objective of this research was to develop faster and more general algorithms for finding perfect hash functions of Cichelli's general form. The cost of the combinatorial search for acceptable integer assignments to letters dictates the maximum size of key sets that Cichelli's method can process. We investigated several heuristic search methods to accelerate the

search. Each produced nearly optimal hash tables.

We developed and implemented three algorithms for finding perfect hash functions in Pascal and APL and evaluated them for performance and results.[7] In this article, we describe the perfect hash function search using Cichelli's original algorithm and briefly discuss the minor heuristics we devised to improve Cichelli's algorithm, resulting in our first two algorithms.

We also describe our third algorithm fully, informally comparing its

---

Our third algorithm resulted in an interactive system that allows applications engineers to experiment with several search parameters.

---

performance to other algorithms, and tabulating experimental results to illustrate how the minimality criterion and execution efficiency can vary when various problem parameters are adjusted. The significance we attach to our third algorithm stems from its implementation and its practical extension of the data set size it can comfortably handle.

Our third algorithm resulted in an interactive system that allows applications designers to experiment with several search parameters before selecting the desired perfect hash function for their application.

Developing perfect hash algorithms

The problem of finding faster and more general algorithms derived from the Cichelli method can be divided into three subproblems:

(1) choosing a hash identifier that will uniquely identify members of a data set;

(2) efficiently finding an assignment of integer values to letters that will map keys into the hash table without collisions; and

(3) finding ways of enforcing or attaining a reasonable degree of the minimality of the solution.

Choosing a hash identifier. Optimally, a hash identifier uniquely identifies each key so that each may be placed in a unique hash table location. The properties of keys that could be used in a hash identifier include the symbols comprising the key, their position of occurrence in the key, and the key length.

The number of keys that can be distinguished is exactly the number of keys in the data set when the occurrence of the same symbol is treated differently in different positions of hash keys. (Examples are the first and second *e* in *keeps* and the different *s*'s in the keys *disk* and *cats*). Including a consideration for letter (symbol) position in the hash identifier improves its representational power. There is no key that cannot be uniquely represented by such a hash identifier.

Assigning associated letter values. Once a hash identifier has been defined, an efficient search must be organized to find an assignment of integer values to the letters that will map the keys into the hash table with no collisions.

A series of integer values must be chosen for assignment to the letters of the keys. An easily generated integer series that guarantees distinct sums would have advantages, but assignment of such values tends to decrease the hash table loading factor. An integer series that grows slowly and produces distinct addresses would map the keys into a compact address space. Since no naturally occurring integer series investigated (including powers-of-two and Fibanocci series) satisfies the requirements for assignment values, we developed procedures to seek an acceptable assignment of values.

For example, in a search tree with three keys ($N=3$), two letter positions in the hash identifier ($S=2$), and a maximum associated value of two ($M=[0,1,2]$, cardinality (M)$=m=3$), the number of different assignments of integers to letters is m^s, the number of leaf nodes in the tree (see Figure 1).

The number of integer values tested as an acceptable integer assignment during the search, m, is the branching factor of the tree. It controls the extent of the search and whether or not a solution is possible. Procedures used to determine the upper bound of the search variable include having the user decide an upper bound, the algorithm decide an upper bound, and having no upper bound placed on the search variable.

An efficient search will lead to an acceptable assignment of associated values that generates as little as possible of the search tree. We have tried both backtracking and nonbacktracking search methods to find an acceptable assignment of integer values to letters in keys.

A nonbacktrack search is preferable if the integer assignment made at any stage of the search is certain not to ultimately cause collisions. During the backtrack search, the validity of all partial solutions is tested against the search predicate. If a partial solution $<x_1, x_2, \ldots, x_i>$, $0<i<N+1$, fails to satisfy the predicate, the subtree under investigation at this stage can be pruned. This pruning process, called preclusion, avoids generating full and partial solutions that have $<x_1, x_2, \ldots, x_i>$ as an initial segment.

Preclusion is most effective when failure to satisfy the search predicate is discovered at a minimum tree depth. Fortunately, the frequency with which the letter a_i occurs is an excellent heuristic to predict how likely it is that a_i will occur in a key that may collide with other keys. The sum (or product) of letter occurrences for one key is likewise an excellent predictor of how likely it is that a key will collide with other keys.

An ideal heuristic ordering strategy for the letters would order the letters by frequency in nonincreasing order, so that a_1 would have the highest frequency of occurrence and a_s would have the lowest, where s is the depth of the search tree. This arrangement tends to occur when the keys are first ordered by sum of letter frequencies. Then, for each key whose letter has not yet occurred, the keys are chosen in decreasing order of their frequency of occurrence.

Ordering the keys by sum of letter frequencies does not, in general, produce a strict ordering of letters.

However, ordering the keys by sum of letter frequencies does not, in general, produce a strict ordering of letters to be assigned values, so, in the interval between when an integer is assigned to a letter and when the hash address is tested, other hash addresses may have been added to the table. When collisions do occur, the program may have to back up and find new addresses for several keys.

For example, the set of keys $K = \{aa, ab, ac, ad, ae, af, ag, bd, cd, ce, de, fg\}$ after first ordering yields $\{aa, ad, ac, ae, ab, af, ag, cd, de, bd, ce, fg\}$. The letter frequencies for K can be ordered into decreasing frequency of occurrence as $<a, d, c, e, b, f, g>$. Although the key cd is determined as

soon as key ac is placed in the hash table, the placement of cd is not tested until four intervening keys (ae, ab, af, ag) have been assigned hash addresses.

Therefore, a key is sought that has at least one unique letter occurrence, since only such a letter will come last in the ordering and still place a single key in the hash table. As a consequence, because we need to place letters that have a unique occurrence at the end of the ordering of letters, the optimal ordering of letters will have all the keys containing a unique letter occurrence at the end of the key ordering.

After the keys are ordered by the sum of the chosen letter frequencies, a second ordering is performed. This second ordering arranges the yet-to-be-determined keys in the data set depending on the partial assignment of integers to letters to this point. Essentially, the keys are reordered from the beginning of the list so, if a key has first and last letters that appeared previously in the list, that key is placed next in the list. Cichelli[5] reports that this step is crucial to the performance of his algorithm, as we shall see.

This reordering process, and ultimately the ordering of all letters that occur in chosen positions (first and last positions for Cichelli), can be modified so that each sublist of words with equal frequency counts can be ordered so that the words with the greatest second-ordering effect will occur first.

Ordering procedures were used that arranged the keys by sum of letter frequencies, then reordered the keys so any key whose hash value is determined by assigning the associated letter values (already determined by previous keys) is placed next. In our earlier example, the key cd would be placed next—after c is assigned a value—so that it would follow the key ac.

The ordering procedures were further refined to include ordering by product frequencies, key grouping, and unique letter appearance within key groups. These procedures are em-

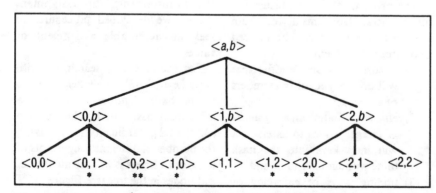

Figure 1. Data set = $\{aa, ab, bb\}$, letters are ordered $\{a,b\}$. Minimal solutions are marked *, nonminimal solutions are marked **.

bodied in algorithm CBK, the details of which are explained later.

Insuring minimality of hash tables. Various methods were used to ensure a minimum loading factor of 0.8.* One heuristic assigns the smallest associated values to those letters that occur most frequently in chosen letter positions, promoting small hash addresses for many keys. All hash addresses fall within the range [least ... least + $(N/0.8)$].

When backtrack search is used to assign associated values, as in Cichelli's algorithm, an LF of at least L can be achieved by simply limiting the size of the hash table to $r = \cdot N/L$, where N is the number of keys. The search procedure will then be forced to backtrack when it encounters any combination of letter values $(x_1, x_2, \ldots, x_i)$ such that for some k_j in K: $H(k_j) > N/L$. All values smaller than x_i in the domain of a_i have been excluded, and any larger values of x_i will surely make $H(k_j)$ greater than N/L.

When backtracking is not used in the search, as in some of the algorithms reported in Cercone et al.,[7] the LF is maximized by careful ordering of search variables and selection and testing of assigned integer values. Although nonbacktracking algorithms produce solutions quickly, the LF tends to diminish as the number of keys increases.

The interactive system reported in this article uses backtracking whenever the hash table becomes too sparsely populated with keys (as determined by the user).

The Cichelli algorithm

Cichelli's perfect hash algorithm uses key length and the first and last letters (without regard to letter position) as the hash identifier. The number of keys that can be distinguished is restricted to $\omega * \Phi(\sigma, 2)$ where ω is the maximum key length, Φ is the familiar choose function, and σ is the cardinality of the symbol alphabet.

*We chose 0.8, rather arbitrarily, as the minimal acceptable LF for our application. The interactive system allows the LF to be set by the user.

Integer assignment values are found using a simple backtracking process. Cichelli proposes no method of choosing a value of m, the size of the domain of associated letter values. This problem is an important parameter since m is the branching factor of the backtrack search tree.

Cichelli uses the two-step ordering heuristic that first arranges the keys in decreasing order of the sum of the first and last letters' frequencies of occurrence. This ordering simply sorts the

---

Cichelli uses the two-step ordering heuristic that first arranges the keys in decreasing order of the sum of the first and last letters' frequencies of occurrence.

---

letters so letters that occur most frequently are assigned integer values first.

During the second step of the ordering, any key whose hash value has already been determined, because both its first and last letters have occurred in keys previous to the current one, is placed next in the list. This double ordering strategy arranges the static set of keys in such a way that hash value collisions will occur and be resolved as early as possible during the backtracking process. Cichelli's algorithm performs the following steps:

(1) [COMPUTE] – Obtain a frequency count of the first and last letters of all keys in the data set.
(2) [SORT] – Order the keys by decreasing sum of frequencies of occurrence of first and last letters.
(3) [REORDER] – Reorder the keys from the beginning of the list so, if a key has first and last letters that appeared previously in the list, that key is placed next in the list.
(4) [SEARCH] – If both critical letters for the current word have been assigned values, TRY to place it in the hash table. If one letter is still unassigned, loop its value from 0 to the maximum value and TRY a placement. If both letters are still unassigned, use two nested loops to assign the letter values and TRY possible placements. Quit if failure.

(5) [TRY] – Given the key, its length, and two letter values, compute its hash table address. Return to SEARCH if there is a collision, otherwise place the word in the hash table. If this was the last word, stop; otherwise SEARCH with the next word on the list.

The CBK perfect hash algorithm

Cook and Oldehoeft[6] and Cercone et al.[7] made successive refinements to Cichelli's algorithm. Several refinements led to the interactive system based on algorithm CBK. One refinement in an earlier algorithm partitioned the original data set into subsets according to the key length and calculated perfect hash functions for each subset, combining the results into one resultant hash table.

The complexity of each subproblem is at least linearly and often exponentially smaller than that of the overall problem, while the increase in the number of problem sets is linear, resulting in a marked reduction in computation. Those letter positions chosen to identify each subset are recorded in a vector of Boolean values and a table is constructed that associates an integer value with each letter that occurs in a chosen position. An offset for each subset is maintained that keeps the subsets' hash addresses separate from those of any of the other hash functions, so the subset of hash functions can be fitted into a single hash table.

Another refinement was our implementation of a procedure that automatically chose, for each set of keys of the same length, the smallest set of letter positions that distinguished each key without regard for when letters occurred within a key. This preprocessing, which made the choice of letter positions, included generation of trial combinations of one position, then two positions, up to P positions, where P is the length of the longest key. When each trial combination was generated, it was tested for its ability to discriminate members of the key set.

Another refinement was to choose an upper bound for each search variable from a naturally occurring integer series that has no pairwise sums among its elements. The upper bound is a solution, though not necessarily the best solution overall, and all associated values with lower potential are tested in hopes of finding a better assignment of integer values.

This method of assigning integer values avoids all backtracking, yielding a rapid search algorithm. This method never needs to undo partial results, but the LF diminishes rapidly for data sets with more than 60 keys. This search procedure relies entirely on the good effects of ordering search variables to achieve a compact solution.

The interactive system based on the CBK algorithm incorporates a further refinement of the nonbacktracking intelligent enumerative search just described. We have implemented an improved version of the search that performs a limited amount of backtracking when a solution has an unacceptable LF (supplied by the user). Our experimental results suggest that this refinement allows minimal-perfect hash tables to be constructed for data sets of about 200 keys and acceptable, almost-minimal-perfect hash tables to be constructed for data sets of more than 200 keys.

By analyzing the occurrence of letters shared among the keys, algorithm CBK eliminates many doomed choices of associated values, streamlining the search process. Cook and Oldehoeft[6] made essentially the same observation when they proposed a letter-oriented perfect hash algorithm.

In the interactive system, the user specifies a set of letter positions and whether or not to include the key length in the hash identifier. The program then tests the user's selection for key discrimination, inviting the user to try again if any two keys cannot be distinguished. The system takes into account the position of occurrence of letters and therefore has the greatest possible discriminatory power of the three algorithms we developed. Any set of distinct lexical keys can be distinguished by this system. Because of the limited backtracking, no upper bound is placed on the size of associated letter values.

The CBK algorithm performs the following steps:

(1) [USER INTERACTION] – The user is prompted to supply two specifications: the set of letter positions used in the hashing and whether or not the key length is a part of the hash function.
(2) [DISTINGUISH] – If any two words cannot be distinguished with the hash function as specified by the user, then report conflicting keys and return to USER INTERACTION; if the hash function is acceptable, then continue with COMPUTE.
(3) [COMPUTE] – Count the number of occurrences of each letter in each position, then subtract one from each sum. For each key, assign a value that is the product of the occurrence counts for the selected letters in this key. Those keys whose assigned values are zero must have at least one unique occurrence of a letter in some chosen position. Place these keys at the head of a list of keys with unique occurrences. Repeat COMPUTE for the nonzero keys until no more keys with unique letter occurrences are found. Keys selected in this process will follow all keys with no unique letter occurrences in the final ordering.
(4) [ORDER] – Order the remaining keys, those with no unique letter occurrences, by decreasing product of their letter frequency counts.
(5) [GROUP] – Form a group by first choosing the key nearest the head of the list that has the fewest letters with no assigned value (new letters); find all the keys whose hash addresses will be determined when the chosen key's new letters are assigned integer values. Repeat GROUP until all keys have been chosen.
(6) [SORT] – Order the keys within each group so that for any two keys k_i and k_j, if we calculate the set differences between the letters from chosen positions in each key [$D_{ij} := L(k_i) - (k_j)$; $D_{ji} := L(k_j) - L(k_i)$, where $L(k_m)$ is the set of letters in chosen positions for k_m], then if k_i precedes k_j in the ordering, all letters in D_{ij} will be assigned values before the last letter in D_{ji} is assigned a value.
(7) [DETERMINE] – For each key, determine which of its chosen letters will be the last to be assigned a value in the search. This letter's value can be manipulated to place the key into an open hash address. When length is the only difference between neighboring keys, the distance back to a key which differs in letters is noted.
(8) [PRECLUDE] – Taking these noted letters in order, we determine for the next letter which of its possible values are precluded by conflict with the hash addresses assigned to previous keys.
(9) [TRY] – Assign letter values. If a single key is being placed, its determining letter value is just the one that places it in the lowest possible open hash address. If the key is part of a group whose hash addresses are determined by assigning the current key's hash address, then we must choose the smallest possible value that maps all the keys into open hash addresses.
(10) [CHECK-LF] – The LF of the partial solution at this point is calculated; if it is acceptable, continue with PRECLUDE. If the LF is too small and the number of allowable backtracks is not exceeded, then proceed to PLACE.
(11) [PLACE] – For the latest group added to the table, determine which keys have the highest and lowest hash addresses; call them k_{max} and k_{min}. Choose a letter from k_{min}, say a_i, that does not affect the hash address of k_{max} and increment the associated value of a_i by one. Reset to zero the associated values of all letters assigned after a_i to zero. Remove from the table all keys that were placed after the value of a_i was assigned, and adjust the sum of assigned letter values for each affected key. Place these keys at the head of the list of keys that have not yet been assigned a hash address. Adjust the order of letters that determine the hash addresses of groups of keys and return to PRECLUDE.

The first two steps handle the user interaction for this perfect hash function system. Until the user specifies an acceptable specification for letter positions (with help from the system), he is unable to continue the search for a perfect hash function.

The third and fourth steps of the CBK algorithm essentially perform the first two steps of Cichelli's algorithm. Completion of step 3 results in two disjoint sets of keys, U and W. The set U contains those keys with unique letter occurrences and W contains those with no such unique letters. In step 4, the W' members of W are sorted in nonincreasing order of their values of t (the product of letter frequencies) so the keys with the highest frequency letters will occur early in the final ordering.

Steps 5, 6, and 7 taken together perform Cichelli's second ordering (Cichelli's step 3). These three steps move keys from W to a new ordering, Y, which, with U appended, forms the final ordering of the keys. In step 5 we choose the next key in the ordering, mark its new letters as used, and finally scan the remaining keys for those whose hash addresses will be newly determined by the choice of values for the chosen key's new letters. These keys are deleted from the old ordering and placed in the new ordering Y as a group. This step is repeated until W is empty.

Step 6 orders the keys within each group so that, when assignments of integers to selected letters are attempted later, collisions can be resolved by adjusting the keys in at most two groups.

The task of step 7 is to find, for each key, in what order the letters that were previously used have their associated values assigned. If the key k_i contains one new letter a_j, then that letter will necessarily be the last of the letters in k_i to be assigned an integer value.

When the key contains more than one new letter, we must choose an order in which they will be assigned values. This step provides us with a strict ordering of the search variables, the letters, as suggested by Cook and Oldehoeft.[6] With each letter a_i, a certain number of keys are associated; for these keys, a_i is the last variable to receive a value when a perfect hash function is being calculated.

In step 8 we analyze the way keys from the current group share letters and the constraints this puts on the choice of associated values. We do not completely analyze the entire set of keys, only a group, because of the preprocessing cost. Consequently, a certain amount of computation may

be undone later. When a possible collision is detected, we choose to alter the associated value of a_k, the letter most recently assigned a value, to leave as much of the partial solution intact as possible.

When we alter this value, we must regroup all keys that have been placed in the hash table since a_k was assigned a value; these groups are placed at the head of the queue of groups waiting to

---

For each letter, information about relationships between letter values must be preserved to preclude choices of associated values that lead to hash value collisions.

---

be mapped into hash addresses. A new value is assigned to a_k, and the search continues. The procedure described here is a specialized sort of backtracking.

Consider a small example at this point. Suppose we have a group of keys whose letters from chosen positions are *rig, fig, fog*, where g is the last unused key for this group and the letters are assigned associated values in the relative order r, f, i, o, g. This assignment agrees with the ordering of the letter combinations above. Some reflection should convince us that before we come to consider a value for g, we must see that none of the partial sums of associated values for the subsets of letters *ri, fi, fo* create collisions.

If any pair of these subsets has equal sums of associated values, then a hash address conflict is inevitable if the three keys have the same length, no matter what value we assign to the letter g. We must therefore look ahead and be certain that, when the letter f is assigned a value, r and f do not have

the same associated value (*rig* and *fig* would otherwise be indistinguishable).

When an assignment is made to o, we must make it different from the value of i to avoid a conflict between *fig* and *fog*. For each letter, information about relationships between letter values must be preserved to preclude choices of associated values that lead to hash value collisions.

We must test for this conflict condition. The question is whether it is done before associated values are assigned or dynamically during the search process. In either case, only keys that follow each key k_i need be examined for this condition, since k_i will have been compared with each key that precedes it in the ordering if the process is done from the first key in the list.

The common characteristic of keys within a group is that the same letter, say a_i, is the last of the letters in chosen positions from these keys to be assigned a value. Step 8 records information that ensures the contributions of the other terms of the hash function are different for each key within a group.

In step 9, we actually choose the least value for letter a_i that will map all d_i members of G_i (the group) into open hash table locations. This step is essentially a kind of pattern matching. In step 8, we recorded the relative values of the partial sums for the keys in each group. The aim is to find the first arrangement of open hash addresses in the table that fits the relative hash values of the keys in the current group.

Consider the set of hash identifiers *abc, adc, abe*, which have the common letter a. Suppose that the current state of the solution is that shown in Figure 2. If $H(a) = 0$, then $H(adc) = 7$; but

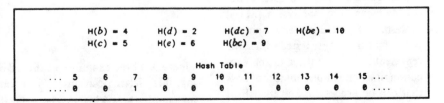

Figure 2. Supposed current solution state in step 9 of the CBK algorithm.

21

that hash address is taken by some previously placed key. If $H(a) = 1$, then $H(abe) = 11$, which is likewise taken. The value 2 is also excluded for a, so 3 is the least value that can be assigned to a that places all three keys in open hash table locations.

When considering a value for a in this example, if we are going to place abc at $H(abc) = x$, then we know from the above relations between the partial hash values for the keys in a's group that we must also find open addresses at $x+2$ and $x+3$ to place all three keys. If X represents a don't-care condition, then our problem is to match the pattern $00X0$ against the array of Boolean values representing the taken property for each hash table location.

Steps 10 and 11 perform final checks to see whether the perfect hash function computed is within the minimal LF set by the user and places the hash keys in the hash table. If for some reason the keys cannot be placed successfully or if the LF is unacceptable, the algorithm backtracks to step 8.

Figure 3 illustrates the CBK algorithm with three examples during a terminal session with the interactive system. The first example shows the results of applying this algorithm to the combined data set consisting of the 76 Pascal reserved words and the Pascal keywords. The two final examples duplicate Cichelli's results for the 12 month abbreviations data set and the 36 Pascal keywords data set, but with much faster computation times.

Comparing performance of perfect hash functions

Cichelli's algorithm was implemented as a Pascal program (Pascal/UBC); the interactive system was written in APL. All programs were run on an IBM 4341 computer under the Michigan Terminal System (MTS) time-sharing operating environment. Both algorithms were tested with some representative key sets, and the execution time, maximum number of keys that can be processed, and the LF of the resulting hash tables were compared.

```
# RUN *APL PAR=D
>   .v3.0  vsapl/aplfs
# EXECUTION BEGINS  00:38:45
>   clear ws
>   wssize  is  46172
> )LOAD  PERFECT  300000
>   saved  12:59:00   06/26/82
>   wssize  is  300124·
>
> HASH                           {preorders data for associated value calculation}
>   WORDS TO BE HASHED: ab        { ab is a variable containing the Pascal IDs }
>   LETTERS TO BE USED: 1 2 4      { for assignment of associated values }
>   IS BLANK TO BE A CHARACTER (Y/N): N { or use last letter of word if approp}
>   IS LENGTH TO BE PART OF FUNCTION (Y/N): Y
>   ORDER BY PRODUCT OR MINIMUM (P/M): P  { product of letter frequencies or
>   CPU SECONDS USED IN HASH IS 1.707              like Cichelli's }
>   THE DATA IN CORRECTED PREORDER FORM:
>
>      round eoln downto do record reset repeat read readln rewrite real for to
>      text set trunc true pred page case ord or write writeln arctan put false
>      cos const not procedure function succ file sin nil then chr char while
>      goto get end and in integer mod eof label in boolean sqr sqrt pack packed
>      maxint begin array until unpack output dispose of it abs div exp new odd
>      var else type with input program otherwise
>
> BASH                           {invoking the second-ordering part}
>   LOADING FACTOR 0.5 TO 1 RANGE:  1
>   NUMBER OF ALLOWABLE BACKTRACKS:  10
>   BASHING STARTED AT  1982 7 12 14 12 52 470
>   TIME DURATION WAS 0 0 0 0 11 914
>   CPU SECONDS USED IN BASH IS  1.551
>   NUMBER OF TIMES THROUGH BASH MAIN LOOP IS  78
>
>   TERMINATION AFTER BACKTRACK 3
>   LETTERS USED 1 2 4
>   OFFSET USED 0
>
>   LETTER VALUES
>   'A'   3  13  35     'I'   8  21  16     'R'   0  11   3
>   'B'  35  29   0     'K'   0   0  36     'S'   3   0  25
>   'C'   2   0  13     'L'  29  64   8     'T'   1  60   9
>   'D'   0  54   5     'M'  38   0   0     'U'   4  11  30
>   'E'   0   1   2     'N'  12  31   0     'V'  50   0  37
>   'F'   8  12  44     'O'   6   0   0     'W'   0   0  51
>   'G'  32   0  57     'P'   0   0  35     'X'   0  27   0
>   'H'   0  29  46     'Q'   0  43   0     'Y'   0  64   0
>
>   HASH TABLE
>    2 DO           3 TO          4 EOLN       5 ROUND      6 DOWNTO    7 RECORD
>    8 RESET        9 REPEAT     10 READ      11 REWRITE   12 READLN   13. REAL
>   14 FOR         15 TEXT       16 SET       17 TRUNC     18 TRUE     19 PAGE
>   20 PRED        21 CASE       22 OR        23 PUT       24 NOT      25 ORD
>   26 WRITE       27 SIN        28 WRITELN   29 ARCTAN    30 COS      31 SUCC
>   32 CONST       33 PROCEDURE  34 THEN      35 FILE      36 GOTO     37 CHR
>   38 CHAR        39 END        40 FUNCTION  41 IN        42 AND      43 WHILE
>   44 NIL         45 GET        46 MOD       47 EOF       48 INTEGER  49 LABEL
>   50 BOOLEAN     51 FALSE      52 SQR       53 PACK      54 ARRAY    55 PACKED
>   56 UNTIL       57 BEGIN      58 OUTPUT    59 SORT      60 ABS      61 DIV
>   62 LN          63 DISPOSE    64 OF        65 EXP       66 IF       67 NEW
>   68 ODD         69 VAR        70 ELSE      71 TYPE      72 WITH     73 MAXINT
>   74 INPUT       75 PROGRAM    76 UNPACK    77 OTHERWISE
```

(a)

Figure 3. Three examples of the CBK algorithm: (a) minimal, backtracking, three letter positions—76 Pascal keywords and identifiers; (b) minimal, nonbacktracking, two letter positions—12 month names; (c) minimal, nonbacktracking, two letter positions—36 Pascal keys.

```
> HASH
>   WORDS TO BE HASHED:  'JAN FEB MAR APR MAY JUN JUL AUG SEP OCT NOV DEC'
>   LETTERS TO BE USED:  2  3
>   IS BLANK TO BE A CHARACTER (Y/N):  N
>   IS LENGTH TO BE PART OF FUNCTION (Y/N):  N
>   ORDER BY PRODUCT OR MINIMUM (P/M):  P
>   CPU SECONDS USED IN HASH IS 0.554
>   THE DATA IN CORRECTED PREORDER FORM:
>
>   jan mar jun may oct feb dec sep nov apr aug jul
>
> BASH
>   LOADING FACTOR 0.5 TO 1 RANGE:  1
>   NUMBER OF ALLOWABLE BACKTRACKS:  0
>   BASHING STARTED AT  1982 7 9 16 16 43 36
>   TIME DURATION WAS 0 0 0 0 0 457
>   CPU SECONDS USED IN BASH IS  0.224
>   NUMBER OF TIMES THROUGH BASH MAIN LOOP IS  16
>
>   TERMINATION AFTER BACKTRACK 0
>   LETTERS USED 2 3
>   OFFSET USED 1
>
>   LETTER VALUES
>    'A'  0  0      'G'  0  8      'P'  8  7      'V'  0  8
>    'B'  0  5      'L'  0  9      'R'  0  1      'Y'  0  3
>    'C'  0  6      'N'  0  0      'T'  0  4
>    'E'  0  0      'O'  0  0      'U'  2  0
>
>   HASH TABLE
>    1 JAN      2 MAR      3 JUN      4 MAY      5 OCT      6 FEB
>    7 DEC      8 SEP      9 NOV     10 APR     11 AUG     12 JUL
>
(b)
```

```
> HASH
>   WORDS TO BE HASHED:  pascalkeys
>   LETTERS TO BE USED:  1  L
>   IS BLANK TO BE A CHARACTER (Y/N):  N
>   IS LENGTH TO BE PART OF FUNCTION (Y/N):  Y
>   ORDER BY PRODUCT OR MINIMUM (P/M):  M
>   CPU SECONDS USED IN HASH IS 0.83
>   THE DATA IN CORRECTED PREORDER FORM:
>
>   to type file then function otherwise do downto in of if for or case else end
>   const procedure packed record repeat not and nil while div mod set var goto
>   with array begin label until program
>
> BASH
>   LOADING FACTOR 0.5 TO 1 RANGE:  1
>   NUMBER OF ALLOWABLE BACKTRACKS:  0
>   BASHING STARTED AT  1982 7 22 12 50 7 138
>   TIME DURATION WAS 0 0 0 0 1 745
>   CPU SECONDS USED IN BASH IS  0.517
>   NUMBER OF TIMES THROUGH BASH MAIN LOOP IS  31
>
>   TERMINATION AFTER BACKTRACK 0
>   LETTERS USED 1 L
>   OFFSET USED 0
>
>   LETTER VALUES
>    'A' 18  0      'F'  1  8      'M' 23 19      'S' 21  0
>    'B' 27  0      'G' 27  0      'N' 14  2      'T'  0  5
>    'C'  8  0      'H'  0  7      'O'  0  0      'U' 23  0
>    'D'  1  2      'I'  4  0      'P' 11  0      'V' 16 23
>    'E' 12  0      'L' 22  8      'R' 13 11      'W' 21  6
>                                                'Y'  0 10
>
>   HASH TABLE
>     2 TC       3 DO       4 TYPE     5 FILE     6 THEM     7 DOWNTO
>     8 IN       9 OTHERWISE 10 OF    11 FUNCTION 12 CASE   13 OR
>    14 IF      15 FOR      16 ELSE   17 END      18 CONST  19 PACKED
>    20 PROCEDURE 21 RECORD 22 NOT   23 AND      24 REPEAT 25 NIL
>    26 WHILE   27 DIV      28 MOD    29 SET      30 VAR    31 GOTO
>    32 WITH    33 ARRAY    34 BEGIN  35 LABEL    36 UNTIL  37 PROGRAM
>
(c)
```

Timing comparisons were gathered via MTS system subroutines that return CPU time in milliseconds. Time-sharing overhead, such as swapping, has been excluded from time totals so that the reported time is the time actually taken to execute the algorithms.

Analytic comparison of the relative performance of backtracking algorithms is difficult, according to Knuth.[8] The number of basic operations of the algorithm and the memory requirements should be considered in algorithm expense. Krause[9] estimates the number of times basic operations are performed by these algorithms.*

Execution time for Cichelli's algorithm rose rapidly with increasing key set size; no results were returned within two hours for key sets larger than 64 (see Table 1).

It is difficult to make direct comparison between the CBK algorithm and the algorithm of Cook and Oldehoeft since we did not implement their algorithm. Their algorithm performed from twice as slow to 10 times as fast. (The most common has key set consisted of 31 English words, 34 ASCII control codes, 40 Pascal reserved words [they used 39 since *odd* conflicted with *ord* in their algorithm], and 36 Pascal reserved words.)

Nevertheless, these results are inconclusive since Cook and Oldehoeft wrote their programs in Pascal running under the NOS 1.4 operating system on a CDC Cyber 720 computer system while we used an IBM 4341 super-minicomputer. The largest hash table they reported was for the 105 PL/I keywords and their abbreviations represented in four partitions to avoid collisions among the identifiers. The CBK algorithm need not resort to Cook-and-Oldehoeft-style partitions until the key sets reach more than 200 keys.

---

*Krause also defines the effective loading factor (ELF) of a perfect hash function as ELF $N = (r+t)$ where r is the range of calculated hash addresses and t is the number of associated letter values stored. ELF is a realistic measure of the amount of memory needed for implementing each algorithm since associated value tables are an essential part of each algorithm and they differ in each algorithm.

Table 1.
Times (T) and loading factors (LF) for some representative key sets.

Hash Key Set	Cichelli's Algorithm		CBK Algorithm	
31 Most Frequent English Words	T=290	LF=0.97	T=1763	LF=1.0
33 Basic Keywords	N/A		T=0.669	LF=1.0
34 ASCII Control Codes	T=1833	LF=1.0	T=1993	LF=1.0
36 Pascal Reserved Words	T=579	LF=1.0	T=2609	LF=1.0
40 Pascal Predefined IDs	T=360641	LF=1.0	T=3060	LF=1.0
42 Algol-W Reserved Words	N/A		T=0.616	LF=1.0
64 Most Frequent English Words	T>>1 hour		T=2933	LF=1.0
76 Pascal Reserved + Predefined Ids	no results		T=3414	LF=0.98
100 Most Frequent English Words	no results		T=5190	LF=0.96
200 Most Frequent English Words	no results		T=8986	LF=0.70
500 Most Frequent English Words	no results		T=33505	LF=0.61

NOTE: Times [T] are given in milliseconds

Table 2.
Table of relative utility (U=N∗LF/T).

N	Cichelli's	CBK Algorithm
31	103.69	70.62
33	N/A	49.33
34	0.04	59.96
36	61.22	60.50
39	1.14	N/A
40	N/A	56.02
42	N/A	68.18
44	N/A	53.04
64	N/A	59.73
76	N/A	62.97
100	N/A	66.10
200	N/A	42.25
500	N/A	20.82

The CBK algorithm found minimal-perfect hash functions for key sets of $N \leq 64$ and returned almost minimal solutions for $N \geq 500$ (see Table 1). (An alternative algorithm we developed earlier returned minimal-perfect hash functions for key sets of up to 200 keys but performed poorly beyond that point.[7])

Utility (U) is proposed as a further measure of relative performance: $U = N * LF/T$, where N represents the number of keys to be hashed, LF is the loading factor, and T is the search time in milliseconds. Larger values of U imply a greater degree of utility. Though an arbitrary measure, utility does reward compact solutions to large problem sets and penalizes algorithms using excessive execution time.

Table 2 presents the relative utility of the two algorithms. Cichelli's algorithm produces spectacular utilities for key sets up to about 36 keys. Cercone et al.[7] have found that when the sizes of the subsets produced by partitioning reach around 50 keys; however, these values decline rapidly. The utility of the CBK algorithm remained relatively constant for all key sets hashed.

To summarize, the two major problems with Cichelli's algorithm are (1) that the LFs of the solutions produced degenerate quickly for key sets of more than 50 keys and (2) that the mechanism used for distinguishing keys is not adequate for many problem sets.

Our refinements led to the development of the substantially different CBK algorithm and addressed these problems directly with moderate success with respect to problem 1 and total success with problem 2. The CBK algorithm outperforms Cichelli's (and others reported to date[3,4,6,9]) and shows great promise for further development. This algorithm does require additional storage to maintain separate associated value tables for each letter position selected.

Some experimental results

Tables 1 and 2 make explicit comparisons between Cichelli's original algorithm and our CBK algorithm. In

Table 3.
Product vs. minimum initial ordering of keys.

Parameters -> Sample data set	Product or Minimum	CPU time (seconds)	Backtracking employed	Perfect Minimum Solution	Letters Used in associated value calcs.
36 Pascal	Product	1.344	No	Yes	first, last
Reserved Words	Minimum	1.357	No	Yes	
39 Pascal	Product	1.321	No	Yes	
Identifiers	Minimum	1.344	No	Yes	
75 Pascal	Product	3.565	No	No	first,
Reserved Words	Minimum	2.430	No	No	second,
+ Predefined	Product	3.244	Yes	Yes	last
Identifiers	Minimum	5.411	Yes	Yes	
31 Most Freq	Product	1.197	No	Yes	first, last
English Words	Minimum	1.232	No	Yes	
40 Most Freq.	Product	1.228	No	Yes	
English Words	Minimum	1.516	No	Yes	
64 Most Freq.	Product	1.670	No	Yes	
English Words	Minimum	5.779	No	Yes	
100 Most Freq.	Product	5.332	No	Yes	first, second,
English Words	Minimum	67.243	No	No	third, fourth
	Minimum	12.783	Yes	Yes	
12 Month	Product	0.847	No	Yes	second, third
Abbreviations	Minimum	0.693	No	Yes	

NOTE: For the tests of all data sets the key length was considered in the hash algorithm; also blank was not considered as a character, keys "wrapped around" (e.g., the 5th character of the key "disk" is "d" as in "diskdisk" this section we present the results of varying several parameters built into the CBK interactive system when the algorithm is tested with different sample key sets.

Table 3 illustrates the effect of using a product of letter frequencies initial ordering (steps 3 and 4 in the CBK algorithm) versus a minimum-letter-frequency initial ordering (as in Cichelli's approach). The product ordering appears to fare slightly better as the sample key set size is increased. Backtracking is necessary to ensure minimal solution in some cases.

The effects of choosing different letter positions for the associated value calculations is demonstrated for several key sets, including the 75 Pascal reserved words plus predefined identifiers and the first and second 100 most frequently used English words. Note that the interactive system immediately ruled out the choice of letters that would not permit conflicts to be avoided. For example, if *beat* and *boat* were in the key set and the chosen letters were 1 and 4, a conflict would arise. Table 4 illustrates these results.

It is apparent from Table 4 that backtracking, which can be controlled with the interactive system, affects both the CPU time to calculate the perfect hash function and the minimality of the resultant hash table. Table 4 also validates the observation that backtracking in this system is no guarantee that the minimality of the resultant hash table will increase.

The final experiment we wish to report is summarized in Table 5. In this case, we generated some non-minimal hash tables using the interactive system for the 500 most frequently used English words.

Applying perfect hash functions

Natural language lexicon design. Retrieval methods usually assume equal likelihood of retrieval for each data item.[2] Cichelli[5] pointed out the utility of perfect hash functions for use in compilers. The literature of lexicography[10] documents that this as-

Table 4.
Effect of choosing different letter positions for associated value computations.

Parameters -> Sample Data Set	Blank a Char	Use Key Length	Product or Minimum	CPU time seconds	Back-tracking employed (Number)	Perfect Minimal Solution	LF	Letters Used in associated value calcs.
75 Pascal	No	Yes	Product	2.709	No(0)	No	.89	1, 2, 4
Reserved	No	Yes	Product	3.258	Yes(3)	Yes	1.0	
Words plus	No	Yes	Minimum	2.537	No(0)	No	.99	
Predeclared	No	Yes	Minimum	2.663	Yes(1)	Yes	1.0	
Identifiers	No	Yes	Product	3.109	No(0)	Yes	1.0	1, 2, 3, 4
	No	Yes	Minimum	3.075	No(0)	No	.82	
	No	Yes	Minimum	15.536	Yes(25)	No	.97	
	No	Yes	Minimum	16.543	Yes(26)	Yes	1.0	
First 100 Most	No	Yes	Product	4.327	No(0)	No	.77	1, 2, 3, 4
Frequently	No	Yes	Product	5.086	Yes(10)	No	.89	
Used English	No	Yes	Product	6.035	Yes(21)	Yes	1.0	
Words	No	Yes	Minimum	3.650	No(0)	No	.64	
	No	Yes	Minimum	8.600	Yes(10)	No	.64	
	No	Yes	Minimum	17.137	Yes(25)	No	.64	
	No	Yes	Minimum	33.164	Yes(50)	No	.71	
	No	Yes	Minimum	68.693	Yes(100)	No	.72	
	No	Yes	Minimum	105.070	Yes(150)	No	.83	
	No	Yes	Minimum	133.440	Yes(200)	No	.72	
	No	Yes	Minimum	146.784	Yes(250)	No	.71	
	No	Yes	Product	4.040	No(0)	No	.92	1, 2, 3, 4, 5
	No	Yes	Product	6.125	Yes(3)	Yes	1.0	
	No	Yes	Minimum	4.128	No(0)	No	.85	
	No	Yes	Minimum	15.193	Yes(10)	No	.78	
	No	Yes	Minimum	31.343	Yes(25)	No	.78	
	No	Yes	Minimum	39.989	Yes(33)	Yes	1.0	
	No	Yes	Product	4.552	No(0)	Yes	1.0	1, 2, 3, 4, 5, 6
	No	Yes	Minimum	4.585	No(0)	No	.92	
	No	Yes	Minimum	9.290	Yes(5)	Yes	1.0	
	No	Yes	Product	4.078	No(0)	No	.92	1, 2, 3, 4, 6
	No	Yes	Product	6.257	Yes(3)	Yes	1.0	
	No	Yes	Product	5.018	No(0)	Yes	1.0	first seven characters
	No	Yes	Minimum	4.906	No(0)	Yes	1.0	
Second 100 Most	No	Yes	Product	6.033	Yes(3)	Yes	1.0	1, 2, 3, 4
Frequently	No	No	Product	5.423	Yes(1)	Yes	1.0	
Used English	Yes	No	Product	16.105	Yes(13)	Yes	1.0	
Words	Yes	No	Minimum	12.783	Yes(16)	Yes	1.0	

Table 5.
Negligible effect of backtracking for large data sets.

Parameters -> Sample Data Set	Blank a Char.	Use Key Length	Product or Minimum	CPU time seconds	Back-tracking employed (Number)	Perfect Minimal Solution	LF	Letters Used in associated value calcs.
First 500 Most	No	Yes	Product	17.318	No(0)	No	.56	1, 2, 3, 4, 10
Frequently	No	Yes	Product	23.772	Yes(3)	No	.55	
Used English	No	Yes	Product	22.698	Yes(4)	No	.61	
Words	No	Yes	Product	194.738	Yes(100)	No	.54	
	No	Yes	Product	22.190	No(0)	No	.64	1, 2, 3, 4, 5, 9
	No	Yes	Product	47.367	Yes(10)	No	.59	
	No	Yes	Product	90.064	Yes(25)	No	.58	

sumption is not valid for the English language (or, presumably, for any natural language).

We propose to use information about how often English words occur and to use a judicious mix of common search and hash encoding techniques to provide an efficient organizational strategy for a natural language lexicon.

If the dictionary is formed by putting properties on Lisp atoms, as is done in many natural language systems, the entire search for lexical entries is performed by a Lisp system. Most Lisp implementations[11] use an object list to access atoms, usually implemented as hash buckets. A built-in general-purpose hash function is provided that distributes the hash values of the complete set of keys in the dictionary (hopefully, equally) among the hash buckets, each of which is searched sequentially. The access time is therefore dependent on the number of buckets and on bucket size.*

In addition to this search for the atom name, the property list must be scanned for dictionary properties. If, for the majority of items in the lexicon, this property is the only one on the property list, the time required for any lexical access is approximately equal to the hash encoding scheme time. Comparatively, the number of words with many properties remains insignificant and will not be considered.

Any desirable search technique can be imposed on an explicitly stored dictionary. When we attempt to organize the lexicon in a way that minimizes retrieval time, many factors affect our choices, such as the size of the lexicon and the need for secondary storage. Some design criteria, however, will improve the access time for any linear search algorithm of a natural language lexicon. One such design feature is to order the dictionary ac-

---

*The retrieval time is dependent on the actual distribution of the keys among the buckets. For any hash function, there exists some set of keys that will produce very uneven distributions. In the worst case, all keys will have the same hash value, so the average cost of a successful search would be $N/2$; for an unsuccessful search, the cost would be N (where N is the number of keys).

Sample session

The following is an interleaved lexicon of the 500 most commonly used English words.

```
# RUN  •APL  PAR=D
>   .v3.0  vsapl/aplfs  # EXECUTION BEGINS  11:44:37
>   clear  ws
>   wssize  is  46172
> )LOAD  PERFECT  300000
>   saved  12:59:00  06/26/82
>   wssize  is  300124
>
> HASH                        {preorders data for associated value calculation}
>   WORDS TO BE HASHED: c1      {c1 is a variable containing the 1st 100 MFEW}
>   LETTERS TO BE USED:  1 2 L        {for assignment of associated values}
>   IS BLANK TO BE A CHARACTER (Y/N): N    {or use last letter if appropriate}
>   IS LENGTH TO BE PART OF FUNCTION (Y/N):  Y
>     THAN CONFLICTS WITH      THEN
>     THERE CONFLICTS WITH     THESE
>   WOULD YOU LIKE TO TRY A DIFFERENT ROUTE: Y
>   LETTERS TO BE USED:  1 2 3 4       {for assignment of associated values}
>   IS BLANK TO BE A CHARACTER (Y/N): N    {or use last letter if appropriate}
>   IS LENGTH TO BE PART OF FUNCTION (Y/N):  Y
>   ORDER BY PRODUCT OR MINIMUM (P/M):  P  {product of letter frequencies or
>   CPU SECONDS USED IN HASH IS 2.518                    like Cichelli's}
>   THE DATA IN CORRECTED PREORDER FORM:
>
>   the then these when she we they there me he were her more be been them than
>   that what war was has some men man this their his time him made say may for
>   first shall would come can could must our one on i in an any or are well
>   will only but out into from who to so not no its it at should before is as
>   your you said had any my by how now of if us a over upon with little do up
>   all two have like such very about every great other which people
>
>   BIND 0        {invoking the second ordering part — nonbacktracking}
>     BINDING STARTED AT  1982 7 30 14 34 36 450
>     TIME DURATION WAS 0 0 0 0 0 2 438
>     CPU SECONDS USED IN BASH IS  1.377
>     NUMBER OF TIMES THROUGH BASH MAIN LOOP IS  75
>
> {at this stage the first of the five tables given below appeared, subsequent
>  invocations of the "HASH" and "BIND n" functions resulted in the other four
>  tables given successively to the right. Note that three different hash
>  functions were utilized to construct this single table of the 500 MFEW      }
>
```

	LETTERS USED 1 2 3 4	LETTERS USED 1 2 3 4	LETTERS USED 1 2 3 4	LETTERS USED 1 3 L	LETTERS USED 1 2 4 L
	OFFSET IS 0	OFFSET IS 95	OFFSET IS 195	OFFSET IS 295	OFFSET IS 390
	LETTER VALUES	LETTER VALUES	LETTER VALUES	LETTER VALUES	LETTER VALUES
A	4 6 14 54	20 0 4 26	26 1 20 0	16 48 56	22 20 13 47
B	9 28 0 0	7 0 6 0	4 0 40 0	15 83 0	16 0 0 0
C	18 0 25 72	6 0 10 43	0 0 57 0	9 47 0	0 23 56 0
D	21 0 16 39	15 0 27 34	2 0 5 7	52 0 1	0 0 2 3
E	30 4 0 0	46 1 5 1	17 0 25 3	63 0 6	22 1 0 20
F	19 0 33 41	4 67 11 78	0 0 76 0	7 52 19	7 27 76 0
G	1 0 0 0	7 53 16 66	4 0 19 50	24 62 15	29 0 0 28
H	6 0 39 44	7 33 25 4	49 26 0 12	3 0 22	0 10 19 44
I	2 12 21 24	0 53 1 2	43 14 36 8	34 31 0	0 30 0 0
K	6 0 34 0	28 0 0 0	0 0 41 28	32 33 60	51 0 51 21
L	43 43 26 13	1 0 35 37	1 17 28 6	22 0 39	15 43 19 33
M	5 0 14 12	24 15 0 34	4 0 0 37	29 0 55	11 65 0 94
N	22 26 14 0	0 0 2 63	35 35 1 4	42 5 45	16 82 0 0
O	14 2 59 0	48 34 0 14	49 7 15 47	23 0 0	26 0 12 0
P	0 0 0 64	24 0 4 37	36 0 85 1	21 48 77	0 50 41 0
R	0 38 3 5	0 0 0 0	68 25 12 36	55 0 0	14 0 0 0
S	4 43 12 0	19 89 2 12	24 47 30	34 26 18	1 3 5 12
T	0 41 19 2	13 0 0 1	7 11 0 2	5 40 1	29 0 44 26
U	20 17 15 0	1 45 2 4	22 46 19 2	0 9 0	0 12 7 22
V	79 57 76 0	32 54 16 59	0 0 104 84	51 33 0	0 33 27 0
W	2 29 0 62	0 14 1 0	3 0 0 0	29 0 55	0 47 46 0
Y	45 44 16 5	19 36 1 48	0 0 45 30	25 32 28	20 0 0 0
		14 0 13 44	60 6 8 33		18 0 40 32
'		0 0 0 76	0 0 5 0		0 2 53 0

26

```
>
> HASH TABLE                    {after c1, the 1st-100 MFEW have been analysed}
>
>      3 THE       4 THEN       5 THESE     6 WHEN      7 SHE
>      8 WE        9 THEY      10 THERE    11 ME       12 HE
>     13 WERE     14 MORE      15 BE       16 THEM     17 BEEN
>                 99 OTHER    100 WHICH   132 FROM    133 PEOPLE
>
> LOADING FACTOR IS:  100/133 = .752
>
> HASH TABLE                    {after c2, the 2nd-100 MFEW have been analysed and added}
>
>      ...        99 OTHER    100 WHICH   101 MONEY   102 POWER
>103 MOST        104 POSSIBLE 105 PART    106 CASE    107 MATTER
>108 CAME        109 HOME     110 HERE    111 BEST    112 GET
>113 PER         114 GOVERNMENT 115 SAME  116 FAR     117 FACT
>118 SEE         119 YET      120 DOES    121 CANNOT  122 GOING
>123 BEING       124 HOUSE    125 LESS    126 SAYS    127 LAST
>128 DAYS        129 DOWN     130 YEAR    131 YEARS   132 FROM
>133 PEOPLE      134 FOUND    135 MAKE       ...
>                199 THOUGHT  203 AWAY    209 SINCE   227 DID
>
> LOADING FACTOR IS:  200/227 = .881
>
> HASH TABLE                    {after c3, the 3rd-100 MFEW have been analysed and added}
>
>      ...       199 THOUGHT  200 SET     201 LET     202 CENT
>203 AWAY        204 LETTER   205 WENT    206 WANT    207 WATER
>208 BATTLE      209 SINCE    210 GENERAL 211 GOT     212 DONE
>213 WOMEN       214 SOMETHING 215 SEVERAL 216 CERTAIN 217 GAVE
>218 CONDITIONS219 FIND       220 SITUATION 221 FORTY 222 BOTH
>223 SIDE        224 MIND     225 SOON    226 FIVE    227 DID
>228 SEEN        229 MEANS    230 MORNING    ...
>      ...       299 NECESSARY 300 THEMSELVES 317 KNOWN  323 OFF
>
> LOADING FACTOR IS:  300/323 = .929
>
> HASH TABLE                    {after c4, the 4th-100 MFEW have been analysed and added}
>
>      ...       299 NECESSARY 300 THEMSELVES 301 SEEMS  302 SEEMED
>303 HELD        304 SOLDIERS 305 SEND    306 TOLD    307 TIMES
>308 TROOPS      309 HANDS    310 THOUSAND 311 CALLED 312 FREE
>313 HOURS       314 SENT     315 CENTS   316 FEET    317 KNOWN
>318 COMPLETE    319 COMMITTEE 320 TRUE   321 ABLE    322 ABOVE
>323 OFF         324 CAUSE    325 FLOUR      ...
>                            395 SUBJECT  396 BEGINNING 397 YESTERDAY
>405 VIEW        407 ASK      408 KEEP    418 DIFFERENT 420 REAL
>
> LOADING FACTOR IS:  400/420 = .952
>
> HASH TABLE                    {after c5, the 5th-100 MFEW have been analysed and added}
>
>                            395 SUBJECT  396 BEGINNING 397 YESTERDAY
>398 POUND       399 HOLD     400 ROAD    401 READ    402 TEN
>403 RECEIVED    404 HEARD    405 VIEW    406 POSITION 407 ASK
>408 KEEP        409 HOWEVER  410 TOGETHER 411 POOR   412 REMEMBER
>413 THIRD       414 MEAN     415 MODERN  416 BEHIND  417 LOAN
>418 DIFFERENT   419 HARD     420 REAL    421 COMES      ...
>498 IMPORTANT   504 UNLESS   519 ELECTRIC 526 GUNS   552 KNOWLEDGE
>
> LOADING FACTOR IS:  500/552 = .906
>
> TOTAL TIME IS:  5 HASHS - 11.913 SECONDS
>                 5 BINDS -  6.789 SECONDS
>
>                 TOTAL - 18.702 SECONDS
>
)OFF
# EXECUTION TERMINATED 11:18:55
```

cording to the relative frequency of letter occurrence in words.

The proposal we explore here divides the dictionary into two or more parts to form dictionary hierarchies. This feature is most interesting when one considers the very high frequency of use of a very small number of words, but it is also important when one needs to consider how to divide a dictionary among different storage media.

For example, 732 items comprise 75 percent of the words used in representative text. A possible three-level hierarchy is one is which 64 items account for 50 percent of the words in the text (see Table 6), 668 items that comprise another 25 percent, and the remainder provide the final 25 percent. A hash into the first level of 64 words followed by a binary search of the second level (which on the average would require about nine accesses),

Table 6.
The 64 most frequently used words (adapted from Dewey).

WORD	REL. FREQ.	TOTAL	WORD	REL. FREQ.	TOTAL
THE	7.310	7.310	FROM	0.433	41.433
OF	3.998	11.308	HAD	0.414	41.847
AND	3.280	14.588	HAS	0.390	42.237
TO	2.924	17.512	ONE	0.389	42.626
A	2.120	19.632	OUR	0.357	43.983
IN	2.116	21.748	AN	0.330	43.313
IT	1.488	23.236	BEEN	0.329	43.642
THAT	1.367	24.603	MY	0.329	43.971
I	1.236	25.839	THERE	0.329	44.300
IS	1.224	27.063	NO	0.321	44.621
FOR	1.035	28.098	THEIR	0.319	44.940
BE	0.956	29.054	WERE	0.307	45.247
WAS	0.850	29.904	SO	0.300	45.547
YOU	0.808	30.712	HIM	0.285	45.832
AS	0.782	31.494	YOUR	0.283	46.115
WITH	0.727	32.221	CAN	0.277	46.392
HE	0.687	32.908	WOULD	0.267	46.659
HAVE	0.658	33.566	IF	0.263	46.922
ON	0.643	34.209	THEM	0.262	47.184
BY	0.600	34.809	WHAT	0.260	47.444
NOT	0.589	35.398	ME	0.257	47.701
AT	0.585	35.983	WHO	0.248	47.949
THIS	0.572	36.555	DO	0.239	48.188
ARE	0.549	37.104	WHEN	0.237	48.425
WE	0.537	37.641	HER	0.234	48.659
HIS	0.517	38.158	TIME	0.232	48.891
BUT	0.504	38.662	WAR	0.217	49.108
THEY	0.495	39.157	ANY	0.210	49.318
ALL	0.467	39.624	MORE	0.210	49.528
WILL	0.464	40.088	NOW	0.210	49.738
OR	0.458	40.546	UP	0.207	49.945
WHICH	0.454	41.000	OUT	0.206	50.151

followed by a trie* search of the third level, would provide a very efficient search.

Lexicon storage is as crucial as the retrieval of lexical information. Common structure sharing and morphological analysis contribute to efficient space use; certain dialects of Lisp use various techniques, such as CDR-encoding, to reduce the representational overhead. The dictionary, represented as a trie, requires less space because letters are not repeated unnecessarily in successive words. Some representational overhead is incurred, however, by the required pointers.

In the previous discussion, we considered how to minimize the space required by the lexicon. We now present a synopsis of some typical lexicon designs. For this discussion, we consider lexicons that contain quantities of information in three representative sizes:

Typically, a small lexicon gains little from complex organization schemes.

- small—500 entries or less;
- medium—1000 to 5000 entries;
- large—10,000 entries or more.

Typically, a small lexicon gains little from complex organization schemes. Our interactive implementation of the CBK algorithm, however, can compute almost-minimal hash functions for most lexicons of small size. One drawback is that we have to store $26*S$ associated values when S letter positions are selected, making this table's size the same order of magnitude as the dictionary itself. Of course, search time would be cut considerably,

---

*Essentially, a trie (derived from the middle letters of "re*trie*val," is an m-ary tree, whose nodes are m-place vectors with components corresponding to digits or characters. Each node on level l represents the set of all keys that begin with a certain sequence of l characters; the node specifies an m-way branch, depending on the $(l+1)$st character.

Interactive terminal sessions

In the sections "Developing Perfect Hash Algorithms" and "Applying Perfect Hash Functions," several examples of terminal sessions where the CBK algorithm was used to find nonminimal- and minimal-perfect hash functions illustrated the system's capabilities, using both non-backtracking and limited backtracking search.

hash value = hash key length +
    associated value of the key's first letter +
    associated value of the key's second letter +
    associated value of the key's four letter

This example is immediately followed by an example of a minimal-perfect hash function with backtracking for the same problem set and a hash function that uses four letter positions in the hash key. The listings are annotated with comments enclosed in set brackets ({}).

The first example is nonminimal, nonbacktracking—hash functions using three letter positions.

```
#  RUN  •APL  PAR=O
 >     v3.0  vsapl/apifs
#  EXECUTION BEGINS  08:48:45
 >   clear  ws
 >   wssize  is  46172
 >   )LOAD  PERFECT  300000
 >   saved  12:59:00  06/26/82
 >   wssize  is  300124
 >
 >  HASH                    {preorders data for associated value calculation}
 >  WORDS TO BE HASHED:  c1      {c1 is a variable containing the 1st 100 MFEW}
 >  LETTERS TO BE USED:  1 2 4        {for assignment of associated values}
 >  IS BLANK TO BE A CHARACTER (Y/N):  N    {or use last letter if appropriate}
 >  IS LENGTH TO BE PART OF FUNCTION (Y/N):  Y
 >         THAN CONFLICTS WITH THEN {1st, 2nd, 4th letters & length are the same}
 >  WOULD YOU LIKE TO TRY A DIFFERENT ROUTE:  N  {new funct with no conflicts?}
 >  ORDER BY PRODUCT OR MINIMUM (P/M):    {product of letter frequencies or
 >  CPU SECONDS USED IN HASH IS 1.951                    like Cichelli's}
 >  THE DATA IN CORRECTED PREORDER FORM:
 >
 >   the she some more time made have then man this these his has that when was
 >   what me he men we were they say may there war her to so who be been before
 >   shall would will well come can could them him must but out our one on only
 >   in into other its it an any at not no or are first for from said had and
 >   there i like little should how now with such your you is as my by of if us
 >   upon a up over do all two very about every great which people
 >
 >  BASH                        {invoking the second ordering part}
 >  LOADING FACTOR  0.5 TO 1 RANGE:  1
 >  NUMBER OF ALLOWABLE BACKTRACKS:  0
 >  BASHING STARTED AT  1982 7 5 12 46 44 529
 >  TIME DURATION WAS 0 0 0 0 1 245
 >  CPU SECONDS USED IN BASH IS  1.114
 >  NUMBER OF TIMES THROUGH BASH MAIN LOOP IS  55
 >  TERMINATION AFTER BACKTRACK 1
 >  LETTERS USED 1 2 4
 >  OFFSET USED 0
 >
 >  LETTER VALUES
 >   'A'   6   2  33      'H'   3   0  61      'R'   0  48  21
 >   'B'  14  72   0      'I'   2   3  60      'S'   1  69   7
 >   'C'  33   0  85      'L'  60  50  32      'T'   0  46  10
 >   'D'  58   0  54      'M'   2   0  44      'U'   4  23  12
 >   'E'  11  19   0      'N'   4  42   6      'V'  50  59   0
 >   'F'  44   0  79      'O'   4   0  30      'W'   8  59  67
 >   'G'  11   0   0      'P'   1   7  73      'Y'  62  56  21
 >
 >  HASH TABLE
 >   3 THE      4 SHE      5 SOME      6 MORE      7 TIME      8 MADE
 >   9 HAVE    10 THEN    11 THIS    12 THESE    13 MAN    14 THAT
```

28

```
>   15 HAS        16 HIS        17 NOT        18 WHEN       19 SHOULD     20 WAS
>   21 UPON       22 WHAT       23 ME         24 HE         25 THEY       26 WHERE
>   27 SAY        28 MAY        29 WE         30 MEN        31 WERE       32 TO
>   33 SO         34 WAR        35 BE         36 NO         37 COME       38 SHALL
>   39 MUST       40 OUT        41 WHO        42 A          43 BEEN       44 CAN
>   45 WOULD      46 HER        47 WILL       48 THEM       49 ONE        50 BUT
>   51 OUR        52 IN         53 HIM        54 ON         55 OTHER      56 AN
>   57 ARE        58 ITS        59 FIRST      60 IT         61 SAID       62 HAD
>   63 WELL       64 AT         65 THEIR      66 I          67 LIKE       68 FOR
>   69 BEFORE     70 COULD      71 ONLY       72 ANY        73 HOW        74 NOW
>   75 OR         76 WITH       77 YOU        78 INTO       79 LITTLE     80 IS
>   81 MY         82 US         83 IF         84 AS         85 OF         86 UP
>   87 YOUR       88 OVER       89 SUCH       90 DO         91 ALL        92 TWO
>   93 BY         94 VERY       95 ABOUT      96 EVERY      97 GREAT      98 WHICH
>   99 PEOPLE    105 AND       140 FROM
```

The second example is minimal, backtracking—hash functions using four letter positions.

```
> HASH
>    WORDS TO BE HASHED:  c1
>    LETTERS TO BE USED:  1  2  3  4
>    IS BLANK TO BE A CHARACTER (Y/N):  N
>    IS LENGTH TO BE PART OF FUNCTION (Y/N):  Y
>    ORDER BY PRODUCT OR MINIMUM (P/M):  P
>    CPU SECONDS USED IN HASH IS 2.162
>    THE DATA IN CORRECTED PREORDER FORM:
>
>    the the these when she we they there me he were her more be been them than
>    that what war was has some men man this their his time him made say may
>    for first shall would come can could must our one on i in an any or are
>    well will only but out into from who to so not no its it at should before
>    is as your you said had and my by how now of if us a over upon with little
>    do up all two have like such very about every great other which people
>
> BASH
>    LOADING FACTOR  0.5 TO 1 RANGE:  1
>    NUMBER OF ALLOWABLE BACKTRACKS:  100
>    BASHING STARTED AT  1982 7 8 9 4 18 989
>    TIME DURATION WAS 0 0 0 0 0 3 923
>    CPU SECONDS USED IN BASH IS  3.17
>    NUMBER OF TIMES THROUGH BASH MAIN LOOP IS  119
>
>    TERMINATION AFTER BACKTRACK 22
>    LETTERS USED 1 2 3 4
>    OFFSET USED 0
>
>    LETTER VALUES
>    'A'   4   6   14   53       'H'   6   0   46   45       'R'   0   38   3   5
>    'B'   9  45    0    0       'I'   2  12   21   24       'S'   4   50  12   0
>    'C'  18   0   24   72       'L'  45  43   26   13       'T'   0   34  19   2
>    'D'  23   0   16   38       'M'   5   0   14   12       'U'  13   17  15  13
>    'E'  31   4    0    0       'N'  22  26   14    0       'V'  79   56  75   0
>    'F'  19   0    9   58       'O'  14   2   29   30       'W'   2   28   0  65
>    'G'   2   0    0    0       'P'  23  34    0   39       'Y'  39   42  16   5
>
>    HASH TABLE
>     3 THE         4 THEN        5 THESE       6 WHEN        7 SHE         8 WE
>     9 THEY       10 THERE      11 ME         12 HE         13 WERE       14 MORE
>    15 BE         16 THEM       17 BEEN       18 THAN       19 WAR        20 THAT
>    21 HER        22 WHAT       23 WAS        24 SOME       25 THIS       26 MEN
>    27 HAS        28 MAN        29 THEIR      30 TIME       31 MADE       32 FOR
>    33 HIS        34 SAY        35 MAY        36 SHALL      37 WOULD      38 COME
>    39 FIRST      40 MUST       41 CAN        42 OUR        43 ONE        44 IN
>    45 ARE        46 AM         47 HIM        48 NOT        49 WELL       50 BUT
>    51 ITS        52 SHOULD     53 COULD      54 ANY        55 OUT        56 ON
>    57 WILL       58 BEFORE     59 IT         60 I          61 AT         62 OR
>    63 TO         64 WHO        65 YOU        66 IS         67 SO         68 AS
>    69 HAD        70 MY         71 IF         72 YOU        73 SAID       74 BY
>    75 ONLY       76 HOW        77 US         78 A          79 OVER       80 UPON
>    81 INTO       82 WITH       83 OF         84 LITTLE     85 NO         86 DO
>    87 AND        88 UP         89 ALL        90 TWO        91 HAVE       92 NOW
>    93 LIKE       94 SUCH       95 VERY       96 ABOUT      97 EVERY      98 GREAT
>    99 OTHER     100 WHICH     101 PEOPLE    102 FROM
)OFF
```

so the storage overhead might still be acceptable.

Medium-size lexicons need to be analyzed differently; if the dictionary can fit in random access memory, a binary search would provide efficient access of items, supplemented by hash encoding into a minidictionary of the most common words. There is no space advantage using a trie structure because the overhead in associated pointers is high and there is little common spelling among so few words.

Another approach, which uses the CBK algorithm, is illustrated in the sample session on page 48. Satisfactory experimental results have shown that 500 words can be placed in a noncolliding hash table in less than 20 seconds. Nevertheless, the LF is only about 0.67, which we feel is unsatisfactory; increasing the LF results in a substantial increase in computation. When more than one hash function is used, an offset can be manipulated to

This technique effectively uses unoccupied spaces from previous CBK algorithm applications.

start the next group of 500 words in the sparse part of the table occupied by the previous group of 500 words, typically resulting in a loss of about only 10 percent of storage space.

In this example, the medium-sized lexicon is divided into group of 500 lexical items (more or less) and the CBK algorithm is applied successively, manipulating the offset to interleave the 500-word pieces to effectively increase the LF to an acceptable level. Our experimental results fit the first 500-word chunk into a table of size 750. The first offset was set to 550, where the application of algorithm CBK began to place items when applied to the second 500-word lexical chunk.

The first 1000 words thus fit into a space of 1340 spaces. We continue this process until we have the dictionary we desire or we exhaust our computer memory. This technique effectively uses unoccupied spaces from previous applications of algorithm CBK. The sample session illustrates this technique using 100-word chunks (because of space limitations) that are nonminimally hashed. If the lexicon cannot fit into memory, it is appropriate to treat the medium-size lexicon as a large lexicon.

Since large lexicons typically require secondary storage, a major concern is to minimize retrievals from secondary storage. The CBK algorithm can include the 732 most frequently used English words in a single almost-minimal hash table, giving one-probe retrieval in 75 percent of the cases.

A second hash function could map the remaining approximately 50,000 words into 50 subsets of about 1000 words each. This second hash function could be based on the ordinal positions of letters in the alphabet, rather than on the machine character code, to preserve machine independence. The 50 subsets of 1000 words each could be stored separately in secondary memory. For each subset, an almost-minimal perfect hash function could be computed, storing the associated values in the same secondary memory location as the lexical information itself.

If the key we are searching for is not in the table of most frequent words, then a hash would be performed to select the proper second-level table from a secondary storage medium; this table would then be searched using its own perfect hash function. This organization would allow us to retrieve any key with three hash calculations and one probe of secondary memory.

Though Cichelli's algorithm provides a useful alternative to numerical approaches to the search for perfect hash functions, the LFs of the solutions produced degenerate quickly for key sets of more than 50 keys. Furthermore, the mechanism used for distinguishing keys is not adequate for many problem sets. Refinements led to the development of the substantially different CBK algorithm.

We have considered improvements along the lines of hash identifier choice, data set partitioning into manageable units, and search methods. In our empirical study of various algorithms,[7] we conclude that the heuristics employed in the CBK algorithm appear to be the most promising for further research.

The introduction of limited backtracking is an important contribution leading to almost-minimal hash tables for large data sets (more than 500 keys). Further analysis of the problem may reveal a better way of performing this limited backtracking.

We are confident that the CBK algorithm can distinguish any distinct set of lexical keys, and the LF will remain adequate for key sets of up to 500 words, although we have presented only a few limited examples. In addition, the CBK algorithm can be used with various lexical organizations to minimize the cost of lexical search and storage. □

Acknowledgements

We thank the reviewers whose many suggestions have helped greatly to make this a more readable and comprehensive article. We also thank Josie Backhouse for reading an earlier draft of this article and Carol Murchison for her extensive editing. This research was supported by the National Science and Engineering Research Council of Canada under Operating Grant No. A4309 and by the Office of the Academic Vice President at Simon Fraser University.

References

1. R. Morris, "Scatter Storage Techniques," *Comm. ACM,* Vol. 11, No. 1, Jan. 1968, pp. 38-44.

2. D. Knuth, *The Art of Computer Programming: Volume 3 Searching and Sorting,* Addison-Wesley, Reading, Mass., 1973.

3. R. Sprugnoli, "Perfect Hashing Functions: A Single Probe Retrieval Method for Static Sets," *Comm. ACM,* Vol. 20, No. 11, Dec. 1978, pp. 841-850.

4. G. Jaeschke, "Reciprocal Hashing: A Method for Generating Minimal Perfect Hashing Functions," *Comm. ACM,* Vol. 24, No. 11, Nov. 1981, pp. 829-833.

5. R. Cichelli, "Minimal Perfect Hash Functions Made Simple," *Comm. ACM,* Vol. 23, No. 1, Jan. 1980, pp. 17-19.

6. C. Cook and R. Oldehoeft, *More on Minimal Perfect Hash Tables,* Technical Report TR-82, Department of Computer Science, Colorado State University, 1982.

7. N. Cercone, M. Krause, and J. Boates, "Minimal and Almost Minimal Perfect Hash Function Search," *Computers and Mathematics with Applications,* Vol. 9. No. 1, Jan. 1983, pp. 215-232.

8. D. Knuth, "Estimating the Efficiency of Backtrack Programs," *Math Comput.,* Vol. 29, No. 2, Feb. 1975, pp. 121-136.

9. M. Krause, *Perfect Hash Function Search,* technical report, masters thesis, Department of Computing Science, Simon Fraser University, 1982.

10. G. Dewey, *Relative Frequency of English Speech Sounds,* Harvard University Press, Cambridge, Mass., 1923.

11. J. Allen, *The Anatomy of Lisp,* McGraw-Hill, New York, 1978.

Nick Cercone is chairman of the School of Computing Science at Simon Fraser University in Burnaby, British Columbia. He also worked for IBM in 1969 and 1971. His research interests include natural language understanding, knowledge representation, knowledge-based systems, artificial intelligence, software engineering, and computing in the humanities.

Cercone received a BS in engineering science from the University of Steubenville in Ohio in 1968, an MS in computing and information science from Ohio State University in 1970, and a PhD in computing science from the University of Alberta at Edmonton in 1975.

He is a member of many professional societies, including IEEE, ACM, AAAI, ACL, and AISB; a past president of the CSCSI/SCEIO, the Canadian Society for Computational Studies of Intelligence; and a member of the Steering Committee of the Canadian Society for Fifth Generation Research.

John Boates is a student in computing science at Simon Fraser University and an employee of Vertigo Graphics in Vancouver, British Columbia. Boates is president of the Computing Science Student's Society at Simon Fraser and a student member of the ACM.

Max Krause is an employee of MacDonald Detweiler and Associates in Richmond, British Columbia. His research interests include artificial intelligence, computational linguistics, and software engineering.

Krause received a BA in psychology from the University of Chicago in 1974 and an MSc in computing science in 1982 at Simon Fraser. He is a member of the IEEE, ACM, and AAAI.

The authors' address is the School of Computing Science, Simon Fraser University, Burnaby, B.C., Canada V5A 1S6.

Binary
Search Trees

Binary Search Trees and File Organization

J. NIEVERGELT*

Binary search trees are an important technique for organizing large files because they are efficient for both random and sequential access of records, and for modification of a file. Because of this, they have received a great deal of attention in recent years, and their properties are now better understood than those of most other file organization methods. This paper surveys the main results which have been obtained.

Key Words and Phrases: Search, search tree, search time, binary search tree, optimal tree, balanced tree, height-balance, weight-balance, file, static file, dynamic file, file organization, file processing, restructuring of file, random access, sequential access, access frequencies.

CR Categories: 2.12, 4.34, 5.30.

INTRODUCTION

Binary search trees are an important technique for organizing large files because they are efficient for both random and sequential access of records, and for modification of a file. Binary search trees are in competition with other methods for organizing files, such as: hash-coding or scatter storage techniques (see e.g. [Mo68]); linear lists, either sequentially allocated or chained (see e.g. [Kn68], pp. 234–251); other kinds of trees, such as "tries" [Fr60], [Su63], or multiway trees of various kinds (see e.g. [Ba72a] and [Ba72b]); and, finally, methods that are based on a combination of such techniques, such as index-sequential file organization [Gh69]. Severance [Se74] presents a survey of the entire field of file organization techniques, and compares their respective properties. Hence this paper discusses file organization techniques only to the extent necessary to motivate the current surge of interest in binary search trees, then concentrates on surveying the recent results in this area.

File organization techniques can be compared according to different criteria, such

* Department of Computer Science, University of Illinois, Urbana, Illinois 61801.

as storage utilization, access time in random and sequential processing, ease of modification, and usability in both one-level and two-level stores. For any *one* of these criteria one chooses to consider, one can usually find a file organization method which is superior to binary search trees. For example, scatter storage techniques lead to shorter average search times; files with sequentially allocated records are optimal from the point of view of storage requirement and sequential processing, and allow a binary search process just as binary search trees do.

However, techniques which are close to optimal in one respect have a tendency to be poor in some other respect. To continue the example above: a hash-coded file needs to be sorted when one wants to process the records sequentially in alphabetic order (if one tries to preserve alphabetic order in a hash-table in order to speed up sequential processing, one is likely to violate the statistical properties that permit fast random access); modification (insertion or deletion of records) is costly in a sequentially allocated file; and random search is slow in a linked linear list.

The importance of binary search trees comes from the fact that they strike a reasonable compromise between the various

CONTENTS

conflicting requirements that must be considered in designing file structures. The table below compares four common techniques for organizing a file of n records by showing how average processing time for three important operations grows as a function of the file size n.

The following comments about this table are appropriate:

a) the insertion/deletion time assumes one already knows (has a pointer to) the record to be deleted, or the place of a new record to be inserted; the time required for search and insertion/deletion is obtained by adding corresponding entries in columns 1 and 3.

b) the entry "constant" means that in first approximation processing time is independent of file size; it may depend on other parameters, as for example, random search time in scatter storage techniques depends primarily on how full memory is.

c) the notation O means "proportional to" or "on the order of" and is mathematically defined as follows: $g(n) = O[f(n)]$ means that there exists a constant c such that, for all sufficiently large values of n, $g(n) \leqslant c \cdot f(n)$. Hence this notation. The notation O hides a constant factor which can be of considerable importance, particularly in small files (for sufficiently small files, sequential allocation is always best); this table shows only trends which come into play with increasing file size.

Note that each of the first three techniques has one entry which is significantly worse than the others in its column (insertion/deletion for sequential allocation, random search for linked lists, sequential processing for scatter storage). Binary search trees, on the other hand, show a reasonable performance in each of the three columns; while they may not be optimal in any one respect, they are "uniformly not bad" in all respects. Further aspects of the comparison between binary search trees and other file organization techniques can be found in [Se74].

Because of their favorable properties as a file organization method, and certainly also because they give rise to interesting mathematical problems (problems which establish

	Random access (search) of single record	Sequential processing (alphabetical listing) of entire file	Insertion/deletion of single record (search time excluded)
Sequentially allocated linear list	$O(\log n)$	$O(n)$	$O(n)$
Linked linear list	$O(n)$	$O(n)$	constant
Scatter storage	constant	$O(n \log n)$	constant
Binary search tree	$O(\log n)$	$O(n)$	constant

connections to other fields, such as information and coding theory, sorting, decision trees, and identification problems), binary search trees have received a great deal of attention in recent years. Due to these investigations, it seems fair to say that the mathematical properties of binary search trees are better understood than those of competitive file organization methods.

This paper attempts to survey the main results which have been obtained about binary search trees. All of the results presented have rather direct implications for file organization, and an attempt will be made to point these out explicitly. No further comparison will be made between binary search trees and other file organization methods.

The problems which have been studied are quite varied, as it is possible to make different assumptions about the file and how one wishes to process it. The main choices are the following:

1. Whether the file is static (i.e., the set of records is given once and for all) or dynamic (i.e., there are frequent insertions and deletions of records). In the first case, one is primarily interested in efficient algorithms for constructing trees which minimize (exactly or approximately) average search time. In the latter case, one is primarily interested in finding classes of trees (whose search time is not too far off from the optimum) which allow efficient insertion and deletion algorithms. The distinction between constructing a tree for a static file, and maintaining a tree for a dynamic file may be blurred in the case where construction is done through repeated insertion.

2. Whether one knows the access probabilities or frequencies (in general according to a nonuniform distribution) for all records, or whether one does not know them. The latter case is usually handled as if one had uniform access frequencies; i.e., all records were accessed equally often. An intermediate approach is to collect data about access frequencies while the file is in use, and to restructure the tree accordingly at certain times. This restructuring is independent of whether insertions and deletions occur.

3. Whether the tree is kept in a random-access central memory (we will call this a one-level store), or whether only a small part of it can be kept in central memory at one time, while the bulk of it must be kept in some back-up store (called the two-level store). For the first case one has been able to obtain statistical estimates of important quantities by analytical means, but for the second one, which is significantly more difficult, what information one has about performance comes primarily from simulation experiments.

These three aspects of files define a classification of file organization design into eight cases. We will not discuss all eight cases, however, because they are not equally important, and also because much more is known about some cases than others. In particular, the important case of using binary search trees in two-level stores is poorly understood compared with the case of the one-level store. Some pertinent results are mentioned in Section 5.

Concerning binary search trees for one-level stores, two cases are of particular importance: that of a static file with known access frequencies, discussed in Section 3, and the case of a dynamic file with unknown access frequencies (Section 4).

The remaining two cases are not discussed for the following reasons. The case of a static file with unknown frequencies is trivial if one makes the almost unavoidable working hypothesis that unknown frequencies are to be treated as uniform frequencies. And the case of a dynamic file with known (nonuniform) access frequencies has hardly received any attention since it is really only in a steady-state situation, when a file does not change much, that one is likely to know access frequencies of individual records.

tively called the left- and the right-subtree of the root ($l \geqq 0$, $r \geqq 0$, $l + r = n - 1$).

A binary search tree over n names X_1, $\cdots$, X_n, is a binary tree T_n each of whose nodes has been labeled with a distinct name chosen from $X_1, \cdots, X_n$, such that for each node N the following property holds: all the names in the left-subtree of N lexicographically precede the name which labels N, and all the names in the right-subtree of N lexicographically follow the name which labels N.

The following picture shows three search trees over the 4 names A, B, C, D, with the roots labeled D, B, and C, respectively.

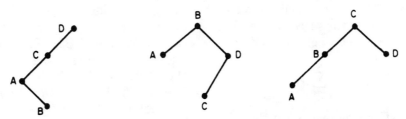

Before continuing this discussion, let us first review the basic concepts involved in binary search trees.

BASIC CONCEPTS AND TERMINOLOGY

For the purpose of this paper, the only relevant property of a file is that its set of records is linearly ordered, according to an order defined on the set of keys associated with the records. In our examples the keys will be strings of letters, and will be called "names" from now on; and the order is the conventional lexicographic one.

A binary tree may be defined recursively as follows: The empty tree T_0 of zero node is a binary tree. A binary tree T_n of $n \geqq 1$ nodes is an ordered triple (T_l, v, T_r), where

A binary search tree allows the following procedure for determining whether a given name X is in the tree, and for finding it when it exists. Compare X to the name at the root, and one of four cases may arise:

1. There is no root (the tree is empty): X is not in the tree, and the search terminates unsuccessfully.

2. X is equal to the name at the root: the search terminates successfully.

3. X precedes the name at the root: the search continues by examining the left-subtree of the root in the same way.

4. X follows the name at the root: the search continues by examining the right-subtree of the root in the same way.

Unsuccessful searches can be illustrated by attaching *leaves* to a tree, indicated by □ in the picture below:

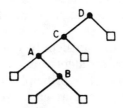 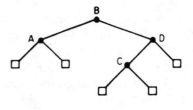

v is a single node called the root of T_n, and T_l, T_r are binary trees of l, r nodes, respec-

Each leaf corresponds to unsuccessful searches for all names X which lie between two consecutive names X_i, X_{i+1} in the tree, with obvious interpretations for the leftmost and the rightmost leaf.

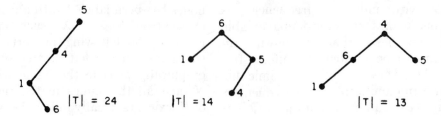

If $\beta_1, \cdots, \beta_n$ denote the access frequencies of the names $X_1, \cdots, X_n$, and $\alpha_0, \alpha_1, \cdots, \alpha_n$ denote the frequencies with which unsuccessful searches terminate at each of the $n + 1$ leaves of a tree T_n, then the average search time (for both successful and unsuccessful searches) can be expressed as

$$\sum_{i=1}^{n} \beta_i l_i + \sum_{i=0}^{n} \alpha_i l_i$$

where the first sum is over all nodes of T_n, the second one over all leaves, and l_i, the *level* of node or leaf i, is the length of the path from the root of T_n to node or leaf i. Two different conventions have been used to measure this length; they amount to defining the level of the root as being either 0 or 1. In this paper we will always assume the root is at level 0. Some formulas and algorithms differ in a trivial way if the other convention is used. The *height* of a tree is the maximal level of any of its nodes.

The quantities β_1, α_i are frequently called node-weights and leaf-weights, respectively, and $\sum \beta_i l_i + \sum \alpha_i l_i$ is also called the *weighted path length* $|T_n|$ of tree T_n. Note that, if one wants to construct trees with minimal weighted path length, it is immaterial whether the weights are normalized to $\sum \beta_i + \sum \alpha_i = 1$. The examples in this paper use unnormalized frequencies or weights. Special cases of interest arise when either the leaf-weights α_i are all zero, or the node-weights β_i are all zero.

With node-weights 1, 6, 4, 5 for the four names A, B, C, D, and with the convention that the level of the root is zero, the weighted path lengths of the three trees shown below are 24, 14, and 13, respectively. The third tree has minimal weighted path length

among all binary search trees over the sequence of node-weights 1, 6, 4, 5, and hence is called *optimal*.

The *root-balance* $\rho(T_n)$ of a binary tree $T_n = (T_l, V, T_r)$ of $n \geq 1$ is $\rho(T_n) = (l + 1/n + 1)$. It ranges over the interval $0 < \rho(T_n) < 1$, and it indicates the relative number of nodes in the left-subtree of T_n. A binary tree T_n is said to be of *bounded balance* α, or in $BB[\alpha]$, for $0 < \alpha \leq 1/2$, if and only if the root-balances $\rho(T')$ of all the subtrees T' of T_n satisfy $\alpha \leq \rho(T) \leq 1 - \alpha$. The trees in $BB[1/2]$ are exactly the completely balanced trees T_n of $n = 2^k - 1$ nodes.

TREES FOR A STATIC FILE WITH KNOWN ACCESS FREQUENCIES

The problem of constructing optimal binary search trees is worked through as follows. Given a sequence $\alpha_0, \beta_1, \alpha_1, \beta_2, \alpha_2, \cdots, \alpha_{n-1}, \beta_n, \alpha_n$ of $2n + 1$ nonnegative real numbers, construct a search tree T_n with node-weights β_i and leaf-weights α_i, which has minimal weighted path length.

It is natural to ask how much work is required to construct an optimal tree on n names. Readers familiar with Huffman trees [Hf52] of coding theory might at first expect that a similarly simple "bottom-up" algorithm might exist (given $n + 1$ weights $\alpha_0, \alpha_1, \cdots, \alpha_n$, join the two smallest ones, say α_0 and α_1, as sons of a newly introduced node whose weight is $\alpha_0 + \alpha_1$; repeat the process on the set of n weights $\alpha_0 + \alpha_1$, $\alpha_2, \cdots, \alpha_n$, until only one weight is left). However, an algorithm, such as Huffman's, based on the principle of choosing the smallest weight at each step, may permute the weights in arbitrary ways, something which is not permissible in binary search trees.

The necessity to preserve the order to the weights appears to require an algorithm significantly more complicated than Huffman's for constructing optimal binary search trees. The most straightforward algorithm is based on the following optimality principle: an optimal binary search tree T_n on weights $\alpha_0, \beta_1, \alpha_1, \cdots, \beta_n, \alpha_n$ has some weight β_i at the root, and an optimal binary search tree T_{i-1} on $\alpha_0, \beta_1, \alpha_1, \cdots, \beta_{i-1}, \alpha_{i-1}$ as left-subtree of the root, and an optimal binary search tree T_{n-i} on $\alpha_i, \beta_{i+1} \cdots, \beta_n, \alpha_n$ as right-subtree of the root.

The difficulty in applying this principle comes from the fact that one cannot choose the root without trying many possibilities, and constructing for each one of them the optimal left- and right-subtrees. This leads to a bottom-up algorithm where, for $i = 1$ to n, one constructs all $n - i + 1$ optimal trees on i consecutive node-weights (and their adjacent leaf-weights), using the optimal trees obtained at step $i - 1$ of this algorithm. The initialization at $i = 1$ is trivial. When the process ends at $i = n$, one has an optimal tree. It is easy to calculate that this algorithm requires a number of operations proportional to n^3, and memory space proportional to n^2.

The figure below shows how this algorithm constructs an optimal tree over four names A, B, C, D with weights 1, 6, 4, 5, respectively. The work required at each step is illustrated explicitly at the last step in the

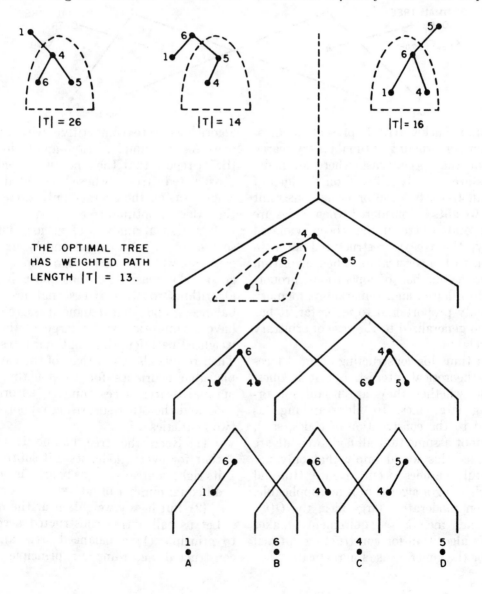

$|T| = 26$ $|T| = 14$ $|T| = 16$

THE OPTIMAL TREE HAS WEIGHTED PATH LENGTH $|T| = 13$.

39

example, where the optimal tree over all four names is selected by comparing its weighted path length with that of three other possible candidates. The subtrees surrounded by dotted lines are optimal trees constructed at earlier steps in the algorithm.

Knuth [Kn71] improved this algorithm to run in time proportional to n^2 by proving that the root of an optimal tree over names $X_1, \cdots, X_n$ need never lie outside the interval bracketed by the two roots of an optimal tree over $X_1, \cdots, X_{n-1}$ and one over $X_2, \cdots, X_n$ (see the figure below).

Since access frequencies are typically not known with great accuracy, it may not be worthwhile to spend much effort on an optimal tree for inaccurate weights, when there might exist simple algorithms for constructing trees whose performance is very near that of optimal trees. Such considerations led various authors (e.g., [Br71], [Wa71], [We71]) to consider heuristic algorithms for constructing near-optimal search trees, and to investigate their performance by simulation experiments. Their conclusion was that trees constructed by heuristic

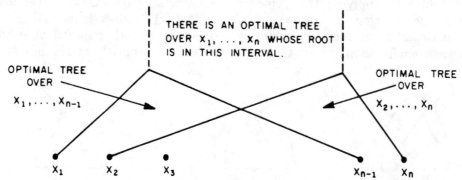

Hu and Tucker [Hu71] present an algorithm for constructing optimal binary search trees for the special case where all node-weights are zero. It is based on the idea of Huffman trees, but the ordering constraint on the weights is considered when nodes are joined; and where it has been violated initially, the tree is restructured later to conform to the constraints. Their algorithm requires a number of operations proportional to $n \log n$, and, remarkably, memory space only proportional to n. So far, it has not been generalized to the case of arbitrary node-weights.

Algorithms for constructing optimal trees are of theoretical interest, but it is questionable whether they are useful for organizing large files. In file searching (as opposed to the construction of codes, say), one cannot assume that all node-weights are zero, since this would imply that only unsuccessful searches occur. Hence Hu and Tucker's $n \log n$ algorithm is not applicable. For even moderately large files, the $O(n^2)$ time and memory requirement makes Knuth's algorithm for constructing optimal trees for the general case impractical.

algorithms were competitive with optimal ones. As an example, Bruno and Coffman in [Br71] report that their heuristic algorithm constructed trees whose weighted path length was on the average only 2.5% larger than that of optimal trees.

A statistical analysis of various kinds of search trees by Nievergelt and Wong [Ni71] explains why heuristic algorithms are so good. The reason is, that most heuristic algorithms construct trees that are nearly balanced, and that balanced search trees have asymptotically (for large n) the same weighted path length as optimal trees have. Their results also show that, of the two most plausible heuristics for constructing near-optimal search trees, one is surprisingly good and the other surprisingly poor. These two heuristics are:

(1) Keep the tree balanced; i.e., so that for every node, its left-subtree and its right-subtree have as nearly as possible an equal number of nodes.

(2) Put heavy weights near the root.

Let us call a tree constructed according to principle (1) a balanced tree, and one constructed according to principle (2) a monotonic tree (because the weights along any path from the root to a leaf form a monotonically nonincreasing sequence). As a basis for comparison, let us also consider random trees on n nodes, defined as follows: every node has equal probability $1/n$ of being chosen as the root; if node i is chosen as the root, then it has a random tree on nodes $1, \cdots, i - 1$ as its left-subtree, and a random tree on nodes $i + 1, \cdots, n$ as its right-subtree.

Now assume that n weights $\beta_1, \cdots, \beta_n$ are drawn in sequence as independent samples from a given probability distribution on nonnegative real numbers, and that E denotes expectation with respect to this distribution (so that $E(\beta)$ denotes the average weight). Denote by O_n, B_n, M_n, R_n the expected weighted path length of optimal, balanced, monotonic, and random trees, respectively, constructed over these n node-weights. Then:

$$O_n = E(\beta)n \log_2 n + O(n)$$
$$B_n = E(\beta)n \log_2 n + O(n)$$
$$M_n = 2 \ln 2\, E(\beta)n \log_2 n + O(n)$$
$$R_n = 2 \ln 2\, E(\beta)n \log_2 n + O(n)$$

(The last result concerning random trees is due to Hibbard [Hi62].)

Hence, averaged over the class of all weight sequences sampled as described above, and asymptotically for large n, balanced trees are as good as optimal trees, and monotonic trees as bad as random trees, the latter having an average search time of $2 \ln 2 \approx 1.4$ times longer than either optimal or balanced trees. These same results hold in the general case where leaf-weights as well as node-weights are present.

The poor showing of the principle of putting heavy weights near the root is surprising. These results indicate that a reasonable heuristic procedure would start from a balanced tree, and use the rule of placing a larger weight nearer to the root than a smaller weight only as a local perturbation, being careful not to unbalance the tree too much in the process. But they also indicate that, if a file is static (i.e., it is irrelevant whether insertions and deletions can be done easily) and each record has equal memory requirements, then a se-quentially allocated linear list has most desirable features: it can be constructed for the cost of sorting, an $O(n \log n)$ operation; it has no storage overhead; and it allows a binary search corresponding to a balanced tree, which for most practical cases is nearly as good as an optimal tree.

Let us also describe briefly a category of algorithms which might be called "tree construction by insertion." One can consider them either to be tree-construction techniques for static files, or maintenance techniques for a file where only insertions occur, but no deletions. They are also strongly related to algorithms of the Quicksort-type (see e.g. [Ho61]). The names are taken in some sequence $X_1, \cdots, X_n$ (usually not in lexicographic order, but in an arbitrary given order), and the tree is constructed by inserting, for $j = 1$ to n, X_j into the tree on names $X_1, \cdots, X_{j-1}$. If this insertion is done in the conventional way (namely, adding X_j as a new leaf in the tree on $X_1, \cdots, X_{j-1}$ at the place where the unsuccessful search for X_j ended), then the resulting tree is entirely determined by the given sequence of names. Under the assumption that all permutations of the sequence of names are equally likely, Hibbard [Hi62] proved that the expected total path length of the resulting tree T_n is $E(|T_n|) = 2 \ln 2 \cdot n \log_2 n + O(n)$; that is, if access frequencies are equal, the average search time will be approximately $1.4 \log_2 n$.

In this construction method, the shape of the resulting tree depends critically on the first name chosen, which constitutes the root. As a consequence, the tree is in general not balanced, which accounts for the factor 1.4 in the average search time. Wong and Chang [Wo72] describe an improved algorithm of construction by insertion, which rebalances from time to time the tree obtained so far. They show that asymptotically for large n, both average construction time and average search time per name are $\log_2 n$, that is, better by a factor of 1.4 than in the conventional construction by insertion.

It is possible to make further assumptions about the sequence $X_1, \cdots, X_n$ in which names are inserted in the tree. Coffman and Bruno [Co70] consider the case where the tree is constructed as the file is being used; that is, a name is inserted at the time when it is first being searched. This technique will generate trees in which names with high access frequencies are likely to be near the root, but no effort to balance the tree is made. On the basis of the statistical analysis mentioned earlier, which shows that balanced trees are superior to monotonic trees, one would expect the technique of [Wo72] to be better.

Another assumption on the insertion sequence is useful in the context of sorting. Assume we are given a sequence $X_1, \cdots, X_n$ which, although not in lexicographic order, is likely to have relatively long subsequences which are ordered. Then it is much more appropriate to insert the names in the se-

about dynamic trees, there are elegant and efficient insertion/deletion algorithms which preserve the trees in reasonably balanced shape. It should be noted here that in the case of a dynamic set of names, the assumption of known access frequencies is not very natural, and the criterion of optimality is to have a tree which is as balanced as possible (this is the same as minimizing the average search time under the assumption of uniform access frequencies). However, keeping a search tree as balanced as possible makes insertions and deletions time consuming, as shown in the following example, where the newly added name A causes the tree to become less well balanced than it can be. The transformation to the completely balanced tree on the right changes all the parts of the tree, and hence requires an amount of work proportional to n.

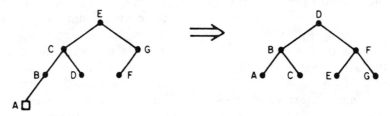

quence $X_{n/2}$, $X_{n/4}$, $X_{3n/4}$, $X_{n/8}$, etc., rather than in the given sequence $X_1, X_2, \cdots, X_n$.

CLASSES OF TREES WHICH ALLOW EASY MODIFICATION

The assumption that the set of names in a search tree changes because of frequent insertions and deletions is a more realistic one in most applications than the assumption of a static file discussed in the preceding section. However, fewer results are known about the case of dynamic trees, simply because the analysis of such trees, and even the stating of meaningful assumptions, is more difficult than in the static case. Among the few theorems in this area, an early result by Hibbard [Hi62] deserves notice: it shows that, in a certain sense, random deletions do not alter the statistical properties of the class of trees constructed by random insertions.

While one has obtained few theorems

The classes of trees we will discuss have the property that, if a transformation is required after an insertion or deletion, it can be carried out by local changes along a single path from root to a leaf, thus requiring an amount of work proportional to log n. To achieve this flexibility, the trees must be allowed to deviate from balanced trees, but they do so to a sufficiently small extent that the average search time is only slightly larger than that of completely balanced trees.

The first class of trees with these properties, due to Adelson-Velskii and Landis [Ad62] (also described in [Fo65], [Kt71], and [Kn73]), might best be called "height-balanced trees." They are defined as follows: T_n is a height-balanced tree if and only if for every node N, the height of the left-subtree of N and the height of the right-subtree of N differ by at most 1. The following picture shows some height-balanced trees and one which is not:

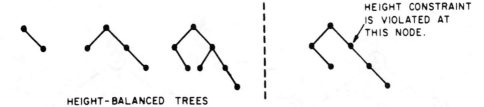

HEIGHT CONSTRAINT
IS VIOLATED AT
THIS NODE.

HEIGHT-BALANCED TREES

The height constraint prevents these trees from being too far away from a completely balanced tree—indeed, the illustration above shows the three "most unbalanced" height-balanced trees of their respective number of nodes.

Despite the fact that height-balanced trees look sparse, the search time they require is only moderately longer than in completely balanced trees, as shown in the following table. Thus height-balanced trees satisfy the requirement of short search time.

	Completely balanced tree of n nodes	Height-balanced tree of n nodes
Worst possible search time	$\log (n + 1)$	$1.44 \log (n + 1)$
Expected average search time (averaged over all trees in class)	$\log (n + 1) - 2$	$\log (n + 1) +$ constant (based on empirical evidence [Kn73])

The more interesting aspect of a scheme for organizing a highly dynamic file is the requirement that insertions and deletions can be performed easily while maintaining the tree within the desired class. The following example shows how this is done for height-balanced trees:

"new" is about to be inserted. Two nodes with names A and B are shown explicitly, along with their condition codes "−" and "/", respectively, which record the fact that, before insertion, the heights of the two subtrees of A are equal, and that the left-subtree of B is of greater height than the right-subtree of B.

After insertion of the new node the height constraint is violated at node B. The transformation shown in the figure above (appropriately called a rotation) restores all tree heights so as to satisfy the height constraint (and, of course, it preserves the lexicographic order of the names).

There is one other case which may arise in updating height-balanced trees, and it is handled by a transformation called "double rotation" shown below. If the new node is inserted at either of the positions indicated by "new" or "new′" on the left, all height constraints will be satisfied, and lexicographic order is preserved, after the tree has been transformed to the form shown at right.

Insertion in height-balanced trees requires at most one rotation or double rotation. Deletion, on the other hand, may require as many as $h/2$ transformations (where h is the height of the tree), but on the average (over all height-balanced trees) the number

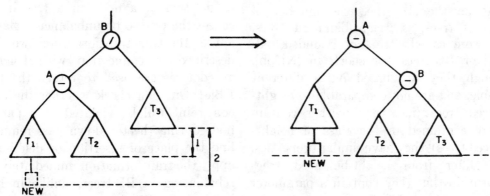

The figure at left shows a subtree of a height-balanced tree, in which a new node of transformations required is a small constant (i.e., independent of tree size). Since

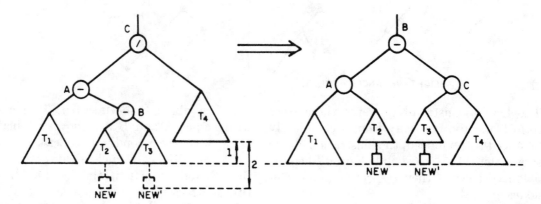

each transformation requires an amount of work which is independent of tree size (i.e., adjusting a few pointers), the amount of work required to update height-balanced trees is indeed small.

Height-balanced trees have been generalized in two different ways. Foster [Fo73] relaxes the height constraint so that the left- and right-subtree of each node may differ by at most δ in height ($\delta = 1$ gives the trees of Adelson-Velskii and Landis). Bayer [Ba72b] considers binary trees with two different kinds of branches, downward pointers, and horizontal pointers. The height constraint he imposes is that every path from the root to a leaf contains the same number of downward pointers, and that there may never be two horizontal pointers in succession. The trees of Adelson-Velskii and Landis can be represented in this way by assigning some branches on long paths to horizontal pointers.

A new class of binary search trees, where the height-constraint is replaced by a constraint on the size (i.e., the number of nodes) of trees, is weight-balanced trees. They were called "trees of bounded balance," or BB-trees, for short, in [Ni73b]. Although they are based on a different principle, and are not comparable to height-balanced trees (i.e., they neither contain nor are contained in the class of height-balanced trees), they have similar properties. They differ from height-balanced trees primarily in that they contain a parameter which can be varied so the compromise between short search time and infrequent rebalancing can be chosen arbitrarily. A tree T is of bounded balance α, or in BB[α],

if and only if, for each subtree T' of T, the fraction of nodes in the left-subtree T_l' of T' lies (approximately; for a precise definition see Section 2) between α and $1 - \alpha$. Thus in a tree of bounded balance $1/4$, one subtree of a node may be up to 3 times the size of the other. The weighted path length $|T_n|$ of a tree in BB[α] is bounded by:

$$|T_n| \leqq \frac{1}{H(\alpha)} (n + 1) \log (n + 1) - 2n,$$

where H is the entropy function $H(\alpha) = -\alpha \log \alpha - (1 - \alpha) \log (1 - \alpha)$ [Ni73a]. For $\alpha = 1/4$, $1/H(1/4) \approx 1.14$, which means that in the worst BB[1/4] tree, average search time is less than 14% longer than in completely balanced trees. However, since most trees in BB[α] are not as "skewed" as they are allowed to be, one would expect that actual search times are considerably better than the bound above indicates, and indeed experimental evidence confirms this.

For any $\alpha < 1 - \sqrt{2/2} \approx .29$, if insertion or deletion of a node in a tree in BB[α] causes the tree to be unbalanced relative to α, then the same transformations which were described in connection with height-balanced trees are used to return the tree to BB[α]. One can check whether the balance constraint will be violated at a particular node during the top-down pass required to find the place of insertion or deletion, and apply the transformation immediately. Thus rebalancing in BB-trees, unlike in height-balanced trees, does not require a bottom-up pass following the top-down pass, and thus does away with the pushdown store conventionally used for the bottom-up pass.

In the case of very large files, the most realistic models are those which explicitly take account of the fact that the largest part of the search tree must reside on a back-up storage device, from which parts of the tree are transferred into main memory when needed. Common back-up storage devices such as disks, drums, and data cells have the characteristics that they normally require a rather long access or wait time, but once the transmission of physically sequential data has been initiated, the data rate is high. Thus, if the tree is allocated properly, rather large parts of it will be brought into main memory in block transfers, and the performance of the tree will be measured not in terms of the average number of comparisons required to locate a name, but in terms of the average number of block transfers.

Muntz and Uzgalis [Mu70] consider the problem of how the nodes of a binary search tree should be allocated to pages (i.e., fixed size memory blocks which are the units in terms of which data is transferred between main memory and secondary storage) so as to minimize the average number of page requests necessary to search the tree. They consider two allocation techniques. The first, called *sequential allocation*, ignores page boundaries, and allocates storage for new names in consecutive locations as they are received. The second method, called *grouped allocation*, takes page boundaries into consideration. If possible, the new node is allocated to the same page as the node which will be the father of the new node. If the father node is on a full page, then the new name is allocated as a "seed node" on a newly opened page. It is clear that by this technique nodes are allocated on a page on the basis of proximity in the search tree, rather than on the basis of proximity in the (arbitrarily given) input sequence. It is plausible that grouped allocation results in a significantly lower number of page requests than sequential allocation, and this is also supported by simulation experiments and some rough analytical estimates. The only consideration which speaks against this scheme is a possibly low memory utilization factor resulting from having many sparsely filled pages. If the total size of the search tree is known or can be estimated a priori, then the following modified group allocation scheme will overcome the problem of low memory utilization, at a moderate increase in the number of page requests: Allocate new pages, as before, as long as they are available; thereafter, a seed node is allocated to the most sparsely filled page.

Other studies of trees for a two-level store have treated primarily multiway trees, where each node may have more than two direct descendants. (For a survey of such trees, see [Kn73], pp. 471–480.) Bayer and McCreight [Ba72a] have studied one such class of trees in detail.

While one knows little about the optimal way of allocating trees to access-limited storage devices, it appears clear from investigations like those described above, that trees can be allocated in reasonably efficient ways. At least there is no reason to assume that trees are less well suited to back-up storage devices than other file organization techniques.

CONCLUSIONS

Binary search trees are one of the most flexible and best understood techniques for organizing large files. Their practical importance comes mainly from the fact that they perform with reasonable efficiency all of the common operations on files: random and sequential processing of a file, insertion and deletion of records, and restructuring of the file. And they can be allocated in reasonable ways on back-up storage devices with restricted access. In addition to their practical importance, they are of theoretical interest because they generate mathematical problems which arise in many other areas of information processing: sorting, coding and information theory, and others.

The main open problems concerning the use of binary search trees for file organization concern their allocation in a two-level store. It would be useful to investigate other allocation schemes, and to understand their statistical properties better.

ACKNOWLEDGMENTS

This work was started while the author was on leave at the Swiss Federal Institute of Technology, Zurich, and at Project MAC, MIT, Cambridge, Massachusetts. It was partially supported also by the National Science Foundation under grant GJ-31222.

REFERENCES

[Ad62] ADELSON-VELSKII, G. M.; AND LANDIS, YE. M. "An algorithm for the organization of information." *Dokl. Akad. Nauk* SSSR 146 (1962), 263–266 (Russian). English translation in *Soviet Math. Dokl.* 3 (1962), 1259–1262.

[Ba72a] BAYER, R., AND MCCREIGHT. "Organization and maintenance of large ordered indexes." *Acta Informatica* 1, 3 (1972), 173–189.

[Ba72b] BAYER, R. "Symmetric binary B-trees: data structure and maintenance algorithms." *Acta Informatica* 1, 4 (1972), 290–306.

[Br71] BRUNO, J.; AND COFFMAN, E. G. "Nearly optimal binary search trees." *Proc. IFIP Congress 71.* North-Holland Publishing Co., Amsterdam 1972, 99–103.

[Co70] COFFMAN, E. G.; AND BRUNO, J. "On file structuring for non-uniform access frequencies." *BIT* 10 (1970), 443–456.

[Fo65] FOSTER, C. C. "Information storage and retrieval using AVL trees." *Proc. ACM 20th National Conf.*, 1965, 192–205.

[Fo73] FOSTER, C. C. "A generalization of AVL trees." *Comm. ACM* 16, 8 (August 1973), 513–517.

[Fr60] FREDKIN, E. "Trie memory." *Comm. ACM* 3, 9 (Sept. 1960), 490–500.

[Gh69] GHOSH, S. P.; AND SENKO, M. E. "File organization: On the selection of random access index points for sequential files." *J. ACM* 16, 4 (Oct 1969), 569–579.

[Hf52] HUFFMAN, D. A. "A method for the construction of minimum redundancy codes." *Proc. IRE*, Vol. 40, (1952), 1098–1101.

[Hi62] HIBBARD, T. "Some combinatorial properties of certain trees, with applications to searching and sorting." *J. ACM* 9, 1 (Jan. 1962), 13–28.

[Ho61] HOARE, C. A. R. "Algorithm 63, partition, and algorithms 64, Quicksort." *Comm. ACM*, 4, 7 (July 1961), 321.

[Hu71] HU, T. C.; AND TUCKER, A. C. "Optimal computer search trees and variable-length alphabetic codes." *SIAM J. Appl. Math.* 21, 4 (Dec. 1971), 514–532.

[Kn68] KNUTH, D. E. *The Art of Computer Programming*, Vol. 1: *Fundamental Algorithms*, Addison-Wesley, Reading, Mass., 1968.

[Kn71] KNUTH, D. E. "Optimum binary search trees." *Acta Informatica* 1 (1971), 14–25.

[Kn73] KNUTH, D. E. *The Art of Computer Programming*, Vol. 3: *Sorting and Searching*, Addison-Wesley, Reading, Mass.. 1973.

[Kt71] KNOTT, G. D. "A balanced tree storage and retrieval algorithm." *Proc. Symp. on Information Storage and Retrieval*, Univ. Maryland, College Park, Md., 1971, 175–196.

[Mo68] MORRIS, R. "Scatter storage techniques." *Comm. ACM* 11, 1 (Jan. 1968), 38–44.

[Mu70] MUNTZ, R.; AND UZGALIS, R. "Dynamic storage allocation for binary search trees in a two-level memory." *Proc. 4th Annual Princeton Conference*, Princeton, N.J., 1970.

[Ni71] NIEVERGELT, J.; AND WONG, C. K. "On binary search trees." *Proc. IFIP Congress 71*, North Holland Publ. Co., Amsterdam 1972, 91–98.

[Ni73a] NIEVERGELT, J.; AND WONG, C. K. "Upper bounds for the total path length of binary trees." *J. ACM* 20, 1 (Jan. 1973), 1–6.

[Ni73b] NIEVERGELT, J.; AND REINGOLD, E. M. "Binary search trees of bounded balance." *SIAM J. Computing* 2, 1 (March 1973), 33–43.

[Se74] SEVERANCE, D. G. "Identifier search mechanisms: a survey and generalized model." *Computing Surveys* 6, 3 (Sept. 1974), 175–194.

[Su63] SUSSENGUTH, E. H. "Use of tree structures for processing files." *Comm. ACM* 6, 5 (May 1963), 272–279.

[Wa71] WALKER, W. A.; AND GOTLIEB, C. C. "A top-down algorithm for constructing nearly-optimal lexicographic trees." R. C. Read (ed.), *Graph Theory and Computing*, Academic Press, New York, 1972, 303–323.

[We71] WEINER, P. "On the heuristic design of binary search trees." *Proc. 5th Annual Princeton Conference*, Princeton, N.J., March 1971.

[Wo72] WONG, C. K.; AND CHANG, S. K. "The generation and balancing of binary search trees." (to appear).

B-Trees

The Ubiquitous B-Tree

DOUGLAS COMER

Computer Science Department, Purdue University, West Lafayette, Indiana 47907

B-trees have become, de facto, a standard for file organization. File indexes of users, dedicated database systems, and general-purpose access methods have all been proposed and implemented using B-trees. This paper reviews B-trees and shows why they have been so successful. It discusses the major variations of the B-tree, especially the B^+-tree, contrasting the relative merits and costs of each implementation. It illustrates a general purpose access method which uses a B-tree.

Keywords and Phrases: B-tree, B^*-tree, B^+-tree, file organization, index

CR Categories: 3.73 3.74 4.33 4.34

INTRODUCTION

The secondary storage facilities available on large computer systems allow users to store, update, and recall data from large collections of information called files. A computer must retrieve an item and place it in main memory before it can be processed. In order to make good use of the computer resources, one must organize files intelligently, making the retrieval process efficient.

The choice of a good file organization depends on the kinds of retrieval to be performed. There are two broad classes of retrieval commands which can be illustrated by the following examples:

Sequential: "From our employee file, prepare a list of all employees' names and addresses," and

Random: "From our employee file, extract the information about employee J. Smith".

We can imagine a filing cabinet with three drawers of folders, one folder for each employee. The drawers might be labeled "A–G," "H–R," and "S–Z," while the folders might be labeled with the employees' last names. A sequential request requires the searcher to examine the entire file, one folder at a time. On the other hand, a random request implies that the searcher, guided by the labels on the drawers and folders, need only extract one folder.

Associated with a large, randomly accessed file in a computer system is an *index* which, like the labels on the drawers and folders of the file cabinet, speeds retrieval by directing the searcher to the small part of the file containing the desired item. Figure 1 depicts a file and its index. An index may be physically integrated with the file, like the labels on employee folders, or physically separate, like the labels on the drawers. Usually the index itself is a file. If the index file is large, another index may be built on top of it to speed retrieval further, and so on. The resulting hierarchy is similar to the employee file, where the topmost index consists of labels on drawers, and the next level of index consists of labels on folders.

Natural hierarchies, like the one formed by considering last names as index entries, do not always produce the best perform-

"The Ubiquitous B-Tree" by D. Comer from *ACM Computing Surveys*, Vol. 11, No. 2, June 1979, pages 121-137. Copyright © 1979 by The Association for Computing Machinery, Inc., reprinted by permission.

CONTENTS

B^+-tree, showing why it has become popular. It surveys the literature on B-trees including recent papers not mentioned in textbooks. In addition, it discusses a general purpose file access method based on the B-tree.

The starting point of our discussion is an internal storage structure called the binary search tree. In particular, we begin with balanced binary search trees because of their guaranteed low retrieval cost. For a survey of binary search trees and other internal storage mechanisms, the reader is referred to SEVE74 and NIEV74. NIEV74 also explains the graph theoretic terms "tree," "node," "edge," "root," "path," and "leaf," which will be used throughout the discussion.

The remainder of this Introduction presents a model of the retrieval process and outlines the file operations to be considered. Section 1 presents the basic B-tree as proposed by Bayer and McCreight, giving the methods for inserting, deleting, and locating items. Then for each type of operation, Section 2 examines the cost and concludes that sequential processing can be expensive. In many cases, changes in implementation can lower the costs; Section 3 shows variations of the B-tree which have been developed to do so. Extending the variations of B-trees, Section 4 reviews the problems of maintaining a B-tree in a multiple user environment and outlines solutions for concurrency and security problems. Finally, Section 5 presents IBM's general purpose file access method which is based on the B-tree.

ance when used in a computer system. Usually, a unique *key* is assigned to each item in the file, and all retrieval is requested by specifying the key. For example, each employee might be assigned a unique employee number which would identify that employee's record. Instead of labeling the drawers of the cabinet "A–G," etc., one would use ranges of employee numbers like "0001"–"3000".

Many techniques for organizing a file and its index have been proposed; Knuth [KNUT73] provides a survey of the basics. While no single scheme can be optimum for all applications, the technique of organizing a file and its index called the B-tree has become widely used. The B-tree is, de facto, the standard organization for indexes in a database system. This paper, intended for computer professionals who have heard of B-trees and want some explanation or direction for further reading, compares several variations of the B-tree, especially the

Operations on a File

For purposes of this paper, we think of a *file* as a set of *n records*, each of the form $r_i = (k_i, \alpha_i)$, in which k_i is called the *key* for the ith record, and α_i the *associated information*. For example, the key for a record in an employee file might be a five-digit employee number, while the associated information might consist of the employee's name, address, salary, and number of dependents.

We assume that key k_i uniquely identifies record r_i. Furthermore, we assume that although the key is much shorter than the

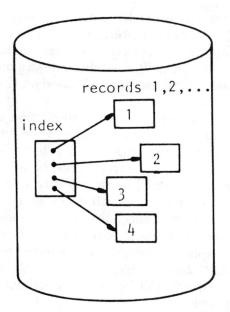

FIGURE 1. A file and its index on a secondary store.

associated information, the set of all keys is too large to fit into main memory. These assumptions imply that if records are to be retrieved randomly using the keys, it would be advantageous to construct an index to speed retrieval. Since the set of all keys does not fit in main memory, the index itself must be external. Finally, we assume that the keys have a natural order, say alphabetical, so we can refer to the *key-sequence order* of a file.

Users conduct *transactions* against a file, inserting, deleting, retrieving, and updating records. In additions, users frequently process the file sequentially, in key-sequence order, starting at a given point. Most often, that starting point is the beginning of the file. A set of *basic operations* which support such transactions are:

insert: add a new record, (k_i, α_i), checking that k_i is unique,

delete: remove record (k_i, α_i) given k_i,

find: retrieve α_i given k_i,

next: retrieve α_{i+1} given that α_i was just retrieved (i.e., process the file sequentially).

For a given file organization, there are costs associated with maintaining the index and with performing each of these operations. Since the index is intended to speed retrieval, processing time is usually taken as the primary cost measure. With current hardware technology, the time required to

access secondary storage is the main component of the total time required to process the data. Furthermore, most random access devices transfer a fixed amount of data per read operation, so that the total time required is linearly related to the number of reads. Therefore, the number of secondary storage accesses serves as a reasonable cost measure for evaluating index methods. Other less important costs include the time to process data once it has been placed in main memory, the secondary storage space utilization, and the ratio of the space required by the index to the space required by the associated information.

1. THE BASIC B-TREE

The B-tree has a short but important history. In the late 1960s computer manufacturers and independent research groups competitively developed general purpose file systems and so-called "access methods" for their machines. At Sperry Univac Corporation (in conjunction with Case Western Reserve University) H. Chiat, M. Schwartz, and others developed and implemented a system which carried out insert and find operations in a manner related to the B-tree method which we will describe shortly. Independently, B. Cole, S. Radcliffe, M. Kaufman, and others developed a similar system at Control Data Corporation (in conjunction with Stanford University). R. Bayer and E. McCreight, then at Boeing Scientific Research Labs, proposed an external index mechanism with relatively low cost for most of the operations defined in the previous section; they called it a B-tree[1] [BAYE72].

This section presents the basic B-tree data structure and maintenance algorithms as a generalization of the binary search tree in which more than two paths leave a given node; the next section discusses costs for each operation. Other general introductions may be found in HORO76, KNUT73, and WIRT76.

---

[1] The origin of "B-tree" has never been explained by the authors. As we shall see, "balanced," "broad," or "bushy" might apply. Others suggest that the "B" stands for Boeing. Because of his contributions, however, it seems appropriate to think of B-trees as "Bayer"-trees.

Recall that in a binary search tree the branch taken at a node depends on the outcome of a comparison of the *query key* and the key stored at the node. If the query is less than the stored key, the left branch is taken; if it is greater, the right branch is followed. Figure 2 shows part of such a tree used to store employee numbers, and the path taken for the query "15."

Now consider Figure 3 which shows a modified search tree with two keys stored in each node. Searching proceeds by choosing one of three paths at each node. In the figure, the query, 15, is less than 42 so the leftmost would be taken at the root. For those queries between 42 and 81 the center path would be selected, while the rightmost path would be followed for queries greater than 81. The decision procedure is repeated at each node until an exact match occurs (success) or a leaf is encountered (failure).

In general, each node in a *B-tree of order d* contains at most $2d$ keys and $2d + 1$ pointers, as shown in Figure 4. Actually, the number of keys may vary from node to node, but each must have at least d keys and $d + 1$ pointers. As a result, each node is at least ½ full. In the usual implementation a node forms one record of the index file, has a fixed length capable of accommodating $2d$ keys and $2d$ pointers, and contains additional information telling how many keys correctly reside in the node.

Usually, large, multikey nodes cannot be kept in main memory and require an access to secondary storage each time they are to be inspected. Later, we will see how, under our cost criterion, maintaining more than one key per node lowers the cost of find, insert, and delete operations.

Balancing

The beauty of B-trees lies in the methods for inserting and deleting records that always leave the tree balanced. As in the case of binary search trees, random insertions of records into a file can leave a tree unbalanced. While an unbalanced tree, like the one shown in Figure 5a has some long paths and some short ones, a balanced tree, like the one shown in Figure 5b, has all leaves at the same depth. Intuitively, B-trees have a shape as shown in Figure 6. The longest path in a B-tree of n keys contains at most about $\log_d n$ nodes, d being the order of the B-tree. A *find* operation may visit n nodes

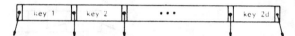

FIGURE 4. A node in a B-tree of order d with $2d$ keys and $2d + 1$ pointers.

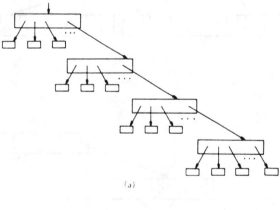

(a)

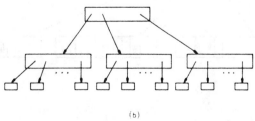

(b)

FIGURE 5. (a) An unbalanced tree with many long paths, and (b) a balanced tree with all paths to leaves exactly the same length.

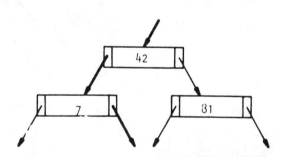

FIGURE 2. Part of a binary search tree for employee numbers. The path taken for query "15" is darkened.

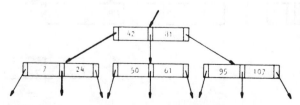

FIGURE 3. A search tree with 2 keys and 3 branches per node. The path taken for query "15" is darkened.

in an unbalanced tree indexing a file of n records, but it never visits more than $1 + \log_d n$ nodes in a B-tree of order d for such a file. Because each visit requires a secondary storage access, balancing the tree has large potential savings. Many schemes to balance trees have been proposed (see NIEV74, FOST65, KARL76 for examples). Each scheme requires some computation time to perform the balancing, so the savings during retrieval operations must be greater than the cost of balancing itself. The B-tree balancing scheme restricts changes in the tree to a single path from a leaf to the root, so it cannot introduce "runaway" overhead. Furthermore, the balancing mechanism uses extra storage to lower the balancing costs (presumably, secondary storage is inexpensive compared to retrieval time). Hence, B-trees gain the advantages of balanced tree schemes while avoiding some of the time-consuming maintenance.

Insertion

To see how balance is maintained during insertion, consider Figure 7a which shows a B-tree of order 2. Since each node in a B-tree of order d contains between d and $2d$ keys, each node in the example has between 2 and 4 keys. Some indicator which is not depicted must be present in each node to mark the current number of keys. Insertion of a new key requires a two-step process. First, a find proceeds from the root to locate the proper leaf for insertion. Then the insertion is performed, and balance is restored by a procedure which moves from the leaf back toward the root. Referring to Figure 7a, one can see that when inserting

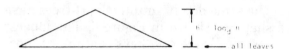

FIGURE 6. The shape of a B-tree of order d indexing a file of n records.

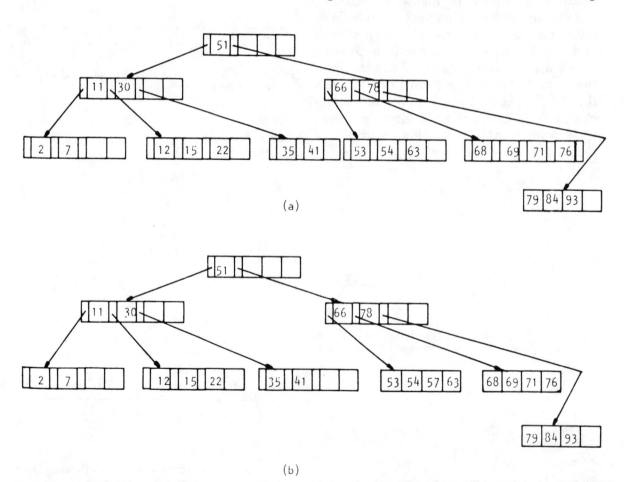

FIGURE 7. (a) A B-tree of order 2, and (b) the same tree after insertion of key "57". Note that the number of keys in the root node may be less than d, the order of the B-tree. All other nodes have at least d keys in them.

the key "57" the find terminates unsuccessfully at the fourth leaf. Since the leaf can accommodate another key, the new key is simply inserted, yielding the tree shown in Figure 7b. If the key "72" were inserted, however, complications would arise because the appropriate leaf is already full. Whenever a key needs to be inserted in a node that is already full, a *split* occurs: the node is divided as shown in Figure 8. Of the $2d + 1$ keys, the smallest d are placed in one node, the largest d are placed in another node, and the remaining value is promoted to the parent node where it serves as a separator. Usually the parent node will accommodate an additional key and the insertion process terminates. If the parent node happens to be full too, then the same splitting process is applied again. In the worst case, splitting propagates all the way to the root and the tree increases in height by one level. In fact, a B-tree only increases in height because of a split at the root.

Deletion

Deletion in a B-tree also requires a find operation to locate the proper node. There are then two possibilities: the key to be deleted resides in a leaf, or the key resides in a nonleaf node. A nonleaf deletion requires that an adjacent key be found and swapped into the vacated position so that it finds work correctly. To locate an adjacent key in key-sequence order, one merely searches for the leftmost leaf in the right subtree of the now empty slot. As in a binary search tree, the needed value always resides in a leaf. Figure 9 demonstrates these relationships.

Once the empty slot has been "moved" to a leaf, we must check to see that at least d keys remain. If less than d keys occupy

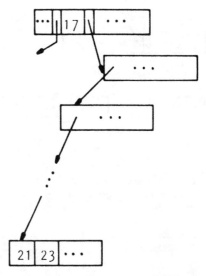

FIGURE 9. Deletion of key "17" requires that the next sequential key, "21" be found and swapped into the vacant position. The next sequential key always resides in the leftmost leaf of the subtree given by the right pointer of the empty position.

the leaf, then an *underflow* is said to occur, and redistribution of the keys becomes necessary. To restore balance (and the B-tree property that each node has at least d keys) only one key is needed—it could be obtained by borrowing from a neighboring leaf. But since the operation requires at least two accesses to secondary storage, a better redistribution would evenly divide the remaining keys between the two neighboring nodes, lowering the cost of successive deletions from the same node. Redistribution is illustrated by Figure 10.

Of course, the distribution of keys among two neighbors will suffice only if there are at least $2d$ keys to distribute. When less than $2d$ values remain, a *concatenation* must occur. During a concatenation, the keys are simply combined into one of the nodes, and the other is discarded (note that concatenation is the inverse of splitting). Since only one node remains, the key separating the two nodes in the ancestor is no longer necessary; it too is added to the single remaining leaf. Figure 11 shows an example of concatenation and the final location of the separator key.

When some node loses a separator key due to concatenation of two of its children, it too may underflow and require redistribution from one of its neighbors. The process of concatenating may force concate-

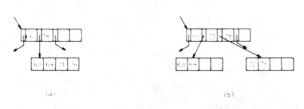

FIGURE 8. (a) a leaf and its ancestor in a B-tree, and (b) the same subtree after insertion of key "72". Each node retains between 2 and 4 keys (d and $2d$).

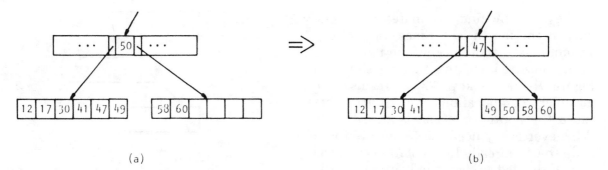

(a)   (b)

FIGURE 10. (a) Part of a B-tree before, and (b) after redistribution of keys among two neighbors. Note the final position of the separator key, "50". Redistribution into equal size nodes helps avoid underflow on successive deletions.

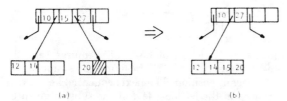

(a)   (b)

FIGURE 11. (a) A deletion causing concatenation, and (b) the rebalanced tree.

nating at the next higher level, and so on, to the root level. Finally, if the descendants of the root are concatenated, they form a new root, decreasing the height of the B-tree by 1.

Algorithms for insertion and deletion may be found in BAYE72. Simple examples programmed in PASCAL are provided by Wirth [WIRT76].

2. THE COST OF OPERATIONS

Since visiting a node in a B-tree requires an access to secondary storage, the number of nodes visited during an operation provides a measure of its cost. Bayer and McCreight [BAYE72] give a precise analysis of the costs of insertion, deletion, and retrieval. They also provide comprehensive experimental results which relate the theoretical bounds to actual devices. Knuth [KNUT73] also derives bounds for the cost of operations in a B-tree using a slightly different definition. The next section gives a simple explanation of the asymptotic bound on costs.

Retrieval Costs

First, consider the cost of a find operation. Except for the root, each node in the B-tree has at least d direct descendants since there

are between d and $2d$ keys per node; the root has at least 2 descendants. So the number of nodes at depths[2] 0, 1, 2, ..., must be at least 2, $2d$, $2d^2$, $2d^3$, ... All leaves lie at the same depth h so there are

$$\sum_{i=0}^{h} d^i = \frac{d^h - 1}{2d - 1}$$

nodes with at least d keys each. The height of a tree with n total keys is therefore constrained so that

$$2d(d^h - 1)/(d - 1) \le n$$

with a little work one can show that

$$2d^h \le n + 1,$$

or

$$h \le \log_d \frac{n + 1}{2}$$

Thus, the cost of processing a find operation grows as the logarithm of the file size.

Table I shows how reasonable logarithmic cost can be, even for large files. A B-tree of order 50 which indexes a file of one million records can be searched with only 4 disk accesses in the worst case. Later we will see that this estimate is too high; simple implementation techniques lower the worst case cost to 3, and the average cost to less.

Aho et al. [AHO74] provide another perspective on the cost of finds in a B-tree. They show that for the decision-tree model of computation, one where searching is based on comparison at each node, no asymptotically faster retrieval algorithm can be devised. Of course, this model does

_____
[2] The root of a tree lies at depth 0; sons of a node at depth $i-1$ lie at depth i.

TABLE I. Upper bound on the number of nodes retrieved in the worst case for various node sizes and file sizes.

Node size \ File size (records)	10^3	10^4	10^5	10^6	10^7
10	3	4	5	6	7
50	2	3	3	4	4
100	2	2	3	3	4
150	2	2	3	3	4

rule out some methods, such as hashing [MAUE75]. Nevertheless, B-trees exhibit low retrieval costs in both a practical and theoretical sense.

Insertion and Deletion Costs

An insert or delete operation may require additional secondary storage accesses beyond the cost of a find operation as it progresses back up the tree. Overall, the costs are at most doubled, so the height of the tree still dominates the expressions for these costs. Therefore, in a B-tree of order d for a file of n records, insertion and deletion take time proportional to $\log_d n$ in the worst case.

The advantage of nodes containing a large number of keys should now be clear. As the branch factor, d, increases, the logarithmic base increases, and the costs of find, insert, and delete operations decrease. There are, however, practical limits on the size of a node: most hardware systems bound the amount of data that can be transferred with one access to secondary storage. Besides, our cost hides the constant factor which grows as the size of data transferred increases. Finally, each device has some fixed track size which must be accommodated to avoid wasting large amounts of space. So, in practice, optimum node size depends critically on the characteristics of the system and the devices on which the file is allocated.

Bayer and McCreight [BAYE72] give some loose guidelines for choosing node sizes based on rotational delay time, transfer rate, and key size. Their experiments verify that the model's optimal values perform well in practice.

Sequential Processing

So far we have considered random transactions conducted by specifying a key. Often, users wish to view the file as a sequential one, using the *next* operation to process all records in key-sequence order. In fact, one alternative to B-trees, the so called Indexed Sequential Access Method (ISAM) [GHOS69], assumes that sequential accesses occur very frequently.

Unfortunately, a B-tree may not do well in a sequential processing environment. While a simple preorder tree walk [KNUT68] extracts all the keys in order, it requires space for at least $h = \log_d(n + 1)$ nodes in main memory since it stacks the nodes along a path from the root to avoid reading them twice. Additionally, processing a next operation may require tracing a path through several nodes before reaching the desired key. For example, the smallest key is located in the leftmost leaf; finding it requires accessing all nodes along a path from the root to that leaf as shown in Figure 12.

What can be done to improve the cost of the next operation? This question and others will be answered in the next section, under the topic "B$^+$-trees."

3. B-TREES VARIANTS

As with most file organizations, variations of B-trees abound. Bayer and McCreight [BAYE72] suggest several implementation alternatives in their original paper. For ex-

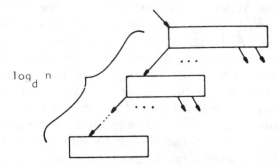

$\log_d n$

FIGURE 12. The location of the smallest key in the leftmost leaf of a B-tree. Reaching it requires $\log_d n$ accesses.

ample, the underflow condition, resulting from a deletion, is handled without concatenation by redistributing keys from neighboring nodes (unless the requisite number of keys cannot be obtained). Applying the same strategy to the overflow condition can delay splitting and eliminate the associated overhead. Thus, instead of splitting a node as soon as it fills up, keys could merely be distributed into a neighboring node, splitting only when two neighbors fill.

Other variations of B-trees have concentrated on improvements in the secondary costs. Clampet [CLAM64] considers the cost of processing a node once it has been retrieved from secondary storage. He suggests using a binary search instead of a linear lookup to locate the proper descendent pointer. Knuth [KNUT73] points out that a binary search might be useful if the node is large, while a sequential search might be best for small nodes. There is no reason to limit internal searching to sequential or binary search; any number of techniques from KNUT73 might be used. In particular, Maruyama and Smith [MARU77] mention an extrapolation technique they call the square root search.

In their general treatment of index creation for a file, Ghosh and Senko [GHOS69] consider the use of an interpolation search to eliminate a secondary storage access. The analysis presented generalizes to B-trees and indicates that it might be cost effective to eliminate some of the index levels just above the leaves. Since a search would terminate with several possible candidate leaves, the correct one would be found by an "estimate" based on the key value and the key distribution within the file. When the estimate produced the wrong leaf, a sequential search could be carried out. Although some estimates might miss, the method would pay off on the average.

Knuth [KNUT73] suggests a B-tree variation which has varying "order" at each depth. Part of the motivation comes from his observation that pointers in leaf nodes waste space and should be eliminated. It also makes sense to have a different shape for the root (which is seldom very full compared to the other nodes). Maintenance

costs for this implementation seem rather high compared to the benefits, especially since secondary storage is both inexpensive and well suited to fixed length nodes.

B*-Trees

Perhaps the most misused term in B-tree literature is B*-tree.[3] Actually, Knuth [KNUT73] defines a B*-tree to be a B-tree in which each node is at least 2/3 full (instead of just 1/2 full). B*-tree insertion employs a local redistribution scheme to delay splitting until 2 sibling nodes are full. Then the 2 nodes are divided into 3, each 2/3 full. This scheme guarantees that storage utilization is at least 66%, while requiring only moderate adjustment of the maintenance algorithms. It should be pointed out that increasing storage utilization has the side effect of speeding up the search since the height of the resulting tree is smaller.

The term B*-tree has frequently been applied to another, very popular variation of B-trees also suggested by Knuth (cf. [KNUT73, WEDE74, BAYE77]). To avoid confusion, we will use the term B⁺-tree for Knuth's unnamed implementation.

B⁺-Trees

In a B⁺-tree, all keys reside in the leaves. The upper levels, which are organized as a B-tree, consist only of an index, a roadmap to enable rapid location of the index and key parts. Figure 13 shows the logical separation of the index and key parts. Naturally, index nodes and leaf nodes may have different formats or even different sizes. In particular, leaf nodes are usually linked together left-to-right, as shown. The linked list of leaves is referred to as the *sequence set*. Sequence set links allow easy sequential processing.

To fully appreciate a B⁺-tree, one must understand the implications of having an independent index and sequence set. Consider for a moment the find operation.

---

[3] An amusing case is the "B* tree search algorithm," which is about a tree-search algorithm named B* [BERL78].

Searching proceeds from the root of a B⁺-tree through the index to a leaf. Since all keys reside in the leaves, it does not matter what values are encountered as the search progresses as long as the path leads to the correct leaf.

During deletion in a B⁺-tree, the ability to leave non-key values in the index part as separators simplifies processing. The key to be deleted must always reside in a leaf so its removal is simple. As long as the leaf remains at least half full, the index need not be changed, even if a copy of the key had been propagated up into it. Figure 14 shows how the copy of a deleted key can still direct searches to the correct leaf. Of course, if an underflow condition arises, the redistribution or concatenation procedures may require adjusting values in the index as well as in the leaves.

Insertion and find operations in a B⁺-tree are processed almost identically to insertion and find operations in a B-tree. When a leaf splits in two, instead of promoting the middle key, the algorithm promotes a copy of the key, retaining the actual key in the right leaf. Find operations differ from those in a B-tree in that searching does not stop if a key in the index equals the query value. Instead, the nearest right pointer is followed, and the search proceeds all the way to a leaf.

We have seen that B-trees, which support low-cost find, insert, and delete operations, may require $\log_d n$ accesses to secondary storage to process a next operation. The B⁺-tree implementation retains the logarithmic cost properties for operations by key, but gains the advantage of requiring at most 1 access to satisfy a next operation. Moreover, during the sequential processing of a file, no node will be accessed more than once, so space for only 1 node need be available in main memory. Thus, B⁺-trees are well suited to applications which entail both random and sequential processing.

Prefix B⁺-Trees

The separation of the index and sequence set in a B⁺-tree is intuitively appealing. Recall that the index part serves merely as a roadmap to guide the search to the correct leaf; it need not contain actual keys at all. When keys consist of a string of characters there is good reason not to use actual keys

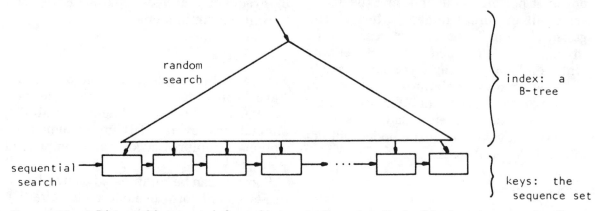

FIGURE 13. A B⁺-tree with separate index and key parts. Operations "by key" begin at the root as in a B-tree; sequential processing begins at the leftmost leaf.

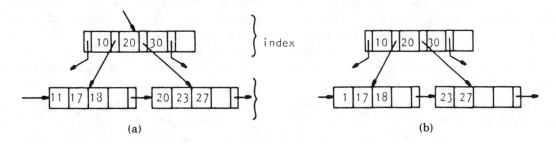

FIGURE 14. (a) A B⁺-tree and (b) the B⁺-tree after deletion of the key "20". Even after its removal, key "20" still serves as a separator value in the index part.

as separators: actual keys require too much space. Bayer and Unterauer [BAYE77] consider an alternative, the Prefix B⁺-tree.

Suppose that the sequence of alphabetic keys "binary," "compiler," "computer," "electronic," "program," and "system" were allocated in a B-tree as shown in Figure 15. The separator value in the index between the keys "computer," "electronic" need not be either of them; any string between suffices. For example, any of the strings "elec," "e," or "d" would do nicely. Since it makes no difference during retrieval, the shortest such separator should be used to save space. As space requirements become smaller, more keys can be placed in each node, the branching factor increases, and the height of the tree decreases. Since shorter trees cost less to search, using shorter separators will decrease access time as well as save space.

The simple technique of choosing the shortest unique prefix of the key to serve as a separator works well. In the example, the shortest prefix of "electronic" which distinguishes it from "computer" is "e." Sometimes, however, the prefix technique does not perform well: choosing the shortest prefix of "programmers" which distinguishes it from "programmer" results in no savings at all. In such cases, Bayer and Unterauer suggest scanning a small neighborhood of keys to obtain a good pair for the separation algorithm. While this may leave the nodes unevenly loaded, having a few extra keys in one of the nodes will not affect the overall costs.

Virtual B-Trees

Many modern computer systems employ a memory management scheme which provides each user with a large virtual memory. The address space of a user's virtual memory is divided into pages which are saved on secondary storage and loaded into main memory automatically when they are referenced. This technique, called *demand paging*, multiplexes real memory among users and, at the same time, affords protection to insure that one user will not interfere with the data of another. Furthermore, special purpose hardware handles the paging so that transfers to and from secondary storage are performed at high speed.

The availability of demand paging hardware suggests an interesting implementation of B-trees. Through careful allocation, each node of the B-tree can be mapped into one page of the virtual address space. Then the user treats the B-tree as if it were in memory. Accesses to nodes (pages) which are not in memory cause the system to "page-in" the node from secondary storage.

Most paging algorithms choose to remove the least recently used (LRU) page when making room for a new one. In terms of a B-tree, the most active nodes are those close to the root; these tend to stay in memory. In fact, Bayer and McCreight [BAYE72] and Knuth [KNUT73] both suggest a LRU mechanism for B-trees even when not using paging hardware. At least, the root should remain in main memory since it is accessed for each search.

Thus, virtual B-trees have the following advantages:

1) The special hardware performs transfers at high speed,
2) The memory protection mechanism isolates other users, and
3) Frequently accessed parts of the tree will remain in memory.

Compression

Several other implementation techniques have been suggested to improve the performance of B-trees. Wagner [WAGN73] summarizes several of them, including the notions of compressed keys and compressed pointers.[4]

Pointers can be compressed using a base/displacement form of node address rather than an absolute address value. A node with compressed pointers has the form shown in Figure 16, where the base address is stored once in the node, and an offset value, or displacement beyond the base, replaces each pointer. To reconstruct an actual pointer value, the base is added to the displacement for that pointer. Compressed pointer techniques are particularly appropriate for virtual B-trees where pointers take on large address values.

Keys, or separator values, can be com-

---

[4] See also AUER76.

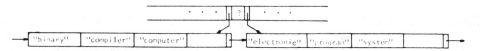

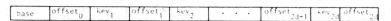

FIGURE 15. Part of a Prefix B$^+$-tree. The index entry "e" is sufficient to separate "computer" from "electronic."

base	offset$_0$	key$_1$	offset$_1$	key$_2$	$\cdots$	offset$_{2d-1}$	key$_{2d}$	offset$_{2d}$

FIGURE 16. A node with compressed pointers. To obtain the ith pointer, the base value is added to the ith offset.

pressed using any one of several standard techniques for removing redundancy [RUBI76]. Both key compression and pointer compression increase the capacity of each node and, therefore, decrease the retrieval costs. The tradeoff for decreased secondary storage accesses is an increase in the CPU time necessary to search a node after it has been read. Thus, complicated compression algorithms may not always be cost effective.

It should be noted that both front and rear compression can be applied to keys. For example Bayer and Unterauer [BAYE77] consider compression of keys for prefix B$^+$-trees.

Variable Length Entries

Many applications require the storage of data with variable length keys. Additionally, variable length entries result from compression techniques mentioned above. McCreight [McCR77] considers the storage of trees with variable length entries and shows how promoting shorter keys during an insertion produces a tree with better storage utilization and faster access times.

Binary B-Trees

Another variation proposed by Bayer [BAYE72a], the Binary B-tree, makes B-trees suitable for a one-level store. Essentially, a Binary B-tree is a B-tree of order 1; each node has 1 or 2 keys and 2 or 3 pointers. To avoid wasting space for nodes that are only half full, a linked representation is used as shown in Figure 17. Nodes with 1 key are represented exactly as in Figure 17a, while nodes with 2 keys are linked as in Figure 17b. Since the right pointer in a node may point to either a

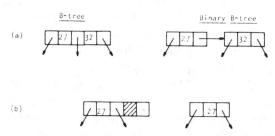

FIGURE 17. Nodes in a B-tree and the corresponding nodes in a Binary B-tree. Each right pointer in the Binary B-tree representation can point to a sibling or a descendent.

sibling or a descendant, one extra bit must be used to indicate its meaning.

Analysis shows that insertion, deletion, and find still take only log n steps as in a B-tree, although searching the rightmost path requires twice as many nodes to be accessed as the leftmost. Using the right pointer for two purposes does complicate the insertion and deletion algorithms, however. To maintain logarithmic cost, care must be taken to insure that there are never two right links pointing to sibling nodes in a row. Detailed algorithms for a rotation process, one that prevents three or more successive sibling links, are given in BAYE72a and WIRT76.

An extension of the Binary B-tree, which allows for both left and right links to point to sibling nodes, exhibits symmetry lacking in the Binary B-tree. Hence, the name Symmetric Binary B-tree has been applied to such a data structure by Bayer [BAYE73], who also reports that Symmetric Binary B-trees contain the well-known class of AVL trees as a subclass [FOST65].

2-3 Trees and Theoretical Results

Hopcroft developed the notion of a 2-3 tree, and explored its usefulness in a one-level store. Each node in a 2-3 tree has 2 or 3 sons (because it contains 1 or 2 keys). Thus, a 2-3 tree is a B-tree of order 1, and vice versa. The small node size makes 2-3 trees impractical for external storage, but quite appropriate for an internal data structure. Rosenbaum and Snyder [ROSE78], and Miller et al. [MILL77] consider the problem of constructing optimal 2-3 trees for a given set of keys. They use the number of comparisons and the number of node accesses, respectively, as the cost criterion. In each case, a linear time algorithm is presented for constructing optimal trees from the sorted list of keys. The results in MILL77 extend to B-trees of arbitrary order.

Yao [YAO78] reports the results of analyzing 2-3 trees built from a uniformly distributed set of n keys. The paper gives both an upper and lower bound on the expected storage utilization. Extending the analysis to B-trees of higher order, Yao has shown that the expected storage utilization is $ln\ 2 \approx 69\%$.

Guibas et al. [GUIB77] consider a B-tree variant for maintaining a list of keys which have highly skewed probability of access. By maintaining a set of *fingers* which point to localities of interest, one can update items within p locations from a finger in $\log_d p$ time. For example, one might allocate a finger at the beginning and end of the list. As locality of activity changes, one of the fingers can be moved to the new locality.

Guibas and Sedgewick [GUIB78] present another B-tree scheme and compare the performance of several balanced tree techniques. Their important contribution shows that no upward splitting is ever required. The trick is to split nodes that are nearly full when traveling down the tree. The next section shows that eliminating bottom-up updating can be crucial to performance.

Also see BROW78 and BROW78a for related theoretical results.

4. B-TREES IN A MULTIUSER ENVIRONMENT

If B-trees are to be used in a general purpose database system, they must permit several user requests to be processed simultaneously. Unless some constraints are applied to synchronize the processes, they may interfere with each other. One process may read a node and follow one of the links while another process is changing it. To further complicate the interaction, find operations begin processing top-down in the B-tree while insertion and deletion require bottom-up access. Samadi [SAMA76] presents one solution to the concurrency problem. Held and Stonebraker [HELD78] argue that concurrency conflicts, which are resolved by giving only one process access to the tree, diminish the advantages of B-trees in a multiuser environment.

Bayer and Schkolnick [BAYE77a] show that a set of locking protocols, enforced by a supervisor process, can insure the integrity of B-tree accesses while allowing concurrent activity. In essence, a find locks, or holds, a node once it has been read so that other processes cannot interfere with it. As the search progresses to the next depth, the find processor releases its lock on the ancestor, allowing others to read it. Thus, readers lock at most two nodes at any time; other reader processes are free to explore (and lock) other parts of the tree simultaneously.

Updating in a concurrent environment presents a more complex problem, one that requires more complex protocols. Since updates may affect higher levels in the tree, an update process leaves a reservation on each node it accesses, reserving the right to lock the node. Later, the reservation may be converted to a lock if the update process determines that its change will propagate to the reserved node. Alternatively, the reservation may be cancelled if the update will not affect the reserved node. Reserved nodes may be read, since readers will always continue to a leaf, but they may not be reserved a second time until the first reservation is cancelled.

Once an update process establishes reservations on a path leading to some leaf, it may convert the reservations to absolute locks, top-down. The absolute lock guarantees that no other process will access the node. Then the update proceeds, changing only nodes on which it holds absolute locks. After all changes have been made, absolute locks are cancelled and the updated path becomes available for other processes.

Reserving an entire path from the root to a leaf prevents other updates from accessing the B-tree. Furthermore, most updates affect only a few levels—those near a leaf—

so reserving an entire path is not desirable. Yet reserving too few nodes might make it necessary to begin again at the root. Bayer and Schkolnick, therefore, propose a generalized locking protocol which represents a tradeoff between the two extremes. They provide a parameterized model and show how reservations can permit enough concurrency to utilize present technology while wasting very little time on restarting reservations.

In contrast, using the top-down splitting suggested in GUIB78 eliminates the need for all but the most simple protocols, since updaters never need to travel back up the tree at all. Thus, only one pair of nodes will ever be locked at a given time. Of course, the price for splitting nodes before they fill completely is a slight decrease in storage utilization and a corresponding increase in access time.

Security

The protection of information in a multi-user environment poses another problem for database designers. Earlier, under the topic Virtual B-Tree, it was indicated that isolation of users could be obtained from the memory protection mechanism of paging. When the contents of a file must be protected outside of the system, some encryption technique must be used. Bayer and Metzger [BAYE76] consider encipherment schemes and possible security threats. They show that encipherment has a relatively high cost unless implemented via hardware. On the other hand, changes to the B-tree maintenance algorithms to accommodate encoded files are minor, especially if the encipherment can be done "on the fly" during data transmission.

5. A GENERAL PURPOSE ACCESS METHOD USING B⁺-TREES

This section presents an example of the use of B⁺-trees—IBM's general purpose B-tree based access method, VSAM [IBM1, IBM2, KEEH72, WAGN73]. Intended to serve in a wide variety of applications, VSAM is designed to support sequential searching as well as logarithmic cost insertion, deletion, and find operations. Compared to the conventional indexed-sequential organization,

the B⁺-trees offer the following advantages: dynamic allocation and release of storage, guaranteed storage utilization of 50%, and no need for periodic "reorganization" of the entire file.

Since VSAM must handle the storage of both keys and associated information, a VSAM file is represented as in Figure 18. The top two sections of the VSAM tree form a B⁺-tree index and sequence set as described earlier; the leaves contain actual *data records*. In VSAM terminology, a leaf is called a *control interval*, and forms the basic unit of data transferred in one I/O operation. Each control interval contains one or more data records as well as *control information* describing the format of the interval. Figure 19 illustrates the fields of a control interval.

Performance Enhancements

Although VSAM presents a logical, or machine-independent, view of data to the user, the file organization must accommodate the underlying devices if transactions are to be conducted efficiently. Therefore, the maximum size of a control interval is limited by the largest unit of data that the hardware can transfer in one operation. In addition, the set of all control intervals associated with one sequence set node (called a *control area*) must fit on one cylinder of the particular disk storage unit used to store the file. These restrictions improve performance and permit even further enhancements described below.

Since all the descendants of a sequence set node are allocated on one cylinder, performance can be improved by allocating the sequence set node on the same cylinder. Then, once the sequence set node has been retrieved, items in the control area can be retrieved without disk arm movement. An extension to the contiguous sequence set node allocation is demonstrated in Figure 20 which shows how the sequence set node can be replicated on one track of the cylinder. Replication reduces disk seek time. VSAM attempts to improve performance in several other ways. Pointers are compressed using the base/displacement method described above, keys are compressed in both the forward (prefix) and

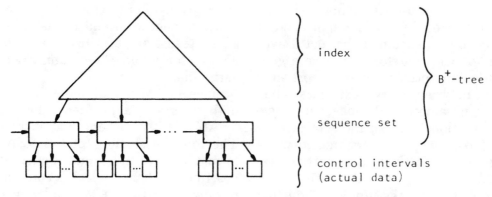

FIGURE 18. A VSAM file with actual data (associated information) stored in the leaves.

Data record 1	Data record 2	· · ·	Data record r	control information about data	control information about control interval

FIGURE 19. The format of a control interval. The control fields describe the control interval itself, and the format of the data fields.

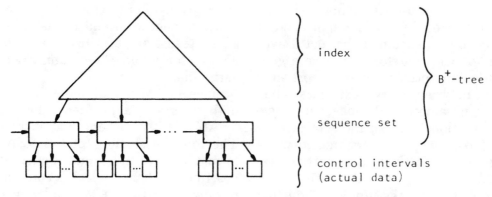

FIGURE 20. The format of a control area with the sequence set node, S, replicated on the first track to minimize latency time.

backward (suffix) directions, index records can be replicated, and the index can be allocated on a separate device to allow concurrent access of index and data. Finally, VSAM allows the index part to be a virtual B-tree, using the virtual memory hardware to retrieve it.

Tree-Structured File Directory

Perhaps the most novel idea in the VSAM implementation is that one data format should be used throughout the system. For example, those routines which maintain a directory of all VSAM files in the system keep the information in a VSAM file, the *master catalog*. Figure 21 shows the master catalog which contains an entry for each VSAM file (or VSAM data set). Since all VSAM files must be entered into the catalog, the system can locate any file automatically given its name. Of course, the catalog is a VSAM data set so it contains an entry describing itself.

If several processes access the master catalog simultaneously, contention occurs, and all but one will have to wait. To avoid lengthy delays caused by such contention, each user can define a local catalog with entries for his VSAM files. The user catalogs, which are VSAM files, must be entered into the master catalog. Once a user catalog has been located by searching the master catalog, further references to files indexed by that catalog do not entail searching the master catalog. The resulting multilevel, tree-structured catalog scheme has a flavor similar to the MULTICS file system [ORGA72].

Other VSAM Facilities

Many facets of VSAM have not surfaced in our brief discussion—the reader is warned that we have only given a quick overview. For example, the VSAM files we discussed are called *key-sequenced*. Another form, the *entry-sequenced* VSAM files allow efficient sequential processing when no key accompanies a record (i.e., no operations are to be performed using the key). Entry-sequenced VSAM files require no index so they are less expensive to maintain.

In addition to the VSAM file maintenance and retrieval procedures, the system provides a mechanism for defining and loading a VSAM file. One must decide how to distribute free space within the file: if the user anticipates many insertions, then

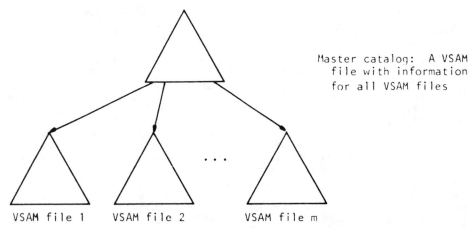

Master catalog: A VSAM file with information for all VSAM files

VSAM file 1   VSAM file 2   VSAM file m

FIGURE 21.   The VSAM Master catalog, which serves as a directory for all VSAM files, is itself a VSAM file.

the file should probably not be loaded with each node 100% full or the initial insertions will be expensive. On the other hand, if the file will remain relatively stable, loading the nodes to only 50% capacity wastes storage. The VSAM file definition facility provides assistance by loading the file according to the parameters chosen.

Finally, VSAM supplies facilities for efficient insertion of a large contiguous set of records, protection of data, file backup, and error recovery, all of which are necessary in a production environment.

SUMMARY

A balanced, multiway, external file organization, the B-tree, is efficient, versatile, simple, and easily maintained. One variation, the B$^+$-tree, allows efficient sequential processing of the file while retaining the desirable logarithmic cost for find, insert, and delete operations. B-tree schemes guarantee 50% storage utilization while allocating and releasing space as the file grows or shrinks. Moreover, B-trees grow and shrink in exactly the opposite manner; massive file "reorganization" is never necessary even after heavy transaction traffic.

Different B-tree implementation techniques provide enhanced performance, generality, and the ability to use B-trees in a multiuser environment. Compression of keys and pointers, careful allocation (and replication) of nodes on secondary storage, and local redistribution of keys during insertion or deletion all improve performance and make B-trees viable in a production environment, while locking protocols, vir-

tual memory protection, and data encryption provide security and mutual exclusion necessary when a B-tree must be shared by several users.

IBM's VSAM demonstrates that it is reasonable to construct a general purpose file access method based on B-trees. In addition to user's B-tree files, the system itself uses a B-tree file to catalog the name and location of all available VSAM files. Using a B$^+$-tree implementation to permit efficient sequential processing, VSAM incorporates many of the techniques available for performance enhancement and protection of data.

ACKNOWLEDGMENTS

The author thanks the referees, especially for providing contacts regarding the history of B-trees, and IBM Corporation for cheerfully making available detailed information on its B-tree based access method when none of its competitors would reveal theirs.

REFERENCES

AHO74   AHO, A., HOPCROFT, J., AND ULLMAN, J. *The design and analysis of computer algorithms,* Addison Wesley, Publ. Co., Reading, Mass., 1974.

AUER76   AUER, R. *Schlusselkompressionen in B*-baumen,* Diplomarbeit, Tech. Universitat, Munich, 1976.

BAYE72   BAYER, R., AND MCCREIGHT, C. "Organization and maintenance of large ordered indexes," *Acta Inf.* 1, 3 (1972), 173–189.

BAYE72a BAYER, R. "Binary B-trees for virtual memory," in *Proc. 1971 ACM SIGFIDET Workshop,* ACM, New York, 219–235.

BAYE73   BAYER, R. "Symmetric binary B-trees: data structure and maintenance algorithms," *Acta Inf.* 1, 4 (1972), 290–306.

BAYE76   BAYER, R., AND METZGER, J. "On enciclopherment of search trees and random access files," *ACM Trans. Database Syst.* **1,** 1 (March 1976), 37–52.

BAYE77   BAYER, R., AND UNTERAUER, K. "Prefix B-trees," *ACM Trans. Database Syst.* **2,** 1 (March 1977), 11–26.

BAYE77a   BAYER, R., AND SCHKOLNICK, M. "Concurrency of operations on B-trees," *Acta Inf.* **9,** 1 (1977), 1–21.

BERL78   BERLINER, H. *The B*-tree search algorithm: a best-first proof procedure,* Tech. Rep. CMU-CA-78-112, Computer Science Dept., Carnegie-Mellon Univ., Pittsburgh, 1978.

BROW78   BROWN, M. "A storage scheme for height-balanced trees," *Inf. Process. Lett.* **7,** 5 (Aug. 1978), 231–232.

BROW78a   BROWN, M. "A partial analysis of height-balanced trees," *SIAM J. Comput.,* to appear.

CLAM64   CLAMPETT, H. "Randomized binary searching with tree structures," *Commun. ACM* **7,** 3 (March 1964), 163–165.

FOST65   FOSTER, C. "Information storage and retrieval using AVL trees," in *Proc. ACM 20th National Conf.,* ACM, New York, 1965, 192–205.

GHOS69   GHOSH, S., AND SENKO, M. "File organization: on the selection of random access index points for sequential files," *J. ACM* **16,** 4 (Oct. 1969), 569–579.

GUIB77   GUIBUS, L., MCCREIGHT, E., PLASS, M., AND ROBERTS, J. "A new representation for linear lists," in *Proc. 9th ACM Symp. Theory of Computing,* ACM, New York, 1977, 49–60.

GUIB78   GUIBAS, L., AND SEDGEWICK, R. "A dichromatic framework for balanced trees," in *Proc. 19th Symp. Foundations of Computer Science,* 1978, 8–21.

HELD78   HELD, G., AND STONEBRAKER, M. "B-trees reexamined," *Commun. ACM* **21,** 2 (Feb. 1978), 139–143.

HORO76   HOROWITZ, E., AND SAHNI, S. *Fundamentals of data structures,* Computer Science Press, Inc., Woodland Hills, Calif., 1976.

IBM1   *OS/VS Virtual Storage Access Method (VSAM) planning guide,* Order No. GC26-3799, IBM, Armonk, N.Y.

IBM2   *OS/VS Virtual Storage Access Method (VSAM) logic,* Order No. SY26-3841, IBM, Armonk, N.Y.

KARL76   KARLTON, P., FULLER, S., SCROGGS, R., AND KACHLER, E. "Performance of height balanced trees," *Commun. ACM* **19,** 1 (Jan. 1976), 23–28.

KEEH74   KEEHN, D., AND LACY, J. "VSAM data set design parameters," *IBM Syst. J.* **3,** (1974), 186–212.

KNUT68   KNUTH, D. *The art of computer programming, Vol. 1: fundamental algorithms,* Addison-Wesley Publ. Co., Reading, Mass., 1968.

KNUT73   KNUTH, D. *The art of computer programming, Vol. 3: sorting and searching,* Addison-Wesley Publ. Co., Reading, Mass., 1973.

MARU77   MARUYAMA, K., AND SMITH, S. "Analysis of design alternatives for virtual memory indexes," *Commun. ACM* **20,** 4 (April 1977), 245–254.

MAUE75   MAUER, W., AND LEWIS, T. "Hash table methods," *Comput. Surv.* **7,** 1 (March 1975), 5–19.

MCCR77   MCCREIGHT, E. "Pagination of B*-trees with variable-length records," *Commun. ACM* **20,** 9 (Sept. 1977), 670–674.

MILL77   MILLER, R., PIPPENGER, N., ROSENBERG, A., AND SNYDER, L. *Optimal 2-3 trees,* IBM Research Rep. RC 6505, IBM Research Lab., Yorktown Heights, N.Y., 1977.

NIEV74   NIEVERGELT, J. "Binary search trees and file organization," *Comput. Surv.* **6,** 3 (Sept. 1973), 195–207.

ORGA72   ORGANICK, E. *The Multics system: an examination of its structure,* MIT Press, Cambridge, Mass., 1972.

ROSE78   ROSENBERG, A., AND SNYDER, L. "Minimal comparison 2-3 trees," *SIAM J. Comput.* **7,** 4 (Nov. 1978), 465–480.

RUBI76   RUBIN, F. "Experiments in text file compression," *Commun. ACM* **19,** 11 (Nov. 1976), 617–623.

SAMA76   SAMADI, B. "B-trees in a system with multiple views," *Inf. Process. Lett.* **5,** 4 (Oct. 1976), 107–112.

SEVE74   SEVERENCE, D. "Identifier search mechnisms: a survey and generalized model," *Comput. Surv.* **6,** 3 (Sept. 1974), 175–194.

WAGN73   WAGNER, R. "Indexing design considerations," *IBM Syst. J.* **4,** (1973), 351–367.

WEDE74   WEDEKIND, H. "On the selection of access paths in a database system," in *Data base management (Proc. IFIP Working Conf. Data Base Management)* J. Klimbie and K. Koffeman (Eds.), Elsevier/North-Holland Publishing Co., New York, 1974, 385–397.

WIRT76   WIRTH, N. *Algorithms + data structures = programs,* Prentice-Hall Inc., Englewood Cliffs, N.J., 1976.

YAO78   YAO, A. "On random 2-3 trees," *Acta Inf.* **9,** 2 (1978), 159–170.

RECEIVED AUGUST 1978; FINAL REVISION ACCEPTED DECEMBER 1978.

Binary Digital
Search Trees

Reprinted from *IEEE Transactions on Software Engineering*, Vol. SE-13, No. 7, July 1987, pages 799-810. Copyright © 1987 by The Institute of Electrical and Electronics Engineers, Inc. All rights reserved.

Two Access Methods Using Compact Binary Trees

WIEBREN DE JONGE, ANDREW S. TANENBAUM, MEMBER, IEEE, AND REIND P. VAN DE RIET

Abstract—It is shown how a highly compact representation of binary trees can be used as the basis of two access methods for dynamic files, called BDS-trees and S-trees, respectively. Both these methods preserve key-order and offer easy and efficient sequential access. They are different in the way the compact binary trees are used for searching. With a BDS-tree the search is a digital search using binary digits. Although the S-tree search is performed on a bit-by-bit basis as well, it will appear to be slightly different. Actually, with S-trees the compact binary trees are used to represent separators at low storage costs. As a result, the fan-out, and thus performance, of a B-tree can be improved by using within each index page an S-tree for representing separators efficiently.

Index Terms—Access method, B-tree, file, searching, tree.

I. INTRODUCTION

IN many applications, files consist of many records, each containing a key by which the record is accessed. Examples are personnel files keyed on employee number, inventory files keyed on part number, and bank files keyed on account number. Typical operations are: given a key, read, write or delete the corresponding record; insert a new record in such a way that it can later be efficiently retrieved by its key; read the entire file sequentially, in key order; and perform a range query. To perform all these operations efficiently, the program (or database system) must be able to map a key onto the disk address of the corresponding record, without this mapping itself requiring many disk accesses.

Several methods for performing the mapping are known, including B-trees [1]–[3], Trie Hashing [12], Extendible Hashing [7], and Linear Hashing [10], [11]. The access methods that will be developed in this paper, are, like B-trees and Trie Hashing, order preserving, which makes sequential access to the records easy. Linear Hashing and Extendible Hashing do not have this property, and will not be considered further. B-trees, Trie Hashing, and our two methods all require some kind of data structure, or index, used to convert keys to disk addresses. This index must be updated as the file changes. The various methods use different data structures for the index. Actually, our methods mainly differ from B-trees and Trie Hashing in the way the index is represented.

In the following sections, we will describe our ideas in detail. In Section II, we present the necessary background information about access methods and keys. Then the bi-

nary digital search tree (BDS-tree), a first method using binary trees, is discussed and illustrated by an example in Section III. In Section IV we turn to a variation, the separator tree (S-tree), which offers better storage utilization. It is this variation that shows how separators can be represented by binary trees. Section V deals with the compact representation of the binary trees and the algorithms using this representation. In Section VI we compare our methods to Trie Hashing [12] and we show how the fan-out of B-trees can be increased by representing the search information within each page by using our S-trees. Finally, in Section VII we summarize our results.

II. KEYS, BUCKETS, SEPARATORS, AND FAN-OUT

As mentioned earlier, every record is assumed to have a (unique) key by which it is accessed. Throughout this paper, we will focus our attention on the key, but every record has a non-key portion as well, of course. A *key* is a string of bits, 0's, and 1's. Keys need not have any fixed maximum length.

Any set of distinct keys can be uniquely arranged in order, from smallest to largest. The ordering we will use is similar to lexicographic order. To compare two keys, examine each from the left, bit by bit, until they differ in some bit position. The key containing a 0 in that position is defined as the smaller of the two. A *prefix* of a key is a substring starting at the left end. Note that if one of the two keys is a prefix of the other, in our scheme zeros must be appended to the shorter until the comparison terminates.

If the actual record keys are integers, reals, characters, etc., to preserve key order, they must be converted to bit strings in such a way as to preserve this ordering. Sixteen bit numbers have the same ordering when viewed as unsigned integers compared numerically as when viewed as bit strings compared lexicographically, but signed integers and reals do not. Long and highly redundant keys lead to less compact search information. Therefore, if possible, also (an order preserving) text compression should be applied to the keys, before using them for an index. (This does not imply that the keys in the data records should be compressed too!) For example, character strings consisting exclusively of letters should be mapped with $a = 0$, $b = 1$, $c = 2$, etc., so each character can be represented in 5 bits, instead of, say, 8 bits.

In most applications, files are too large to be kept in main memory. Therefore, they are kept on disk or other random access secondary storage medium. We will call the unit of data transferred between memory and disk in

Manuscript received December 28, 1984; revised March 29, 1985.
The authors are with the Department of Mathematics and Computer Science, Vrije Universiteit, Amsterdam, The Netherlands.
IEEE Log Number 8714556.

a single operation a *bucket*, page, or disk block. Typically a bucket is a sector or a track. We will use *b* to denote the capacity of a bucket, i.e., the number of records that can be stored in one bucket. Each bucket has a unique symbolical or physical address. A basic assumption beyond all access methods is that the time necessary to access a data structure in main memory is negligible compared to the time necessary to access a bucket on secondary storage.

While presenting our two methods in Sections III and IV we will assume, just for our convenience, that the index entirely fits in main memory. Since our way of representing the search information is very compact, this assumption may be realistic even for quite large files.

Still, despite our compact representation, an index may become too large to be entirely kept in main memory. An efficient way to structure such large indexes in a paged, multilevel index organization is offered by B$^+$-trees [3]. A B$^+$-tree organizes the data into a multilevel index part, containing search information, and a file with the records themselves. Within each page of the index, the search information consists of pointers and *separators* [2]. The performance of B$^+$-trees can be improved by increasing the number of (separator, pointer)-pairs per index block, i.e., the fan-out of each index block since a higher fan-out leads to a smaller depth for the index tree of a certain file, and hence to fewer disk accesses to fetch the data.

Since our so-called S-trees of Sections IV and V will appear to be a very compact way of representing (separator, pointer)-pairs, the fan-out, and thus performance, of a B$^+$-tree can be increased by using an S-tree for representing the search information within each index page (see Section VI). Thus, the reader has to keep in mind that the assumption about the index entirely fitting in main memory is not crucial for the usefulness of the ideas to be presented.

III. BINARY DIGITAL SEARCH TREES

The method to be presented in this section uses a binary tree to map keys onto bucket addresses. We have chosen to call this access method a Binary Digital Search Tree (BDS-tree), since a key is examined bit-by-bit during the search rather than being compared in its entirety to other keys [9]. As customary with binary trees we distinguish between *internal nodes*, which have exactly two descendants, and external nodes or *leaves*, which do not have descendants. Internal nodes are used to discriminate during the search, while only leaves may correspond to buckets on disk. For convenience, we assume that *each leaf corresponds to a bucket*. Therefore, we need to distinguish between buckets that contain at least one record, and those that are completely empty, since no actual disk storage will be allocated for the latter, even though they occur in the access tree. Empty buckets (and their corresponding leaves) will be called *dummies*.

Fig. 1 illustrates a small binary tree with four internal nodes and five leaves, one of which is a dummy. A known property concerning binary trees is that the number of

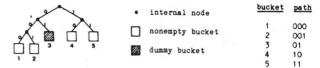

	bucket	path
• internal node	1	000
☐ nonempty bucket	2	001
▨ dummy bucket	3	01
	4	10
	5	11

Fig. 1. A binary tree showing the paths.

leaves is one more than the number of internal nodes. This property underlies our search algorithm, as explained in Section V-D.

Another thing to note about Fig. 1 is the labeling of the edges. Left edges are labeled 0; right edges are labeled 1. Using these numbers, every bucket can be labeled by its *path* from the root. Bucket 1 has path 000, bucket 2 has path 001, bucket 3 (a dummy) has path 01, etc.

A. Searching

Given a tree of the kind shown in Fig. 1 and a record key, it is possible to determine which bucket the record belongs in. The algorithm is simple: starting from the root of the tree, the key is examined bit-by-bit from the left end. Each time a 0 is encountered, go left. Each time a 1 is encountered, go right. When a leaf is reached, stop. The corresponding bucket is where the record belongs. In other words, the key belongs in the bucket whose path is a prefix of the key. For example, key 00101 belongs in bucket 2 and key 110011 belongs in bucket 5.

Observe that *bucket numbers* are different from *bucket addresses*. The bucket numbers go from 1 to some maximum in tree-traversal order, that is, in the order the leaves would be encountered when traversing the entire tree. The issue of how to convert bucket numbers to bucket addresses will be discussed in detail later. For the time being just assume the existence of a table indexed by bucket number that contains the address of each bucket (with a special bucket address, say 0, for dummies). By simply scanning this table, it is possible to find all the buckets in order, and therefore read the file sequentially starting at the beginning or at an arbitrary bucket.

B. Insertions

When a new record is to be inserted, we can distinguish three cases:
- the required bucket is partially filled.
- the required bucket is a dummy (i.e., this is the first entry).
- the required bucket is full.

In the first case, insertion is trivial: the required bucket is read in, the new record inserted into it, and the bucket is rewritten to the disk. In the second case, the dummy bucket is converted into a real one. Since dummy buckets do not have disk space allocated to them, inserting a record in a dummy bucket will require allocating a new disk bucket. If a record with key 01100 were inserted into the tree of Fig. 1, the result would be Fig. 2(a).

The case of inserting a record into an already full bucket is more involved. The bucket must be split into two buckets, and all *b* + 1 keys (the *b* keys that previously filled

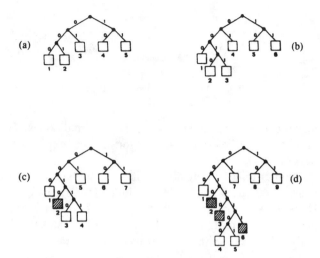

Fig. 2. Insertions.

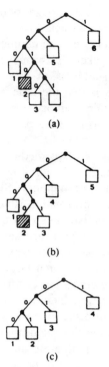

Fig. 3. Deletions.

the bucket, plus the new one to be inserted) are distributed over the two new buckets. As an example, consider what would happen if an insertion was executed in bucket 2 of Fig. 2(a) when this bucket is already full. The node would be converted to an internal node, with two buckets under it, as shown in Fig. 2(b). (Note that a split causes all subsequent buckets to be renumbered.) Whereas prior to the split, all keys starting with 001 went into bucket 2, after the split, those keys beginning with 0010 go into bucket 2, and those keys beginning with 0011 go into bucket 3. This redistribution applies both to the $b + 1$ keys of bucket 2 just prior to the split, and keys occurring subsequently.

In most cases, roughly half the keys will go into bucket 2 and the other half into bucket 3. However, in the worst case, all the keys might go into one of the buckets. For example, suppose $b = 4$, and prior to the split bucket 2 contained keys 0011000, 0011001, 0011011, and 0011110. Now key 0011101 is to be inserted. When all five keys are redistributed into buckets 2 and 3 of Fig. 2(b), unfortunately all five of them fall into bucket 3, which must itself be split, yielding Fig. 2(c). Fortunately, three of these go into bucket 3 and two go into bucket 4. Bucket 2 becomes a dummy. If the five keys had all started with 001110, bucket 4 in Fig. 2(c) would also have to be split (making bucket 3 a dummy), and its left child would have to have been split too, making its right child into a dummy as well [see Fig. 2(d)].

In general, if all the keys in a bucket to be split have long identical prefixes, many new levels may have to be created in the access tree to distinguish them, since each level corresponds to a single key bit. This tendency may or may not be of any importance in practice. In any event, Section IV deals with a variant of the BDS-tree that can guarantee a 50–50 split every time.

C. Deletions

In principle, deletions can be handled by just removing the record in question without changing the access tree structure. In practice, doing so might lead to many buckets with a utilization of less than 50 percent, thus wasting

disk storage. A simple way to pursue a more acceptable degree of disk utilization is to make a check after each deletion as to see if the bucket being deleted from still is more than, say, half full. If not, it may be possible to combine the bucket with its immediate sibling. As an example, consider the effect of a deletion from bucket 6 in Fig. 2(c). If buckets 6 and 7 can now be merged into a single bucket, one bucket can be freed, and the tree reorganized as shown in Fig. 3(a). If a subsequent deletion from bucket 4 allows buckets 3 and 4 to be merged, we get Fig. 3(b), which in turn can be converted in Fig. 3(c) by merging bucket 3 with dummy bucket 2.

From Figs. 2 and 3 it can be seen how the access tree dynamically changes its shape as records are inserted and deleted from the file.

D. Some Properties of BDS-Trees

Assuming that the access tree can be kept in main memory, a successful search always takes exactly one disk access, since the search process yields the correct bucket every time. When searching for a key not present in the file, no disk access at all will be needed if the search terminates in a dummy bucket. When the search terminates in a nonempty bucket, exactly one disk access is needed to determine that the key is not present. Depending on what fraction of the (unsuccessful) searches end in dummy buckets, the mean number of disk accesses per read request will be between 0 and 1.

With BDS-trees a high storage utilization cannot be guaranteed. If every split would put exactly half the keys in one of the new buckets and the other half in the other new bucket, storage utilization in these new buckets will be 50 percent initially. As they subsequently fill up, the efficiency will rise toward 100 percent. The mean efficiency would fall somewhere between these limits, typically about 70 percent [13].

However, if many bad splits occur, some buckets will be nearly empty, and storage utilization may be lower. For example, a 90–10 percent split would still yield a 50 percent storage utilization on the average, initially, but if the nearly full bucket is filled up and then split again, we have $1.1b$ entries spread over three buckets, for a 37 percent efficiency. Thus, a nonuniform key distribution usually leads to a storage utilization lower than 70 percent.

Note that a nonuniform key distribution does not always have a bad influence on the storage utilization or on the compactness of the tree. Suppose, for example, that a huge number of records whose keys begin with 00110 were to be inserted into Fig. 3(a). If these keys were randomly distributed starting at bit 6, few dummies would occur in the search tree, even though it is severely unbalanced. Furthermore, the storage utilization would be just the usual 70 percent. Put in other words, even if the key distribution exhibits large clusters, the storage utilization does not suffer. Also the storage costs of the search tree would not be affected, since the representation of an unbalanced tree costs no more bits than of a balanced one with the same number of leaves. To result in many "bad" splits, the key distribution must be more pathological; ordinary clustering is not enough.

It is also worth noting the effect of dummy buckets on the performance. As mentioned above, they make it possible to determine that certain keys are *not* present without making any disk accesses at all. Therefore, a higher percentage of dummies will usually lead to a lower average number of disk accesses required for an unsuccessful search. Since no disk storage is allocated for dummies, they do not waste disk space, but their negative effect is to increase the size of the access tree. However, as we will discuss later, this effect can be reduced to 3 bits per dummy.

As a final remark, we mention that, assuming some fixed bucket capacity, a certain set of keys has only one corresponding BDS-tree. Insertion of a certain set of keys in an initially empty BDS-tree will always result in the same, final BDS-tree, irrespective of the order in which these keys were inserted.

IV. SEPARATOR TREES

Although, in practice, the load factor for BDS trees may suffer from highly skewed key distributions, a modification of the method can guarantee that all splits are close to 50–50, for all key distributions, no matter how bad. The trees used here will be called S-trees (separator trees) to distinguish them from the BDS-trees used above.

A. Searching

With BDS-trees, each bucket is effectively assigned a range of keys, namely all the keys that begin with its path. Thus in Fig. 1, bucket 1 gets all keys beginning with 000, bucket 2 gets all keys beginning with 001, bucket 3 gets

bucket	from	to
1	00000...	00011...
2	00100...	00111...
3	01000...	01111...
4	10000...	10111...
5	11000...	11111...

(a)

bucket	from	to
1	00000...	00011...
2	00100...	01111...
3	-	-
4	10000...	10111...
5	11000...	11111...

(b)

Fig. 4. Bucket ranges for Fig. 1. (a) As a BDS-tree. (b) As an S-tree.

all keys beginning with 01, etc., as shown in Fig. 4(a). In an S-tree, only each nonempty bucket has a range, namely from its path up to but not including the path of the next nonempty bucket (or to 11111 . . . for the rightmost nonempty bucket). To reiterate for emphasis, in an S-tree, unlike in a BDS-tree, the dummy buckets do not have ranges assigned to them. If a search leads to a dummy, the nearest nonempty bucket to the left must be inspected instead. A dummy always has a nonempty bucket to its left, since the insertion algorithm guarantees that the leftmost bucket (i.e., bucket 1) is nonempty. Fig. 4(b) shows the ranges assigned to each bucket of Fig. 1 when this figure is interpreted as an S-tree.

To make this point clearer, consider how a record with key 010 would be inserted into the S-tree of Fig. 1. As indicated in Fig. 4(b), this key falls within the range of bucket 2 and thus would go into that bucket instead of going into bucket 3, as would occur if the tree of Fig. 1 was interpreted as a BDS-tree. The reason is intuitively clear: to achieve a high storage efficiency, we want to prevent situations like this—a bucket with just one record.

Put in other terms, due to the way ranges are assigned to buckets, in any S-tree the union of the ranges of the currently existing nonempty buckets exhausts the entire key space. Barring overflows, no new buckets are ever created, since every key belongs in some existing bucket. Only when an overflow occurs is a new bucket created, and then, as we shall see shortly, the records can be evenly divided between the two buckets.

With BDS-trees, the union of the nonempty bucket ranges does not exhaust the key space, since dummy buckets "own" the keys starting with their paths. Hence, a dummy bucket must be converted to a real one when even one record falls in its range. By not assigning any range to the dummies in an S-tree, this problem is avoided.

B. Insertions

From the above reasoning, we can see that in S-trees new buckets are only created upon bucket overflow. Now we will show how it is possible to guarantee that the keys are evenly divided between the two buckets.

First, sort all $b + 1$ keys belonging to the overflowing

$$k_0 = 10110000$$
$$k_1 = 10110001$$
$$k_2 = 10110010$$
$$k_3 = 10110101$$
$$k_4 = 10110111$$

(a)

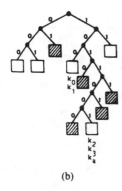

(b)

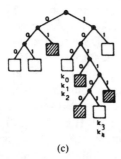

(c)

Fig. 5. (a) Five keys. (b) Split using 1011001 as separator. (c) Split using 101101 as separator.

bucket. Then find the median key K_m. Next find the *median separator* S_m, defined as the shortest prefix of the median key such that $K_{m-1} < S_m \leq K_m$. In effect, the median separator divides the sorted keys in two subsets, with all keys prior to the median key remaining in the overflowing bucket, and it and its successors being put in a newly created bucket. In other words, the median separator divided the original range of the overflowing bucket into two parts. The first part becomes the new range of the overflowing bucket and the other part becomes the range of the new, nonempty bucket to its right.

As an example of how this works, consider what would happen if the five keys of Fig. 5(a) landed in bucket 4 of Fig. 1, thereby causing an overflow (for $b = 4$). The median key in the sorted list is K_2 (10110010). The median separator is 1011001 because $10110001 < 1011001 \leq 10110010$ and no shorter prefix of K_2 (e.g., 101100) has this property. A path is then created for this separator, and it is inserted into the tree, as shown in Fig. 5(b). Note that it makes no difference here if K_0 would have been chosen to be 10001000 instead of 10110000.

A split does not always lead to the substitution of the overfull node by a subtree with two nonempty buckets. Consider, for example, the situation of Fig. 6(a) with bucket 2 containing the keys 00110, 10010, 10100, and 10111. If key 10110 has to be inserted, an overflow oc-

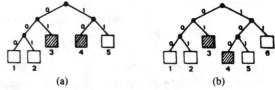

(a)   (b)

Fig. 6. Second kind of splitting.

curs. Then the median key is 10100, with separator 101. The result is that 00110 and 10010 stay in bucket 2, while the others go into the new bucket 5 as indicated in Fig. 6(b).

In the above examples the keys of the overflowing bucket were evenly divided by using the median separator. A variant of this idea is not to use the median key for determining the separator, but instead another key from some interval around the median key. (We apply here the idea proposed in [2].) In our example of Fig. 5, choosing K_3 instead of K_2 leads to a shorter separator (101101) and a tree [see Fig. 5(c)] with fewer dummies, although in both cases the keys split equally good. In general, a trade-off must be made between a potentially worse division of the keys between the buckets, which eventually leads to a lower load factor, and a longer separator, which means more dummies.

If the interval is chosen to cover the entire bucket, then the algorithm produces the shortest possible separator, just as the split algorithm of the BDS-tree actually does. Thus, the S-trees generated then will have the "shape" of the corresponding BDS-trees. A difference will be that some nonempty buckets in the BDS-tree correspond to dummies in the S-tree, since in an S-tree these dummies will not be converted to a nonempty bucket until the nearest nonempty bucket to their left overflows (see also Section IV-D).

C. Deletions

The only possible merge in a BDS tree is to combine two siblings (that is, two nodes having the same parent. In Fig. 6(a), buckets 1 and 2 are siblings, but 2 and 3 are not.) and replace them and their common parent with a single bucket. In an S-tree a bucket can be merged with the nearmost nonempty bucket to its left or right (i.e., its left or right nonempty neighbor), even if they are not siblings. A merge in an S-tree is performed by adding the records of the right-hand bucket to the left-hand one, and converting the right-hand bucket to a dummy, which results in extending the range of the left-hand bucket as required.

If in Fig. 6(b), the records of buckets 2 and 4 fit together in one bucket, the merge will be performed by adding the records of bucket 5 to bucket 2. Then bucket 5 is converted to a dummy. Since buckets 4 and 5 both are dummies now, the tree can be reduced and will become as in Fig. 6(a). Note that, unlike in BDS-trees, it is impossible to reduce the tree further, since reducing buckets 4 and 5 of Fig. 6(a) to one nonempty bucket would unintentionally change the ranges of buckets 2 and 5.

D. Comparison to BDS-Trees

If the entire S-tree can be kept in main memory, exactly one disk access is needed, both for successful and unsuccessful searches. This performance is slightly worse than with BDS-trees, where some unsuccessful searches can be completed without any disk accesses at all. With S-trees, no key range is assigned to dummies, so if a key leads to a dummy, the nonempty bucket to its left must be inspected anyway.

Unlike with BDS-trees, a certain set of keys has (assuming some fixed bucket capacity) usually more than one corresponding S-tree. Precisely which S-tree will result from the insertion of a certain set of keys in an initially empty tree, depends on the order these keys are inserted.

If the split interval used is not too large, it is guaranteed that an overflow leads to two (approximately) half full buckets. Thus, in case of pure insertions, bucket utilization will be between 50 and 100 percent and mean load factor will be about 70 percent [13]. This situation is equal to that of B-trees and usually better than that of BDS-trees (see results below). In addition, it is possible for S-trees (as for B-trees) to achieve a utilization even higher than 70 percent by merging buckets with more than one adjacent neighbor, and by only performing a split if an overflow cannot be resolved by reallocating some keys to the neighboring buckets. (Of course, if some keys are reallocated to a neighboring bucket, the corresponding separator must be adapted.) However, doing so makes insertions and deletions slightly more expensive because overflows and merges then require more work.

Another difference is that S-trees tend to have more dummies than BDS-trees, depending on how large an interval around the median key is chosen. If a large interval around the median key is chosen, a larger choice of separators is available. This makes it possible to choose a short one. Since a short separator corresponds to a shallow tree, it will, in general, require fewer dummies than a long separator, which corresponds to a deep tree. Thus, the larger the interval inspected, the shorter the separator, and the fewer the dummies. We have made measurements on the percentage of dummies as a function of the interval searched (expressed as a fraction of the bucket capacity). As an example, Fig. 7(a) shows the results for a list of 50 000 Dutch words when using a bucket capacity of 50 (i.e., $b = 50$) and a 5-bit-per-character encoding. The 50 000 words were inserted in random order.

On the other hand, the larger the interval searched for a separator, the worse the split can be, and the lower the load factor. If the interval searched is 20 percent of the bucket (10 percent on either side of the median key), for example, the worst possible split is 60–40 percent. With a 50 percent interval, the split can be as bad as 25–75 percent. Finally, if 100 percent of the bucket is searched for the shortest separator, in the worst case one of the resulting two nonempty buckets has only one record. Experimental results show that with split intervals up to about 40 percent there is almost no degradation of the load fac-

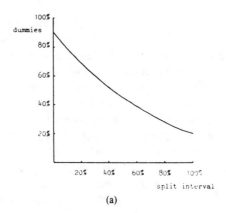

(a)

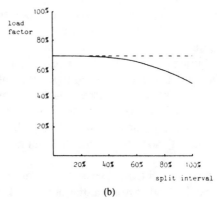

(b)

Fig. 7. (a) Percentage of dummies as a function of the split interval. (b) Load factor as a function of the split interval.

tor from the 70 percent derived in [13], but with larger intervals, the load factor drops off. As an example, Fig. 7(b) shows the results for the list of 50 000 words. For the same list the BDS-tree gave a load factor of 46 percent and a percentage of dummies of almost 14 percent.

When inserting random numbers as keys, both BDS-trees and S-trees gave the expected average load factor of 70 percent. Of course the size of the split interval had in this case no influence on the average load factor of the S-tree. The percentage of dummies was negligible (i.e., much less than 1 percent) for BDS-trees. For S-trees a split interval of 40 percent appeared to be sufficient to make the percentage of dummies negligible too. But, for a 20 percent split interval the percentage of dummies was roughly 25 percent and for 0 percent split interval this percentage was even about 77 percent.

As we already mentioned before, when a 100 percent split interval is used with an S-tree (i.e., the whole bucket is searched for the shortest separator), the resulting tree is similar, but not identical to the BDS-tree corresponding to the same keys. If at a certain moment a key lands in a dummy, the action taken differs for a BDS-tree and an S-tree. In the former case, the dummy is simply converted into a real bucket. In the latter case, the key is put into the nearest real bucket to the left of the dummy, assuming there is room for it. Thus the shape of BDS-tree and the corresponding S-tree using a 100 percent split interval will be identical, only some of the leaves of the tree that are buckets in the BDS-tree may be dummies in the S-tree. Therefore, an S-tree used with a 100 percent split interval will have a better load factor, but also a higher percentage of dummies than the corresponding BDS-tree. For the example of Fig. 7 the BDS-tree gave a load factor of 46 percentage and a percentage of dummies of 13 percent, whereas these numbers for the S-tree using a 100 percent split interval were 50 and 20 percent, respectively.

By way of illustration, consider the insertion of the keys of Fig. 5(a) into bucket 4 of Fig. 1 again. If an S-tree with a 100 percent split interval is used, the tree of Fig. 5(c) is produced. If a BDS-tree is used the resulting tree would have the same shape, but the bucket with path 100 would be a dummy and the bucket with path 101100 would be nonempty. More difference shows up if the next key to be stored is 10111100. For both methods the search algorithm reaches the dummy with path 10111. With an S-tree, the key is put into the nearest nondummy bucket to the left, alongside K_3 and K_4, since there is sufficient room. With a BDS-tree, the dummy with path 10111 would just be converted to a real bucket immediately. After insertion of this key, the BDS-tree thus has one dummy less than the corresponding S-tree, but uses one nonempty bucket more for storing the same number of keys.

In summary, by adjusting the split interval of an S-tree, one can vary the load factor and the number of dummies. Up to about 40 percent split interval leaves the load factor about 70 percent, while lowering the percentage of dummies (and thus the size of the index). With a larger split interval, still fewer dummies are created, but the load factor deteriorates. With a 100 percent split interval an S-tree almost approximates the behavior of a BDS-tree.

V. Representation of BDS- and S-Trees

Up until now, we have been completely silent about how the binary trees should be encoded. The obvious representation of an internal node as two pointers is not, in general, the best one. Similarly, we have said nothing about how (or even where) bucket addresses are represented. They obviously could be kept in the leaves of the tree, but this is not the only place; nor is it necessarily the best one. In the following sections, these issues will be discussed in detail. A compact representation for BDS- and S-trees will be developed, and search algorithms using this representation will be presented.

A. How to Represent Binary Trees Compactly

The straightforward way to represent a binary tree, such as that of Fig. 1, is to have each internal node consist of two pointers. The sign bit of each pointer could distinguish between a pointer to an internal node and a bucket address. The root node of Fig. 1 would then contain two internal pointers; its left child would contain one internal pointer and one external pointer (to the dummy bucket); its right child would contain two external pointers. However, this *standard representation* is not compact enough, since too many bits (namely, two pointers) are needed for each bit of a separator in the tree.

A completely different, and much more compact, rep-

tree	linear representation
Fig.1	000111011
Fig.2(a)	000111011
Fig.2(b)	00010111011
Fig.2(c)	0010010111011
Fig.2(d)	00010101001111011
Fig.3(a)	00010101111
Fig.3(b)	000101111
Fig.3(c)	0001111
Fig.5(b)	0001110010100011111
Fig.5(c)	000111001010011111
Fig.6(a)	000111011
Fig.6(b)	00011100111

Fig. 8. Linear representation of binary trees.

resentation of a binary tree can be obtained by a preorder tree traversal, emitting a 0 for every internal (split) node visited and a 1 for every bucket (dummy or not) visited. When traversing the tree of Fig. 1, we first encounter three internal nodes (including the root), then buckets 1 and 2, then the dummy 3, then the remaining internal node, and finally buckets 4 and 5, for a bit string of 000111011. Since every binary tree has one more bucket than internal nodes, the bit string will always have one less 0 bits than 1 bits. Fig. 8 shows the bit strings corresponding to all the example trees we have used so far. We will call this representation of a binary tree the *linear representation*. In this linear representation the first 1 bit corresponds to bucket number 1, the second 1 bit corresponds to bucket number 2, and so on.

B. Where to Represent Bucket Addresses

Bucket addresses can be stored in one of two ways. In the first way, the bucket address is included in the bit string itself, directly following the 1 bit corresponding to the bucket. For example, if aaaa, bbbb, cccc, etc. represent bucket addresses, the tree of Fig. 1 would be represented as

0001aaaa1bbbb1cccc01dddd1eeee.

This representation requires fixed-size bucket addresses, although any size can be used. Dummies can be represented by any convenient bit pattern of the same length as a bucket address (e.g., all 0's).

A more convenient way of storing the bucket addresses is in a separate table, indexed by bucket number. In Fig. 9(a) we show the linear representation of the tree of Fig. 6(b). Fig. 9(b) shows the *address table* used to convert a bucket number, 1 to 6, to a bucket address. A bucket number is just the position of its leaf bit in the linear representation when zeros (internal nodes) are neglected, whereas the bucket address is a physical or symbolical address. When the tree is modified, the bucket numbers may change, but the bucket addresses assigned to the various buckets do not change. If bucket 2 fills up and splits, buckets 3, 4, 5, and 6 will be renumbered 4, 5, 6, and 7, respectively, and their entries in the address table will have to be shifted downward one slot to reflect this renumbering, and to make room for the new bucket address. We will come back to this point later.

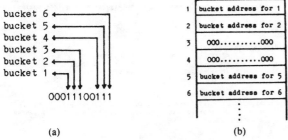

(a)

Fig. 9. (a) Linear representation for the tree of Fig. 6(b). (b) The accessory address table.

Fig. 10. Representation for the tree of Fig. 6(b) when using a bit map.

In the address table of Fig. 9(b), slots are also reserved for dummy buckets. An alternative representation that does not need entries in the address table for dummies is as follows. Associated with each tree is a bit map with as many bits as the tree has leaves. For each leaf (bucket) the corresponding bit is set to 0 if the bucket is empty, otherwise the bit is set to 1.

When a tree search terminates, the bucket number of the bucket found (how to get this number will be explained in Section V-D) is used to index into the bit map to fetch the corresponding bit. If that bit is a 1, the bucket found exists; if it is a 0, the bucket is a dummy. For example, the bit map for Fig. 6(b) is 110011. By scanning the bit map up to and including the bucket found, one can determine how many nondummy buckets exist prior to the one found. This number that will be called the *index number*, can be used as an index into a table that now contains only for each nondummy bucket a slot with its disk address. Fig. 10 shows the linear representation, the bit map and the address table for the tree of Fig. 6(b). In this tree the buckets 1–6 yield the index numbers: 1, 2, 2, 2, 3, 4. Always the first nonempty bucket has index number 1, the second nonempty bucket has index number 2, and so on. Each dummy has the same index number as the rightmost nonempty bucket to its left.

C. Storage Requirements

It is straightforward to calculate the number of bits required in the index per bucket in the file. If a tree has N buckets (including dummies), it will have $2N - 1$ nodes total, and thus $2N - 1$ bits are needed for its linear representation. Thus, each leaf (bucket) requires approximately 2 bits.

If the bit map is not used, then every bucket, dummy or not, has a slot in the address table. Slots corresponding to dummies will contain a string of 0's and slots corresponding to nonempty buckets contain its disk address ($\neq 0$). If we assume that a bucket address needs A bits for its representation, then the number of bits required per bucket is $A + 2$. If a fraction d of all the buckets are dummies, the number of bits per nondummy bucket is $(A + 2)/(1 - d)$.

If the bit map is used, the number of bits per leaf is increased from 2 to 3, but only nondummy buckets need a slot in the table for their disk addresses, so the total number of bits per nondummy bucket is $A + 3/(1 - d)$.

Clearly, the bit map scheme is to be preferred whenever:

$$A + 3/(1 - d) < (A + 2)/(1 - d)$$

which occurs whenever $d > 1/A$. For typical values of $A = 16$ or 32, if more than 6 or 3 percent of the buckets are dummies, which is nearly always the case, the bit map method is better.

By way of example, suppose that the bit map method is used for an S-tree. As can be seen from Fig. 7, using a split interval of 30 percent of the bucket capacity typically leads to about 60 percent dummies, while the load factor will be the usual 70 percent. Thus, if a bucket address costs 2 bytes (i.e., for files up to about 65 000 buckets), the total cost per bucket would be about 3 bytes.

D. Search Algorithms

Now we will present in detail the BDS- and S-tree search algorithms operating on the above developed, compact representation using the bit map. The reader can easily derive from our description the algorithms for the variant without the bit map.

It may already be clear how a search proceeds once the bucket number has been found. The bucket number is used as an index in the bit map. If the bit map has a 0 for the bucket, it is a dummy; if it has a 1, it is a useful bucket.

For a BDS-tree, a dummy means the key is not present and the algorithm terminates. If the bit map entry is a 1 for a BDS-tree, the program must count the number of 1 bits in the bit map from the first bit up to and including the bit corresponding to the bucket found to determine the index number of that bucket. This index number indicates which slot in the table contains the required disk address.

For S-trees, the same procedure is followed as for BDS-trees, except that the count is applied no matter what the bit map value is since finding a dummy when searching an S-tree does not mean that the key is absent. One must look in the first nonempty bucket to the left of this dummy to find out. Since a dummy has the same index number as this first nonempty bucket to its left, always counting 1's up to its own bit in the bit map is justified.

It is now time to describe in detail how the bucket number can be found. This part of the search process has two inputs: the key to be found, and the linear representation of the tree. Two markers are used, one to mark the current position in the tree as it is traversed, and one to mark the current position in the key as it is scanned. Initially, the tree marker is at the root of the binary tree and the key marker is at the first bit of the key.

Each time the bit pointed to by the tree marker is a 0 (i.e., an internal node), the bit pointed to by the key marker is used to decide whether to advance the tree marker to the left subtree or to the right subtree. If this bit of the key is a 0 the tree marker must go to the left, and if it is a 1, to the right subtree.

Advancing the tree marker to the left subtree can simply be accomplished by advancing it to one position further, since in the linear representation a left subtree is represented directly following the 0 bit of its parent. To advance the tree marker to the right subtree, the left subtree must be skipped. The fact that any subtree contains one more 1 than 0's, can be used to find the end of a subtree easily.

The above described search goes on until the bit pointed to by the tree marker finally is a 1 (i.e., a leaf). This 1 bit corresponds to the bucket found (which is possibly a dummy). Instead of afterward counting all 1 bits left to it in the linear representation to determine its bucket number, one can simply keep track of the number of ones passed-by while skipping subtrees.

Fig. 11 shows Pascal functions illustrating the algorithms for the representation using a bit map. The search algorithm spends its time mainly on skipping subtrees and on converting a bucket number to an index number. Since both these operations are very simple, it should be easy to build special hardware for it (or to microprogram these operations). Without special hardware, the searching process can still be made relatively fast (in software) by using two 256-entry tables. For example, computing the index number from a bucket number using the bit map can be done much faster by using a table giving the number of 1's for each possible bit configuration in a byte. Similarly, two other tables can help to make the skipping process work bytewise instead of bitwise for all but a few bits of each subtree. One of these tables gives the difference between the number of ones and zeros within each byte. For example, the byte 00101100 has a difference of −2. (Since this table is equally good for the computation of the index number, a separate table giving the number of ones for each possible byte is not required.) The other table contains the maximum difference between ones and zeros found when traversing the byte bit-by-bit from left to right. For example, the byte 01011100 has as maximum 2. This second table is used to check whether the last bit of the subtree is present in the current byte. If the maximum difference achievable within the current byte is greater than or equal to the difference to be searched for, then the end of the subtree is in this byte. Otherwise it is not, and the difference to be searched for must be adapted by subtracting the total difference in this byte, as given by the first table, before going on with the next byte. Without the check described above, the algorithm would skip too much if the last bit of the subtree is followed by more zeros than ones within the same byte.

The reason to keep the linear representation, the bit map

```
const dummyaddress = 0;
      maxkey      = ....;     { Pascal, not the algorithms, requires maximum sizes }
      maxtree     = ....;
      maxmap      = ....;
      maxtable    = ....;

type diskaddress = integer;
     table       = array [1..maxtable] of diskaddress;
     map         = array [1..maxmap]  of (dummy, nonempty);
     treetype    = array [1..maxtree] of (split, leaf);
     keytype     = array [1..maxkey]  of 0..1;

function skipandcount (var treeptr :integer; tree :treetype) :integer;
                       { skips a subtree and returns the number of leaves in it }
var diff, oldptr :integer;
begin
   diff := 0;
   oldptr := treeptr;
   repeat
      treeptr := treeptr + 1;
      if tree [treeptr] = leaf
         then diff := diff + 1
         else diff := diff - 1;
   until diff = 1;
          { the number of leaves can be computed from the size of the subtree }
   skipandcount := (treeptr - oldptr + 1) div 2;
end;

function findbucketnr (key :keytype; tree :treetype) :integer;
var keyptr, treeptr, bucketnr :integer;
begin
   bucketnr:= 1;
   keyptr  := 1;
   treeptr := 1;
   while tree [treeptr] = split do
   begin
      if key [keyptr] = 1
         then bucketnr := bucketnr + skipandcount (treeptr, tree);
      keyptr  := keyptr + 1;
      treeptr := treeptr + 1;
   end;
   findbucketnr := bucketnr;
end;

function findindexnr (bucketnr :integer; bitmap: map) :integer;
var i, indexnr :integer;
begin
   indexnr := 0;
   for i := 1 to bucketnr do
      if bitmap[i] = nonempty then indexnr := indexnr + 1;
   findindexnr := indexnr;
end;

function findaddress (bdstree      :boolean;
                      key          :keytype;
                      tree         :treetype;
                      bitmap       :map;
                      addresstable :table)    :diskaddress;
var bucketnr :integer;
begin
   bucketnr := findbucketnr (key, tree);
   if bdstree and (bitmap [bucketnr] = dummy)
      then findaddress := dummyaddress
      else findaddress := addresstable [findindexnr (bucketnr, bitmap)];
end;
```

Fig. 11. Pascal version of the algorithms.

and the address table separated, was just to be able to use the relation between the number of ones and zeros in a subtree to skip it, and to use the improvements presented above.

E. Linearity of the Algorithms

From the description above it follows that the computational cost of the search algorithm is linear in the size of the tree. During a search the algorithm reads from the linear representation all bits up to and including the 1 bit representing the bucket (dummy or not) finally found. This means that on the average about half the bits of the linear representation will be read. Clearly, also half the bit map will be scanned on the average.

A separator will have to be added (deleted) only when a bucket overflows (underflows). A little thought reveals that the algorithms for adding or deleting separators are linear too. For example, in case of adding a new separator, it usually will be necessary to replace one leaf by a small, new subtree. To make room for this subtree, on the average about half of the bits of the linear representation need to be shifted to the right. A similar shift is required in the bit map to make room for the dummy-or-not bits corresponding to the leaves of the new subtree. Finally, on the average half the table must be shifted one place to make room for the address of the newly created nonempty bucket.

Although the algorithms presented can be made to run reasonably fast, they are all linear, and thus our compact representation will be useful only for representing binary trees of limited size. As will be explained in the next section, large indexes will have to be divided into parts of restricted size anyway. Therefore, the linearity of the algorithms usually does not cause serious problems.

VI. COMPARISON TO TRIE HASHING AND B-TREES

What we did until now was in fact nothing more than developing a compact representation of search information (i.e., separators and pointers). We showed that separators can be represented in a binary tree, that binary trees can be represented in a compact way, and that rather fast, but linear algorithms exist that operate on this compact representation of search information.

A. Comparison to Trie Hashing

The variant of Trie Hashing using binary digits [12] is in many respects equal to BDS-trees, although they were developed independently. One difference is that Trie Hashing uses a so-called "digit number" in each node. As a result, for files up to 32K buckets and keys of at most 256 bits, Trie Hashing uses 5 bytes per node, while for such files BDS-trees would need in the *standard representation* only 4 bytes per node. Besides, in our case keys may also be longer than 256 bits, since BDS-trees impose no restriction on the length of the keys.

However, this is still not compact enough. Our experiments have convinced us that compactly implemented B$^+$-trees are better than Trie Hashing, BDS-trees, and S-trees using the standard representation. Happily enough, we have shown how a much more compact *linear representation* of our trees can be implemented efficiently. A sequential representation is described in [12] for Trie Hashing too. But, that representation seems to be less compact than ours, and, more importantly, it is doubtful whether it is possible to make algorithms operating on it that are as simple and efficient as ours.

Also, our representation has the advantage that the address table is kept separate. For example, Trie Hashing simply has to fail if the file is so large that the search information cannot be kept in main memory. However, in our case one could put the address table on disk at the cost of an extra disk reference. Note that the address table then has become somewhat similar to the directory of Extendible Hashing [7]. (Still, in our opinion, it is better to page and structure large indices in the multilevel organization of a B$^+$-tree, as described below.)

It was shown already that the storage utilization offered by BDS-trees (and thus also offered by Trie Hashing with binary digits) may be hardly acceptable. Therefore, for most applications S-trees seem to be superior to both BDS-trees and Trie Hashing (see also Section IV-D).

B. Comparison to B-Trees

Although the comparison in [12] between Trie Hashing and B-trees is in favor of Trie Hashing, it does not suffice to have shown that S-trees compare favorably to Trie Hashing. There are several reasons for making a separate comparison between S-trees and B-trees.

First, the comparison in [12] was made assuming that the percentage of nil pointers will be negligible. However, nil pointers obviously have the same bad influence on the cost per effective node in Trie Hashing, as dummies have with BDS- and S-trees, and our experience is that the percentage of dummies (nil pointers) may be significant.

Furthermore, the comparison in [12] was made assuming that with Trie Hashing the whole index (trie) was in core, while with B-trees only the root page of the index was assumed to be there. A more fair comparison can be made in two ways. Either both methods may use the same amount of main memory, and the comparison shows which method needs less disk accesses than the other, or it is assumed that both methods have their index entirely in core, and the comparison shows which method needs less space for its index.

Still, even such a comparison would not be totally fair, since B-trees have a nice property not (yet) present with Trie Hashing and S-trees. Namely, with B-trees it is easy to trade main memory for access performance by having few or many of the index pages resident on disk. Below we will show that an index based on S-trees can be paged into the same multilevel organization as a B$^+$-tree, and that the resulting method will give better performance than a Prefix B$^+$-tree [2].

1) Using the B$^+$-Tree Index Organization: Although an S-tree can be used for representing an index very compactly, it still may happen that a large index does not fit a certain prescribed amount of main memory. Therefore, it should be possible to have (part of) an index on disk.

Since the index organization of B$^+$-trees has proven to be worthwhile, an easy way to get the ability to handle also very large indexes is to use the same paged, multilevel index organization for S-trees. (A somewhat different, but perhaps better way of structuring the index pages in a multilevel organization is described in [5].) Note that this proposal amounts to using S-trees for the representation of the (separator, pointer)-pairs within each index page and structuring the index pages in the organization of a B$^+$-tree. So, the only difference with other compact variants of a B$^+$-tree, such as the Simple Prefix B$^+$-tree (SPB-tree) and the Prefix B$^+$-tree (PB-tree) [2], then lies in the way the (separator, pointer)-pairs are represented.

2) Compactness of S-Trees: Some experiments were run to see how compact the representation of separators in an S-tree really is. In the comparison we assumed the separators in the SPB- and PB-tree to be variable length bit strings represented by a one byte length field and the bit string. The length of a prefix was also expressed in bits, not bytes. Thus the implementation we assumed for the SPB- and PB-trees was squeezed as much as possible. (Using bit stuffing to make it possible to denote the end of the variable length bit string by a special bit pattern, requires about the same number of bits.) Still, it was found that representing separators in an S-tree needs roughly half as many bits as with PB-trees. As expected, the representation used with PB-trees appeared to be only slightly more compact than that of SPB-trees.

The data used were the list of 50 000 words mentioned before and a list of 200 000 names which we got from the Dutch PTT. Both experiments were run once with a 5-bit-per-character encoding and once with the characters in an 8 bit ASCII encoding. For both encodings S-trees appeared to be almost two times as compact as PB-trees.

In Section V-C we mentioned already that the representation of a separator in an S-tree typically may cost one byte. If 3 bytes are used for bucket addresses (i.e., for files up to 16 million buckets), the total cost per (separator, pointer)-pair is typically 4 bytes. Assuming that the size of a page is 1K byte, this means that, when using S-trees, index pages may have a maximum fan-out of about 250, and that the average fan-out can be roughly 175. (Remember that the average load factor of index pages will be about 70 percent too.) Thus, if only the root index page is kept in main memory, records of files up to roughly 44 Mbytes can be accessed in two disk accesses. In general, the same access performance is accomplished if all index levels except the lowest one are kept in core. Thus, each record in a file of $N * 30$ Mbytes can be accessed in two disk accesses if $N + 1$ index pages are kept in main memory. These figures would even be better if a pointer compression scheme would be used. In [5] it is shown how, in case of bucket addresses of 4 bytes, the actual cost per bucket address easily can be reduced to 2 bytes.

VII. Summary and Conclusion

We have shown how a highly compact representation of binary trees can be used for representing search information. Two access methods using this representation were developed, BDS-trees and S-trees. With both methods the index is represented so compactly that it usually will fit in main memory, which means that records usually can be retrieved in one disk access. Each of these two methods may have its own class of applications where it is better than the other. A point in favor of S-trees is, that its behavior can be influenced by varying the size of the split interval used. When a maximum split interval is chosen, S-trees behave almost as BDS-trees. Furthermore, we have shown how the fan-out of a B-tree can be improved by using S-trees for the representation of the (separator, pointer)-pairs.

In this paper the emphasis was on building indexes. However, the techniques presented can also be used, for example, for storing pictures more efficiently than with current methods [5], [6], [8].

Acknowledgment

We would like to thank W. Litwin for his comments on a previous version [4], W. Koot for performing some simulations, the Dutch PTT for some test data, P. Scheuermann for his stimulating interest, and the referees for their valuable comments.

References

[1] R. Bayer and E. McCreight, "Organization and maintenance of large ordered indexes," *Acta Inform.*, vol. 1, no. 3, pp. 173–189, 1972.
[2] R. Bayer and K. Unterauer, "Prefix B-trees," *ACM Trans. Database Syst.*, vol. 2, no. 1, pp. 11–26, Mar. 1977.
[3] D. Comer, "The ubiquitous B-tree," *Comput. Surveys*, vol. 11, no. 2, pp. 121–137, June 1979.
[4] W. de Jonge, A. S. Tanenbaum, and R. P. van de Riet, "A fast, tree-based access method for dynamic files," Vrije Univ., Inform. Rep. IR-70, July 1981.
[5] ——, "A fast, tree-based access method," Vrije Univ., Inform. Rep. IR-85, July 1983.
[6] W. de Jonge, Short note sent to P. Scheuermann, June 1984, 7 pp.
[7] R. Fagin, J. Nievergelt, N. Pippenger, and H. R. Strong, "Extendible hashing—A fast access method for dynamic files," *ACM Trans. Database Syst.*, vol. 4, no. 3, pp. 315–344, Sept. 1979.
[8] I. Gargantini, "An effective way to represent quadtrees," *Commun. ACM*, vol. 25, no. 12, pp. 905–910, Dec. 1982.
[9] D. Knuth, *The Art of Computer Programming, Vol. 3: Sorting and Searching.* Reading, MA: Addison-Wesley.
[10] P. Larson, "Linear hashing with partial expansions," in *Proc. 6th Int. Conf. Very Large Data Bases*, Montreal, Canada, Oct. 1980, pp. 224–232.
[11] W. Litwin, "Linear hashing—A new tool for file and table access," in *Proc. 6th Int. Conf. Very Large Data Bases*, Montreal, Canada, October 1980, pp. 212–223.
[12] ——, "Trie Hashing," in *Proc. ACM-SIGMOD Int. Conf. Management of Data*, Ann Arbor, MI, 1981, pp. 19–29.
[13] A. Yao, "On random 2-3 trees," *Acta Inform.*, vol. 9, no. 2, pp. 159–170, 1978.

Wiebren de Jonge was born in 1954 in Amsterdam, The Netherlands. He received the Bachelor's, Master's, and Ph.D. degrees from Vrije Universiteit in Amsterdam. His dissertation contains articles about statistical databases, keeping secrets, and digital signatures.

Besides being (co)author of several published papers concerning security and privacy, he is also (co)author of two published papers in the database field. Currently, he is mainly interested in this last field and has a tenure position at the Department of Computer Science of Vrije Universiteit.

Dr. de Jonge is a member of the Association for Computing Machinery and NGI.

Andrew S. Tanenbaum (M'75) was born in New York City and raised in White Plains, NY. He received the Bachelor's degree from Massachusetts Institute of Technology, Cambridge, and the Ph.D. degree from the University of California at Berkeley.

He is currently on the faculty at the Vrije Universiteit in Amsterdam, The Netherlands, where he teaches and does research in the areas of computer architecture, operating systems, networks, and distributed systems. He is currently involved in two major research projects, on advanced compiler technology and on distributed operating systems. The compiler project has led to the development of the Amsterdam Compiler Kit, which is a tool kit for building compilers for (at the moment) half a dozen languages and 10 different target machines. The kit is currently being used at more than 100 universities and companies around the world. The operating system research has led to the development of the Amoeba distributed operating system, which will soon be running at five sites in three countries, interconnected by a wide-area network. He is the author of three books (on computer organization, computer networks, and operating systems), and more than 40 published papers on a variety of subjects. He has also lectured in a dozen countries, and has worked for IBM and AT&T Bell Laboratories.

Dr. Tanenbaum is a member of the Association for Computing Machinery, the IEEE Computer Society, and Sigma Xi.

Reind P. van de Riet was born in Groningen, The Netherlands, on April 22, 1939. He received the Bachelor's degree in mathematics from Vrije Universiteit, Amsterdam, The Netherlands, in 1962, and the Ph.D. degree from the Universiteit van Amsterdam in 1968.

Since 1970 he has been Professor of Computer Science in the Department of Mathematics and Computer Science, and Chairman of the Computer Science Group, at Vrije Universiteit. He is the author of about 50 scientific papers. His current research interests include information systems, knowledge-based systems, and fifth generation computer systems.

Dr. van de Riet is Chairman of the Dutch Foundation for Research in Computer Science (SION), European regional Editor of *Data and Knowledge Engineering*, and Consulting Editor of *Future Generation Computer Systems*. He was Chairman of the Conference on Fifth Generation and Super Computers, Rotterdam, The Netherlands, in December 1984.

Digital Search Trees

An Efficient Digital Search Algorithm by Using a Double-Array Structure

JUN-ICHI AOE, MEMBER, IEEE

Reprinted from *IEEE Transactions on Software Engineering*, Vol. 15, No. 9, September 1989, pages 1066-1077. Copyright © 1989 by The Institute of Electrical and Electronics Engineers, Inc. All rights reserved.

Abstract—An efficient digital search algorithm is presented in this paper by introducing a new internal array structure, called a *double-array*, that combines the fast access of a matrix form with the compactness of a list form. Each arc of a digital search tree, called a *DS-tree*, can be computed from the double-array in $O(1)$ time; that is to say, the worst-case time complexity for retrieving a key becomes $O(k)$ for the length k of that key. The double-array is modified to make the size compact while maintaining fast access and algorithms for retrieval, insertion and deletion are presented. Suppose that the size of the double-array is $n + cm$, n being the number of nodes of the DS-tree, m being the number of input symbols, and c a constant depending on each double-array. Then it is theoretically proved that the worst-case times of deletion and insertion are proportional to cm and cm^2, respectively, independent of n. From the experimental results of building the double-array incrementally for various sets of keys, it is shown that the constant c has an extremely small value, ranging from 0.17 to 1.13.

Index Terms—Database systems, data structure, dictionary, digital search, dynamic internal storage, key retrieval algorithm.

I. INTRODUCTION

IN many information retrieval applications, it is necessary to be able to adopt a fast digital search, or trie search [2], [21], [23], [25], [30], for looking at the input character by character. Examples include a lexical analyzer [3], [24] and a local code optimizer [3] of a compiler, a bibliographic search [1], a spell checker [26], a filter for the most frequently used words [27], and a morphological analyzer [12] in natural language processing, and so on. It is important that a dictionary of natural language processing be able to be built incrementally, because one needs to append additional words to the established basic vocabulary from time to time. The algorithm presented here is suitable for information retrieval systems in which the frequency of appending keys is higher than that of deleting keys, allowing the redundant space created by the deletion to be exhausted by the subsequent insertion.

Key retrieval strategies can be roughly classified into two categories, depending on whether a set of keys is variant or invariant. The first category, called the "*dynamic method*" permits the retrieval table to be modified. Several dynamic methods are known, including hashing [2], [23], binary trees [23], [30], B$^+$-trees [2], [30], extensible hashing [20], and trie hashing [19]. The second, the "*static method*," does not allow this modification. Perfect hashing [14]-[16], [18], [27], sparse table representation [5], [9], [22], [29], and a compressed trie [25] are included in this category. When using the static method, we can concentrate our efforts on the retrieval speed and compactness of the data structure, but when using the dynamic method, extra space must be taken into consideration in order to update the items quickly. The retrieval method presented here can be categorized as falling between the static and dynamic methods, so it is called the "*weak static method*." Extending the static method to the weak static method while maintaining the useful points of the former is ideal but difficult task. The extension of perfect hashing has been presented by Cormack *et al.* [16], but they could not determine the upper bound of the insertion time. The aim of this paper is to present a digital search algorithm incorporating the speed and compactness of the static method with the updating ability of the dynamic method.

Instead of basing a search method on comparisons between keys, a digital search [19], [23] makes use of their representation as a sequence of digits or alphabetic characters. Each node of the DS-tree on level h represents the set of all keys that begin with a certain sequence of h characters; the node specifies branches, depending on the $(h + 1)$st character. The basic concept of this paper is to compress a trie structure [2], [21], [23], [30] representing the DS-tree into two one-dimensional arrays BASE and CHECK, called a *double-array*, and to present the updating algorithm. Each node of the trie is an array indexed by the next "item." The element indexed is a final-state flag, plus a pointer to a new node (or a null pointer). Retrieval, deletion and insertion on the trie are very fast, but it takes lots of space because most of the nodes in the trie are empty; that is to say, the trie is sparse. So we shall try to compress node r into CHECK by giving a mapping from locations in r to locations in CHECK such that no two nonempty locations in each node are mapped to the same position in CHECK. Our mapping is defined by BASE[r] for each node r.

In the following sections, we will describe our ideas in detail. In Section II, we formalize the DS-tree as a string pattern matching machine and define the double-array

Manuscript received December 16, 1987; revised February 7, 1989. Recommended by T. Murata. This work was supported in part by a subsidy from the Japanese Ministry of Education for promoting scientific research.

The author is with the Department of Information Science and Systems Engineering, Faculty of Engineering, University of Tokusima, Minami-Josanjima-Cho, Tokusima-Shi 770, Japan.

IEEE Log Number 8929446.

structure computing an arc in $O(1)$ time. In order to apply the double-array to a large set of keys, the double-array is modified while maintaining the fast access, and a retrieval algorithm for the modified double-array is provided. The principal innovation is to store into the double-array only as much of the prefix in the DS-tree as is necessary to disambiguate the key, and to store the tail of the key not needed for further disambiguation in a compact form in a string array. Algorithms for insertion and delection are discussed and illustrated through an example in Section III. When an insertion of a new nonempty location of node r is blocked by a nonempty location of another node k in CHECK, an insertion algorithm solves the conflict by redefining BASE$[r]$ or BASE$[k]$. In this selection of an r or k node, priority is given to the one with fewest nonempty locations, to reduce space and time. In Section IV each worst-case time complexity of the presented algorithms is theoretically determined and supported by results of experimentation with various sets of keys. Partial matching and a key-order search [19] by the double-array are also discussed. Finally, in Section V we summarize our results.

II. RETRIEVAL ALGORITHM USING THE DOUBLE-ARRAY

A. Formalization of a Digital Search Tree

In the DS-tree, each path from the root to a leaf corresponds to one key in the presented set. This way, the nodes of the DS-tree correspond to the prefixes of keys in the set. To avoid confusion between words like THE and THEN, let us add a special *endmarker* symbol, #, to the ends of all keys, so no prefix of a key can be a key itself. In this paper, a set of these keys is denoted as K. There is a remarkable relationship between the DS-tree and the string pattern matching machine [1], [7] [8], [10], which locates all occurrences of a finite number of keys in a text string. Hence, the DS-tree will be defined in terms of the matching machine in this paper.

The DS-tree for K is formally defined by a 5-tuple (S, I, g, s_1, A), where
1) S is a finite set of *nodes*.
2) I is a finite set of *input symbols*.
2) g is a function from $S \times I$ to $S \cup \{$fail$\}$ called a *goto function*.
3) s_1 is the *initial node, or the root* in S.
4) A is a finite set of *accepting nodes*.

In other words, s_r is in A if and only if a path from s_1 to s_r spells out some $x\#$ in K. The arc labeled a in I from s_r to s_t indicates that $g(s_r, a) = s_t$. The absence of an arc indicates *fail*. The following (usual) conventions hold in this paper:

$$a, b, c, d, e \in I \cup \{\#\}; x, y, z \in (I \cup \{\#\})^*.$$

Let ϵ be the empty string. The notation of the goto function for K is extended to strings by the conditions

$$g(s_r, \epsilon) = s_r, g(s_r, ax) = g(g(s_r, a), x).$$

B. A Double-Array Structure and Its Modification

A triple-array structure using one-dimensional arrays BASE, CHECK, and NEXT was defined by S. C. Johnson [17] (the details are found in Aho et al. [3]) as a static implementation scheme for transition tables of YACC [3], [17] and LEX [3], [24]. Aoe et al. [7], [10] improved this structure by restricting the applicable transition table to that of a static string pattern matching machine. The improved structure, or a double-array, uses only two arrays BASE and CHECK, indexed by node numbers, and maintains the configuration represented in Fig. 1 below.

For s_r and s_t in S, $g(s_r, a) = s_t$ if and only if the double-array for K holds

$$t = \text{BASE}[r] + a \text{ and CHECK}[t] = r.$$

Note that each node s_r in S corresponds to an *index* r, or *node number*, of the double-array and that each input symbol a is treated as a numerical value. In the double-array structure, the subsequent governing node number t can be computed by BASE$[r]$ and the current input symbol a, so the array NEXT can be removed from the triple-array. One of the valuable features in this paper is to make the triple-array structure reduce to two arrays, but it is a more significant originality to apply the double-array to a compact and fast key retrieval table; and to extend the static use with the double-array inherited from the triple-array to the dynamic use.

The DS-tree has many nodes for a large set of keys, so it is important to make the double-array more compact. In the interest of space saving, we define the following terms on the DS-tree.

Definition 1: The following nodes are defined on the DS-tree.
1) For key xay in K, we define node s_r such that $g(s_1, xa) = s_r$, as a *separate node* if a is a sufficient symbol for distinguishing the key xay from all others in K.
2) Each node in a path from the initial node to the separate node is called a *multinode*.
3) Each node in a path from the separate node to the accepting node is called a *single-node*.

Let S_P, S_M, and S_I be sets of separate nodes, multinodes and single-nodes, respectively. Note that $S_P = S_M \cap S_I$.

Definition 2: A string x such that $g(s_r, x) = s_t$ for s_r in S_P and for s_t in A is called a *single-string* for the separate node s_r, denoted by STR$[s_r]$.

We propose that the arcs from $S_M \times (I \cup (\#))$ to S_M be stored in the double-array and that those from $S_I \times (I \cup (\#))$ to S_I be stored as the single-string in a string memory, called a *TAIL*. There is, however, a problem in how to determine the following:
1) Whether a given node is a separate node or not.
2) A location for taking a single-string from TAIL.

This problem can be easily solved by using additional arrays, but it can take up too much space. The following modified double-array and TAIL enable us to solve the problem without using extra space.

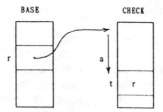

Fig. 1. A double-array structure for $g(s_r, a) = s_t$.

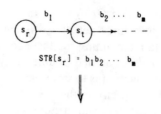

$$STR[s_r] = b_1 b_2 \cdots b_m$$

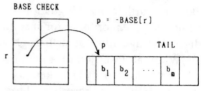

$$p = -BASE[r]$$

Fig. 2. The double-array and TAIL.

Definition 3: We define the double-array and TAIL as being valid for K if the following conditions are satisfied for the DS-tree.

1) For s_r, s_t in S_M, $g(s_r, a) = s_t$ if and only if $BASE[r] + a = t$ and $CHECK[t] = r$.

2) For s_r in S_P, suppose that $STR[s_r] = b_1 b_2 \cdots b_m$ ($0 \leq m$). Then, $BASE[r] < 0$ and for $p = -BASE[r]$,

$$TAIL[p] = b_1, \quad TAIL[p + 1]$$

$$= b_2, \cdots, TAIL[p + m - 1] = b_m.$$

In this elaborate structure as depicted in Fig. 2, $BASE[r]$ has two values to indicate a separate node number and locate the single-string in TAIL. Generally, the double-array can be used as an internal retrieval table, and TAIL may include the essential single-string and a record associated with the retrieval key, or alternatively a pointer locating the record in a file. Thus, in TAIL we use the symbol "\$" as a one-byte information item concerning the record and the symbol "?" as a garbage symbol.

Example 1: Consider a set $K' = \{baby\#, bachelor\#, back\#, badge\#, badger\#, badness\#, bcs\#\}$, where bcs means BCS(Bachelor of Computer Science). Figs. 3 and 4 show the DS-tree, and the double-array and TAIL for K', respectively. In Fig. 3 the multinodes are $s_1 \sim s_{20}$ and the single-nodes $s_4, s_9, s_{10}, s_{13}, s_{15}$ and $s_{19} \sim s_{35}$. The separate nodes and single-strings are as follows:

$$STR[s_4] = y\#, \quad STR[s_{10}] = elor\#, \quad STR[s_{13}] = \#,$$

$$STR[s_{20}] = \epsilon, \quad STR[s_{19}] = \#, \quad STR[s_{15}] = ess\#,$$

$$STR[s_9] = s\#.$$

In this example, the numerical values for $a, b, c, \cdots, r$ are regarded as $1, 2, 3, \cdots 18$, respectively. # is treated as 19. For the double-array and TAIL shown in Fig. 4, arc $g(s_7, b) = s_4$, and separate node s_4, satisfy Definition 3 as follows.

$$BASE[7] + b = 2 + 2 = 4 = t \text{ and } CHECK[4] = 7,$$

$$BASE[4] = -17 < 0, \text{ and } VALUE[17] = y$$

$$\text{and } VALUE[18] = \#.$$

C. Retrieval Algorithm

In order to keep a node number from exceeding the maximum index of the double-array, we define the size, denoted by *DA-SIZE*, of the double-array as the maximum index of the nonzero entries of CHECK, and DA-SIZE is stored in CHECK[1] for the dynamic double-array. Al-

gorithm 1 of retrieving a key is summarized below, where it utilizes the following functions.

FETCH_STR(p): Return a string $TAIL[p]TAIL[p + 1] \cdots TAIL[p + k]$ such that $TAIL[p + k] = \#(0 \leq k)$.

STR_CMP(x, y): Return -1 if a string x is equal to string y, otherwise return the length of the longest prefix of x and y.

Algorithm 1. Retrieval Algorithm.

Input: A string $x = a_1 a_2 \cdots a_n a_{n+1}$, $a_{n+1} = \#$; and BASE, CHECK and TAIL for K.

Output: If $x \in K$, then the output is TRUE, otherwise FALSE.

Method:
  begin
    Initialize the current node number r and the input position h to 1 and 0, respectively;
    repeat
      $h := h + 1$;
      Set the next node number t to $BASE[r] + a_h$;
(1-1)   **if** t exceeds DA-SIZE or $CHECK[t]$ is unequal to r **then** return(FALSE)
      /* $g(s_r, a_h) = s_t$ is undefined*/
      else Set r to t
    until $BASE[r] < 0$; /* s_t is a separate node*/
(1-2) **if** h reaches the last position $n + 1$
    then return(TRUE)
    else Set S_TEMP to the single-string FETCH_STR($-BASE[r]$);
(1-3) **if** $STR\_CMP(a_{h+1} \cdots a_n a_{n+1}, S\_TEMP) = -1$
    then return(TRUE)
    /* $a_{h+1} \cdots a_n a_{n+1}$ is the remaining input string*/
    else return(FALSE)
  end

In Algorithm 1, line(1-1) returns FALSE when a mismatch is detected on the double-array and line (1-2) returns FALSE for a mismatch on TAIL. The repeat-loop terminates if $BASE[r]$ is negative, that is, s_r is a separate node. The remaining input string is compared with S_TEMP corresponding to the single-string $STR[s_r]$ to determine whether x is in K or not. Only if $a_h = \#$ at line

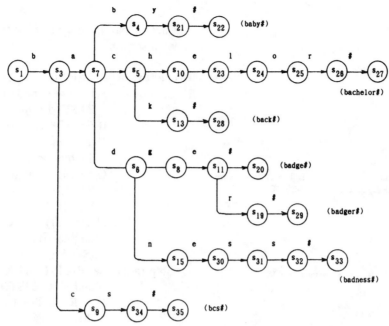

Fig. 3. The DS-tree for K'.

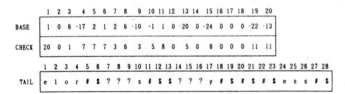

Fig. 4. A double-array for K'.

(1-2), then TRUE is immediately returned because of $STR[s_r] = \epsilon$. Suppose that the double-array and TAIL are valid for K. From the observation and Definition 3, it is clear that Algorithm 1 returns TRUE if the input string x is in K, otherwise FALSE.

Example 2: Consider the retrieval of key *badness#* $\in$ K' by using the double-array and TAIL shown in Fig. 4. Algorithm 1 returns TRUE by the following computations

(1-1): $t = BASE[r] + a_1 = BASE[1] + b = 3$
    $t = 3 < DA\text{-}SIZE = 20$ and $CHECK[t]$
    $= CHECK[3] = 1$
    $BASE[r] = BASE[3] = 6 > 0$
(1-1): $t = BASE[r] + a_2 = BASE[3] + a = 7$
    $t = 7 < DA\text{-}SIZE = 20$ and $CHECK[t]$
    $= CHECK[7] = 3$
    $BASE[r] = BASE[7] = 2 > 0$
(1-1): $t = BASE[r] + a_3 = BASE[7] + d = 6$
    $t = 6 < DA\text{-}SIZE = 20$ and $CHECK[t]$
    $= CHECK[6] = 7$
    $BASE[r] = BASE[6] = 1 > 0$
(1-1): $t = BASE[r] + a_4 = BASE[6] + n = 15$
    $t = 15 < DA\text{-}SIZE = 20$ and $CHECK[t]$
    $= CHECK[15] = 6$
    $BASE[r] = BASE[15] = -24 < 0$
(1-2): $h = 4 \neq n+1 = 8$,
    $S\_TEMP = FETCH\_STR(24) = ess\#$.
(1-3): $STR\_CMP(ess\#, ess\#) = -1$

III. ALGORITHM OF UPDATING THE DOUBLE-ARRAY

A. Insertion Algorithm

In order to understand an insertion algorithm, called Algorithm 2, we will illustrate the insertion process by means of the DS-tree. Suppose that Algorithm 2 uses the same input and output as Algorithm 1. Then, Algorithm 2 can be obtained by modifying return(FALSE) of the lines (1-1) and (1-3) of Algorithm 1 as follows.

a) For return(FALSE) of line (1-1):

begin
    A_INSERT(r, $a_h a_{h+1} \cdots a_n a_{n+1}$);
    return(FALSE)
end

b) For return(FALSE) of line (1-3):

begin
    B_INSERT(r, $a_{h+1} \cdots a_{h+k}$, $a_{h+k+1} \cdots a_n a_{n+1}$,
    $b_1 \cdots b_m$);
    return(FALSE)
end;

The parameters r and $a_h a_{h+1} \cdots a_n a_{n+1}$ of A_INSERT represent the current node number and the remaining input string, respectively. Thus, A_INSERT appends an arc $g(s_r, a_h) = s_t$ to the double-array and stores the single-string $STR[s_t] = a_{h+1} \cdots a_n a_{n+1}$ in TAIL as shown in Fig. 5. When B_INSERT is invoked there must be different symbols b_1 and a_{h+k+1} for $S\_TEMP = STR[s_r]$ $= a_{h+1} a_{h+2} \cdots a_{h+k} b_1 \cdots b_m$ ($0 \leq k \leq n - h + 1$, $1 \leq m$) and for the remaining input string $a_{h+1} \cdots$ $a_{h+k} a_{h+k+1} \cdots a_n a_{n+1}$ as shown in Fig. 6(a). The first parameter r of B_INSERT stands for the current node number and the other parameters are:

• $a_{h+1} \cdots a_{h+k}$ is the longest prefix of the remaining input string and S_TEMP.

83

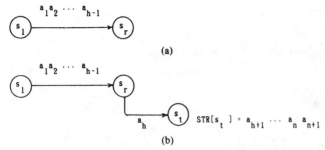

Fig. 5. Illustration of the procedure A_INSERT. (a) The DS-tree before A_INSERT. (b) The DS-tree after A_INSERT.

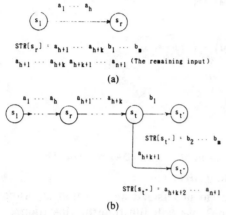

Fig. 6. Illustration of the procedure B_INSERT. (a) The DS-tree before B_INSERT. (b) The DS-tree after B_INSERT.

• $a_{h+k+1} \cdots a_n a_{n+1}$ is the string removed this prefix from that input string.

• $b_1 \cdots b_m$ is the string removed this prefix from S_TEMP.

Thus, B_INSERT appends arcs $g(s_r, a_{h+1} \cdots a_{h+k}) = s_t$, $g(s_t, b_1) = s_{t'}$ and $g(s_t, a_{h+k+1}) = s_{t''}$ to the double-array, and stores $STR(s_{t'}] = b_2 \cdots b_m$ and $STR[s_{t''}] = a_{h+k+2} \cdots a_n a_{n+1}$ into TAIL as shown in Fig. 6(b).

The double-array can be built incrementally using Algorithm 2. We assume that the initial double-array has only two nonzero entries, BASE[1] = 1 and CHECK[1] = 1, and has enough zero entries to insert a new key. Algorithm 2 utilizes the following functions and variables.

Set_LIST(r): Return a set of symbols a such that CHECK[BASE[r] + a] = r.

R-LIST, K-LIST, LIST, ADD, ORG: A subset of $I \cup \{\#\}$.

N(LIST): Return the number of entries in LIST.

POS: A global variable which indicates the minimum index of available entries of TAIL, and which has an initial value of 1.

X_CHECK(LIST): Return the minimum q such that $q > 0$ and CHECK[$q + c$] = 0 for all c in LIST.

STR_TAIL(p, y): Store the string y in the location p of TAIL and return POS incremented by the length of y if p = POS, otherwise return the original POS.

The procedures A_INSERT and B_INSERT are summarized below, but we use the same formal parameters as

the actual parameters in order to aid comprehension of these insertions.

procedure A_INSERT($r, a_h a_{h+1} \cdots a_{n+1}$)
Step (a-1). Set the next node number t to
BASE[r]+a_h.
If CHECK[t] = 0, then goto Step (a-3).
/* $g(s_r, a_h) = s_t$ can be defined on the double-array*/
Otherwise change either BASE[r] or BASE[k] for k = CHECK[t] at the next Step (a-2).
/* $g(s_r, a_h) = s_t$ cannot be defined on the double-array because $g(s_k, b) = s_t$ (See Fig. 7)*/
Step (a-2). Set R-LIST and K-LIST to SET_LIST(r) and SET_LIST(k), respectively.
If N(R-LIST)+1 is less than N(K-LIST) then
Call a function MODIFY($r, r, \{a_h\}$, R-LIST) to determine BASE[r] such that
CHECK[BASE[r]+b] = 0 for all b in R-LIST $\cup \{a_h\}$.
Otherwise call MODIFY(r, k, ϕ, K-LIST) to determine BASE[k] such that
CHECK[BASE[r]+a_h] $\neq$ CHECK[BASE[k]+b] for all b in K-LIST, and set r to the returned node number by this MODIFY.
/* ϕ is the empty set*/
Step (a-3). Call INS_STR($r, a_h a_{h+1} \cdots a_{n+1}$, POS) to define $g(s_r, a_h)$ on the double-array and to store $a_{h+1} \cdots a_{n+1}$ in TAIL.

Since N(R-LIST) and N(K-LIST) designate the numbers of arcs drawing out nodes s_r and s_k, respectively, changing BASE[k] instead of BASE[r] is reasonable in terms of time efficiency when N(R-LIST) + 1 > N(K-LIST), where the value 1 corresponds to $g(s_r, a_h)$. In MODIFY(r, k, ϕ, K-LIST) to change BASE[k], we must consider a special case such that BASE[k] + d = r for d in K-LIST, because the current node number r is changed along with BASE[k] as shown in Fig. 8. To solve the problem, MODIFY has the first parameter indicating the current node number r and returns the valid current node number.

function MODIFY(current_s, h ADD, ORG)
Step (m-1). Copy BASE[h] to *old_base* and determine a new BASE[h] as
X_CHECK(ADD $\cup$ ORG).
Step (m-2). For each c in ORG,
repeat Steps (m-3 ~ m-5).
Step (m-3). Set an old node number t to
old_base + c.

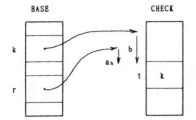

Fig. 7. A double-array for $g(s_k, b) = s_t$ and $g(s_r, a_h) = s_t$.

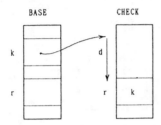

Fig. 8. A double-array such that BASE$[k] + d = r$.

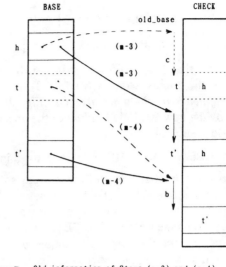

------> Old information of Steps (m-3) and (m-4)

⟶ New information of Steps (m-3) and (m-4)

Fig. 9. Illustration of the function MODIFY.

Set a new node number t' to
  BASE$[h] + c$.
Copy the original BASE$[t]$ into BASE$[t']$
  and set CHECK$[t']$ to h.
/* $g(s_h, c) = s_t$ is redefined by
  $g(s_h, c) = s_{t'}$ as shown in Fig. 9 */
Step (m-4). If BASE$[t] > 0$, then set CHECK$[q]$ to
  t' for each q such that
  CHECK$[$BASE$[t]+b]=t$ and
  $q = $ BASE$[t]+b$.
  /* Replace an old node number t in
  CHECK by a new t' as shown in
  Fig. 9 */
  Set t' to $current\_s$ if $t = current\_s$.
  /*The situation described in Fig. 8
  happens.*/
Step (m-5). Initialize BASE$[t]$ and CHECK$[t]$ to 0,
  respectively.
Step (m-6). Return $current\_s$.

Note that a new arc $g(s_r, a_h)$ is defined on the double-array by Step (a-3) after MODIFY.

procedure INS_STR($h, e_1e_2 \cdots e_q, d\_pos$)
  Step (s-1). Set the next node number t to
    BASE$[h]+e_1$;
  Step (s-2). Set BASE$[t]$ and CHECK$[t]$ to $-d\_pos$
    and h , respectively.
    /* $g(s_h, e_1) = s_t$ is defined on the
    double-array*/
  Step (s-3). POS := STR_TAIL(d_pos,
      $e_2e_3 \cdots e_q\$$).
procedure B_INSERT(r , $a_{h+1} \cdots a_{h+k}$, a_{h+k+1}
      $\cdots a_na_{n+1}$, $b_1 \cdots b_m$)
  Step (b-1). Copy -BASE$[r]$ to old_pos

Step (b-2). Define a sequence of arcs for each a_{h+1}
  for $1 \leq i \leq k$ on the double-array by
  repeating the following statements:
  Determine a new BASE$[r]$ as
  X_CHECK($\{a_{h+i}\}$);
  Set CHECK$[$BASE$[r] + a_{h+i}]$ to r ;
  Set the next node number r to
    BASE$[r] + a_{h+i}$;
Step (b-3). Determine a new BASE$[r]$ as
  X_CHECK($\{a_{h+k+1}, b_1 \}$);
Step (b-4). INS_STR(r, $b_2 \cdots b_m, old\_pos$);
  /* $b_2 \cdots b_m$ is overwritten in the original
  position old_pos of TAIL*/
Step (b-5). INS_STR(r, $a_{h+k+2} \cdots a_na_{n+1}$, POS)
  /* $a_{h+k+2} \cdots a_na_{n+1}$ is written in the
  new POS of TAIL*/

Theorem 1: Suppose that the double-array and TAIL are valid for K and that the input x of Algorithm 2 is not in K. Then, the modified double-array and TAIL by Algorithm 2 are valid for $K \cup \{x\}$.

Proof: For $x = a_1a_2 \cdots a_{n+1} \notin K$, consider the configurations shown in Figs. 5 and 6.

1) Procedure A_INSERT: If CHECK$[t] = 0$ in Step (a-1), then it is clear that Steps (s-1, s-2) of INS_STR invoked at Step (a-3) store an arc $g(s_r, a_h) = s_t$ in the double-array without changing BASE$[r]$. Moreover, node s_t always becomes a separate node, so BASE$[t]$ determined at Step (s-2) and TAIL stored at Step (s-3) hold 1) and 2) of Definition 3. As for the case of CHECK$[t] \neq 0$, we assume that MODIFY$(r, r, \{a_h\}$, R-LIST) was invoked at Step (a-2). It is necessary to prove the following three points.

a) Redefinition of arcs by new BASE$[r]$: From $h = r$, ORG = R-LIST, ADD = $\{a_h\}$, the function

85

X_CHECK of Step (m-1) determines the new BASE[r] such that

$$\text{CHECK}[\text{BASE}[r] + b] = 0$$

$$\text{for all } b \in \text{R-LIST} \cup \{a_h\},$$

so it is clear that $g(s_r, c)$ for all c in R-LIST can be redefined on the double-array by Step (m-3).

b) Influence on the other arcs (see Fig. 9): The arcs defined by the new BASE[r] influence the arcs associated with node s_t such that

$$t = \text{old\_base} + c \text{ and CHECK}[t] = r \text{ for } c \text{ in R-LIST.}$$

This old node number t is no longer used, so BASE[t] must be copied into BASE[t'] for the new node number $t' = \text{BASE}[r] + c$. As for the old arc $g(s_t, b)$, it is necessary to change CHECK[BASE[t] + b] with the old node number t into the new node number t', but it is unnecessary if s_t is a separate node, that is, BASE[t] < 0.

It is clear that these processes are carried out correctly by Steps (m-3, m-4).

c) Deletion of the old arc: From Step (m-5), the validity is straightforward.

As for MODIFY(r, k, ϕ, K-LIST), there is no confusion since a new BASE[k] is determined as X_CHECK(K-LIST) in Step (m-1) and since the current node number r can be replaced by a new number t' in Step (m-4) whenever $r = \text{BASE}[k] + d$ for d in ORG as shown in Fig. 8. When changing BASE[k], CHECK[BASE[r] + a_h] becomes available, so $g(s_r, a_h) = s_t$ can be stored in the double-array at INS_STR invoked by Step (a-3).

Hence, it is clear that the modified double-array and TAIL by A_INSERT are valid for $K \cup \{x\}$.

2) Procedure B_INSERT: From Steps (b-1 ~ b-3), it is clear that B_INSERT defines $g(s_r, a_{h+1} \cdots a_{h+k}) = s_t$, $g(s_t, b_1) = s_{t'}$ and $g(s_t, a_{h+k+1}) = s_{t''}$ to the double-array. By using Steps (s-2, s-3) in INS_STR invoked at Step (b-4), the STR[$s_{t''}$] = $b_2 \cdots b_m$ is overwritten in the original position *old_pos* (copied by Step (b-1)) of TAIL. By using Steps (s-2, s-3) in INS_STR invoked at Step (b-5), the single-string STR[$s_{t'}$] = $a_{h+k+2} \cdots a_n a_{n+1}$ for the remaining input string is written in the first available position POS of TAIL. In this process, it is clear that the positions *old_pos* and POS are stored by Step (s-2) as BASE[t'] = $-\text{old\_pos}$ and BASE[t''] = $-\text{POS}$, respectively. Hence, the modified double-array and TAIL by B_INSERT are valid for $K \cup \{x\}$. Therefore, the theorem is proved. Q.E.D.

Example 3: Consider each insertion of keys *bachelor#, bcs#, badge#, baby#, back#, badger#, badness#* for the initialized double-array. For the first four keys, the results of the double-array and TAIL, and the corresponding DS-trees are shown in Figs. 10 and 11, respectively. These final results have been shown in Figs. 4 and 3, respectively.

(a) bachelor#.

From $t = \text{BASE}[1] + b = 3$ and CHECK[3] = 0 ≠ 1, A_INSERT(1, *bachelor#*) is computed as follows.

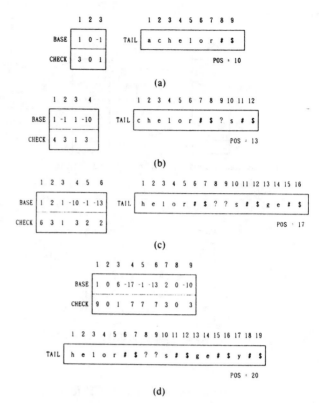

Fig. 10. An example of insertion process on the double-array. (a) The result by A_INSERT (1, *bachelor#*) for *bachelor#*. (b) The result by B_INSERT (3, ϵ, *cs#*, *achelor#*) for *bcs#*. (c) The result by B_INSERT (2, ϵ, *dge#*, *chelor#*) for *badge#*. (d) The result by A_INSERT (2, *by#*) for *baby#*.

(a-1): $t = \text{BASE}[1] + b = 3$, CHECK[3] = 0,
(a-3): INS_STR(1, *bachelor#* , 1),
 (s-1,s-2): CHECK[3] = 1, BASE[3] = −1,
 (s-3): POS = STR_TAIL(1, *achelor#\$*) = 10.
(b) *bcs#*.

The retrieval is unsuccessful because
$t = \text{BASE}[1] + b = 3$, CHECK[3] = 1,
BASE[3] = −1 < 0, $h = 1 \neq n + 1 = 3$,
S_TEMP = FETCH_STR(1) = *achelor#*,
STR_CMP(*cs#*, *achelor#*) = 0.
Then, B_INSERT(3, ϵ , *cs#*, *achelor#*) is computed as follows.
(b-1): *old_pos* = −BASE[3] = 1,
(b-3): BASE[3] = X_CHECK({c, a}) = 1,
(b-4): INS_STR(3, *achelor#*, 1),
 (s-1,s-2): CHECK[2] = 3, BASE[2] = −1,
 (s-3): POS = STR_TAIL(1, *chelor#\$*) = 10,
(b-5): INS_STR(3, *cs#*, 10),
 (s-1,s-2): CHECK[4] = 3, BASE[4] = −10,
 (s-3): POS = STR_TAIL(10, *s#\$*) = 13
(c) *badge#*

The retrieval is unsuccessful because
$t = \text{BASE}[1] + b = 3$, CHECK[3] = 1,
$t = \text{BASE}[3] + a = 2$, CHECK[2] = 3,
BASE[2] = −1 < 0, $h = 2 \neq n+1 = 3$,
S_TEMP = FETCH_STR(1) = *chelor#*,
STR_CMP(*dge#*, *chelor#*) = 0.
Then, B_INSERT(2, ϵ , *dge#*, *chelor#*) = 0 is computed as follows.

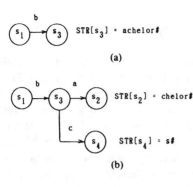

(a)

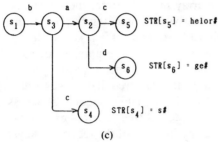

(b)

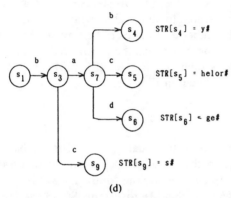

(c)

(d)

Fig. 11. An example of insertion process on the DS-tree. (a) The DS-tree for *bachelor#*. (b) The DS-tree for *bachelor#* and *bcs#*. (c) The DS-tree for *bachelor#*, *bcs#*, and *badge#*. (d) The DS-tree for *bachelor#*, *bcs#*, *badge#*, and *baby#*.

(b-1): $old\_pos = -BASE[2] = 1$,

(b-3): $BASE[2] = X\_CHECK(\{d, c\}) = 2$,

(b-4): $INS\_STR(2, chelor\#, 1)$

(s-1,s-2): $CHECK[5] = 2$, $BASE[5] = -1$,

(s-4): $POS = STR\_TAIL(1, helor\#\$) = 13$,

(b-5): $INS\_STR(2, dge\#, 13)$,

(s-1,s-2): $CHECK[6] = 2$, $BASE[6] = -13$,

(s-3): $POS = STR\_TAIL(13, ge\#\$) = 17$

(d) *baby#*.

The retrieval is unsuccessful because

$t = BASE[1]+b = 3$, $CHECK[3] = 1$,

$t = BASE[3]+a = 2$, $CHECK[2] = 3$,

$t = BASE[2]+b = 4$, $CHECK[4] = 3 \neq 2$.

Then, $A\_INSERT(2, by\#)$ is invoked as follows.

(a-1): $t = BASE[2] + b = 4$, $CHECK[4] = 3 \neq 0$

(a-2): $R\text{-}LIST = SET\_LIST(2) = \{c, d\}$,

$K\text{-}LIST = SET\_LIST(3) = \{a, c\}$,

$N(R\text{-}LIST) + 1 = 3 > N(K\text{-}LIST) = 2$,

$MODIFY(2, 3, \phi, \{a, c\})$ is called.

(m-1): $old\_base = BASE[3] = 1$

$BASE[3] = X\_CHECK(\{a, c\}) = 6$

For a in ORG,

(m-3): $t = old\_base + a = 2$,

$t' = BASE[3] + a = 7$,

$CHECK[7] = 3$, $BASE[7] = BASE[2] = 2$,

(m-4): $BASE[t] = BASE[2] = 2 > 0$,

$CHECK[5] = CHECK[6] = 7$ because of

$CHECK[5] = CHECK[6] = 2$.

$current\_s = 2$ is changed by $t' = 7$ because

of $current\_s = t = 2$.

(m-5): $BASE[2] = 0$, $CHECK[2] = 0$.

For c in LIST,

(m-3): $t = old\_base + c = 4$, $t' = BASE[3]+c = 9$,

$CHECK[9] = 3$, $BASE[9] = BASE[4] = -10$,

(m-4): $BASE[4] = -5 < 0$,

(m-5): $BASE[4] = 0$, $CHECK[4] = 0$.

(m-6): Returns $current\_s = 7$ as the new current node number.

(a-3): $INS\_STR(7, by\#, -17)$

(s-3): $POS = STR\_TAIL(17, y\#\$) = 20$.

B. Deletion

Suppose that a deletion algorithm, called Algorithm 3, uses the same input and output as Algorithm 1. Then, Algorithm 3 can be obtained by modifying two instructions return(TRUE) of Algorithm 1.

Modification of return(TRUE)
   begin
   $BASE[r] = 0$; $CHECK[r] = 0$;
   return(TRUE)
end

Algorithm 3 deletes the arc prior to a separate node s_r and consequently the single-string $STR[s_r]$ of TAIL becomes garbage symbol "?".

Theorem 2: Suppose that the double-array and TAIL are valid for K and that the input x of Algorithm 2 is in K. Then, the modified double-array and TAIL by Algorithm 3 are valid for $K - (x)$.

Proof: From $CHECK[r] = 0$, it is clear that the arc $g(s_t, a_h) = s_r$ entering into a separate node s_r is undefined. A mapping from K to S_p is a bijection (one-to-one correspondence), so the resulting double-array never define $g(s_1, a_1a_2 \cdots a_h)$ for $1 \leq h \leq n + 1$. Therefore, the theorem is proved. Q.E.D.

While the entries initialized by the deletion are available for the next insertion, it is difficult to remove them dynamically. Because of this, we can say that the presented scheme is well suitable for a weak static method as mentioned in Section I.

IV. EVALUATION

A. Theoretical Observations

The worst-case time complexity of the presented insertion algorithm depends on the procedure MODIFY invoked in A_INSERT. Moreover, the time complexity of MODIFY is related to the size, or DA-SIZE, of the double-array, because the function X_CHECK invoked in

MODIFY travels on the all indexes of the double-array. Since the computation of X_CHECK is similar to that of the row displacements proposed by Tarjan *et al.* [29], it is difficult to evaluate theoretically DA-SIZE by using external parameters n (the number of nodes) and m (the number of input symbols). However, because of the sparse relations on the nodes and input symbols of the goto function, we can assume that DA-SIZE is $n + cm$ for a constant c concerning each double-array, where cm is equal to *the number of available indexes on the double-array*. The value c will be determined through empirical observations.

From the above observation, it is clear that the worst-case time complexity of X_CHECK(LIST) is proportional to the product $nm + cm^2$ of DA-SIZE $n + cm$ and the maximum number m of entries in LIST, but we do not expect to include n in this complexity because n is proportional to the number of keys. Thus, we show that n can be removed from this complexity by modifying the structure of the array CHECK.

Definition 4: Let $r_1, r_2, \cdots r_{cm}$ be the increasing order of the available indexes on the double-array. We define a link, called a G-link, such that

$$\text{CHECK}[r_i] = -r_{(i+1)}; \qquad 1 \leqq i \leqq cm-1,$$
$$\text{CHECK}[r_{cm}] = -1,$$

where the value -1 represents the tail of the G-link, but the head of the G-link is represented by G_HEAD. Note that available entries in CHECK must be confirmed by negative integers instead of zeros.

By traveling the G-link in X_CHECK, it is clear that the worst-case time complexity of X_CHECK becomes $O(cm \cdot m) = O(cm^2)$. From two loops concerning "for each c in ORG" in Step (m-2) and "for each q" in Step (m-4), the worst-case time complexity of Steps (m-2 ~ m-5) in MODIFY becomes $O(m^2)$. Hence, the worst-case time complexity of the insertion algorithm becomes $O(cm^2 + m^2) = O(cm^2)$. The double-array realizes random storing of the nodes for the DS-tree, so there is little effect concerning different orders of inserting keys.

Consider the other time complexities. The worst-case time complexity of the deletion algorithm becomes $O(1)$, but the index of the initialized entry in CHECK must be appended to the G-link, so the precise time complexity is $O(cm)$. It is clear that the worst-case time complexity of the retrieval algorithm is $O(k)$ for the length k of a given key.

As for TAIL, the garbage symbol "?" created by the deletion algorithm and the procedure INS_STR invoked in Step (b-4) can be removed by shifting all symbols in TAIL and rewriting the BASE entries for the separate nodes. This time is proportional to $h + (n + cm)$, h being the total length of TAIL. If keys are inserted in alphabetical order, or in numerical value order, then TAIL can be built without creating any garbage symbols because:

1) the single-string x to be rewritten by INS_STR of Step (b-4) must be shorter than the previous single-string y, and

2) the single-string y of 1) always exists in the tail of TAIL.

To do this, the number of created garbage symbols must be subtracted from POS obtained by Step (s-3).

Here, consider a partial matching problem by the double-array. For a key $x * y\#$ with a dummy symbol "*" indicating one unknown symbol, there are at most m arcs $g(s_r, b) = s_t$ for s_r such that $g(s_1, x) = s_r$, and all arcs $g(s_t, y\#) = s_{t'}$ for each s_t must be confirmed on the DS-tree. Since each arc on the DS-tree can be retrieved from the double-array in $O(1)$ time, the worst-case time complexity of this partial matching is proportional to hm for the length h of $y\#$. Thus, for a key with e dummy symbols. the worst-case time complexity of partial matching by the double-array becomes $O(m^e)$.

Essentially, the DS-tree has a key-order preserving property [19] which enables sequential access to keys. In this search on the DS-tree, all arcs $g(s_r, a) = s_t$ for each node s_r existing in range of the requested key-order should be confirmed. Thus, the worst-case time complexity of a sequential search by the double-array becomes $O(dm)$ for the total number d of nodes to be traveled by this search. This time complexity can be greatly reduced by introducing buckets such as a B^+-tree [2], [23], [30]. This modification is shown in Fig. 12.

B. Empirical Observations

A retrieval system, called a *DOUBLE*, based on the presented method, was written using about 2300 lines of C, and implemented on the following workstations: DEC Micro VAX-II, Sun Microsystems Sun-3, SONY NEWS, TOSBAC UX-700, IBM6100, and various personal computers. DOUBLE has the following two routines plus the main routine based on the presented algorithm:

1) design routine,
2) memory management routine.

In routine 1), we can select the sets of the input symbols (i.e., ASCII, EBCDIC, Katakana, or Hiragana in Japanese, Chinese characters, etc.) and design a form of the record plus the essential single-string in TAIL. For example, a bibliographic search [1] and a spell checker [26] require only the single-strings. A local code optimizer [3] of a compiler has a sequence of codes to be replaced. In a machine translation system [12], the basic morphological and syntax data are stored in TAIL and the detailed knowledge translation data is stored in the other file accessible by the pointer in TAIL.

When the maximum node number exceeds a two-byte integer for a large number of keys, the double-array should be divided for appropriate subsets of K if one needs to maintain space efficiency. This division is also useful for a computer with a small main memory, such as a personal computer, because it enables us to read the one appropriate divided double-array from the auxiliary memory. In routine 1), we can set up the number of the divisions and determine whether the double-array and/or TAIL are placed on a main or an auxiliary memory. The routine 2)

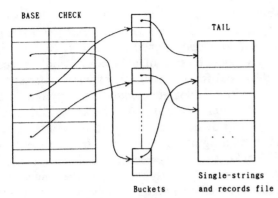

Fig. 12. A double-array with buckets.

TABLE I
SIMULATION RESULTS

	K1	K2	K3	K4	K5
Numbers and Length					
KNUM	35	310	1,480	23,976	32,344
MNUM	17	301	981	16,518	13,039
INUM	109	947	7,281	59,741	43,436
TNUM	161	1,558	9,742	100,233	88,801
KLEN	5.1	7.5	9.5	8.2	5.6
Storages(kilo-bytes)					
SBCT	0.36	3.63	17.17	221	226
SBC	0.25	2.69	9.89	161	182
STAIL	0.11	0.95	7.28	60	44
SSOURCE	0.18	2.33	14.08	196	183
C-VALUE(ordered)	0.17	0.94	0.32	0.23	1.13
C-VALUE(random)	0.19	0.96	0.34	0.24	1.14
Counts					
AVE-cm(ordered)	2.4(6)	6.2(48)	4.8(46)	3.6(64)	11.3(93)
AVE-m^2(ordered)	16.9(65)	97.5(325)	117.2(520)	91.3(650)	136.5(975)
AVE-cm^2(ordered)	1.1(3)	4.7(31)	3.6(37)	3.1(44)	19.5(255)
AVE-cm(random)	2.3(6)	5.9(49)	4.9(47)	3.5(63)	12.7(99)
AVE-m^2(random)	16.3(64)	99.3(398)	125.3(531)	96.7(668)	145.9(997)
AVE-cm^2(random)	1.1(3)	4.9(33)	3.7(39)	3.9(48)	20.7(256)
Times(milli-second)					
TSEARCH	0.38(0.40)	0.39(0.41)	0.42(0.43)	0.39(0.45)	0.38(0.43)
TINSERT	31.4(44.4)	30.6(53.7)	29.1(49.1)	36.7(78.6)	35.5(77.1)

manages dynamic storage of the divided double-array and TAIL by means of a first-fit strategy [2], [23], [30].

Table I represents the experimental results of building the double-array and TAIL incrementally for the following sets of keys.

K1, K2: The reserved words for Pascal and Cobol, respectively.

K3: Main city names in the world.

K4: Words for an English dictionary.

K5: Katakana for a Japanese word dictionary.

Note that, in each case, the number *m* of the input symbols equals 65 and that each double-array for *K4* and *K5* is divided into five. In order to see the effect on space and time of different orders of inserting the keys, the double-array was incrementally built in alphabetical order and in three kinds of random orders. Thus, the value specified by "(ordered)" stands for the result of alphabetical order and that specified by "(random)" for the worst-case result of three random orders. Each single-string in TAIL constructed by random order is shifted to reduce space. These times were about nine and six seconds for all keys in *K4* and *K5*, respectively. It more important to evaluate empirically space and time of the double-array because the single-strings in TAIL should be controlled, together with the records, by a memory management routine in actual information retrieval systems. In Table I, KNUM, MNUM, INUM, and TNUM represent each number of keys, nodes in $S_M - S_P$, nodes in $S_I - S_P$, and all nodes, respectively. That is, TNUM = MNUM + INUM + KNUM because the KNUM is equal to the number of the separate nodes. KLEN is the average length of keys. SBCT stands for storage of both the double-array and TAIL; SBC for storage of the double-array; STAIL for storage of TAIL; and SSOURCE for storage of a source file of all keys with a delimiter between keys. Note that TAIL has no symbol "$" indicating one-byte record information. C-VALUE represents *c* for the size $n + cm$ of the final double-array, but each C-VALUE for *K4* and *K5* is the average value for the divided double-array. As may readily be seen in the results, there is no difference between C-VALUE(ordered) and C-VALUE(random). It depends on the random storing of node numbers in the double-array. From the results, it turns out that the size

of the double-array is independent of different orders of inserting the keys.

From the results in Table I, it turns out that TAIL is useful for the space-saving of the double-array since INUM occupies 50 ~ 70 percent to TNUM, 60 ~ 70 percent if *K5* is ignored. The result of the storage shows that SBCT is just 1.1 ~ 1.2 times larger than SSOURCE for large sets *K3*, *K4*, and *K5*. This depends on the extremely small C-VALUE and DS-tree structure being allowed to merge the common prefixes into the same arc.

In order to estimate the length *cm* of the G-link, the time cost m^2 of Steps (m-2 ~ m-5), and the time cost cm^2 of X_CHECK, the terms of Counts are provided as being the results of all key insertions from *K1* to *K5*. AVE-*cm*, AVE-m^2, and AVE-cm^2, respectively, represent the average length of the G-link; the product of the average number of entries of ORG in Step (m-2) and the time cost *m* in Step (m-4); and the average count of confirming whether the CHECK's entry in X_CHECK is available or not. The values in ( ) represent the maximum value of each count. From these results, it turns out that the length of G-link, the time cost spent at Steps (m-2 ~ m-5) and the time cost spent by X_CHECK are reasonable. From the values specified by "(ordered)" and "(random)," it turns out that the building time of the double-array is independent of different orders of inserting the keys.

Let us compare the space of the double-array with those of an open hash [2], [23] and a binary tree [23], [30]. Since the keys are of varying length, the cells of the buckets of the hash and the node of the tree should not contain the keys themselves. Let *p* be a pointer to the beginning of a key in the key-file and let *q* be a pointer to link the cells of the bucket or the nodes. Thus, the cell of the bucket has pointers *p* and *q*, and the nodes of the binary tree have one pointer p and two pointers q. We assume that q and p are two-byte pointers for the same condition as the two-byte entries of the double-array and that the hash table has $0.5 \times$ KNUM two-byte entries. Then, for $K3$, $K4$, and $K5$, the total sizes of the hash method become from 1.7 to 2.2 times larger than SSOURCE and the total sizes of the binary tree become from 1.8 to 2.4 times larger than SSOURCE. So, it is evident that the double-array can be very compact.

TSEARCH and TINSERT respectively represent average retrieval and insertion times by SONY NEWS (2.3MIPS), for the double-array and TAIL in the main memory. The values in ( ) represent the worst-case times based on the longest key for the retrieval, and the key with the maximum cost of AVE-m^2 plus AVE-cm^2 for the insertion, respectively. As may readily be seen in the results, it turns out that the retrieval is very fast and that the insertion is about one hundred times in the case of average value, about two hundred times in the worst-case, slower than the retrieval, but it is still a reasonable speed. The worst-case retrieval of the above hash method requires searching two keys even if conflicts on the hash table are uniform, and that of the binary tree requires searching $\log_2 x$ keys for $x =$ KNUM even if the tree is balanced. So, it is evident that the retrieval by the double-array is very fast. There are no appropriate empirical data to compare the insertion time of the double-array and those of the two methods under the same condition, but it seems that the double-array is faster than the two methods for a large static set of keys that keeps increasing because of the worst-case time complexity $O(cm^2)$, independent of x, of the double-array and those $O(x)$ of the two methods.

As shown in the experimental results, the storage SBC of the double-array (except TAIL) occupies at most 160 ~ 180K bytes for $K4$ with 23 976 keys and $K5$ with 32 344 keys; thus the presented method enables us to build a compact and fast internal retrieval table if the double-array is placed in a main memory and if TAIL is placed in the auxiliary memory along with the single-strings and the records. That is to say, it enables us to retrieve a key in only one disk access. If one megabyte is available for the double-array, then about 100 000 keys can be stored in the internal retrieval table.

VI. Conclusions

A new internal array structure for a digital search tree, a double-array, has been introduced and the updating algorithm presented. The presented method contains the following features.

1) Any key can be retrieved and deleted in constant time.

2) There is a practical upper bound of the insertion time.

3) Space efficiency is very high if the frequency of insertions is greater than that of deletions.

4) A retrieval table can be constructed for arbitrary sets of keys.

The presented double-array has been used for about 50 sets of static keys (i.e., a lexical analyzer like LEX [24] and a local code optimizer of a compiler, Roman–Hiragana conversion routine of a Japanese word processor [12], etc.), and for about 40 sets of weak static and dynamic keys (i.e., dynamic command interpreters, a bibliographic search [7], [8], [10], Japanese and English morphological dictionaries for a machine translation system [12], filtering of highly frequent English words, and a spell checker emitting correctable candidates, etc.). The double-array can efficiently manipulate the longest applicable match based on a digital search, so it is well suited for the analysis of Japanese sentences without a delimiter between words.

It would be a very interesting study to apply the algorithm presented here for updating the double-array to a pattern matching machine with failure function [1], [7], [10], the reduction of static sparse matrices by using a row displacement [9], [29], the compression of a directed graph [2], a finite state machine [4], [11] associated with a parsing table [3], [6] like YACC [17], and so on.

The developed system will be provided on request to any readers. Please feel free to contact me.

Acknowledgment

The author is grateful to Mr. S. Yasutome for the implementation of the information retrieval system presented.

References

[1] A. V. Aho and M. J. Corasick, "Efficient string matching: An aid bibliographic search," *Commun. ACM*, vol. 18, pp. 333–340, June 1975.

[2] A. V. Aho, J. E. Hopcroft, and J. D. Ullman, *Data Structures and Algorithms.* Reading, MA: Addison-Wesley, 1983.

[3] A. V. Aho, R. Sethi, and J. D. Ullman, *Compilers Principles, Techniques, and Tools.* Reading MA: Addison-Wesley, 1986, ch. 2.

[4] J. Aoe, Y. Yamamoto, and R. Shimada, "An efficient method for storing and retrieving finite state machines" (in Japanese), *IECE Trans.*, vol. J65-D, pp. 1235–1242, Oct. 1982; (in English), *Electronica Japonica*, vol. 13.

[5] ——, "A practical method for reducing sparse matrices with invariant entries," *Int. J. Comput. Math.*, vol. 12, pp. 97–111, Nov. 1982.

[6] ——, "A method for reducing weak precedence parsers," *IEEE Trans. Software Eng.*, vol. SE-10, pp. 25–30, Jan. 1983.

[7] ——, "An efficient method for storing and retrieving pattern matching machines" (in Japanese), *Trans. IPS Japan*, vol. 24, pp. 414–420, July 1983.

[8] ——, "A method for improving string pattern matching machines," *IEEE Trans. Software Eng.*, vol. SE-10, pp. 116–120, Jan. 1984.

[9] ——, "An efficient algorithm of reducing sparse matrices by row displacements" (in Japanese), *Trans. IPS Japan*, vol. 26, pp. 211–218, Mar. 1985.

[10] ——, "An efficient implementation of static string pattern matching machines," in *Proc. First Int. Conf. Supercomputing*, Dec. 1985, pp. 491–498; also in *IEEE Trans. Software Eng.*, vol. 15, pp. 1010–1016, Aug. 1989.

[11] J. Aoe, "An efficient implementation of finite state machines using a double-array structure" (in Japanese), *IECE Trans.*, vol. J70-D, pp. 653–662, Apr. 1987.

[12] J. Aoe and M. Fujikawa, "An efficient representation of hierarchical semantic primitives—An aid to machine translation systems," in *Proc. Second Int. Conf. Supercomputing*, May 1987, pp. 361–370.

[13] J. Aoe, S. Yasutome, and T. Sato, "An efficient digital search algorithm by using a double-array structure," in *Proc. Twelfth Int. Computer Software and Applications Conf.*, Oct. 1988, pp. 472–479.

[14] F. Berman, E. Bock, E. Dittert, M. J. O'Donnelland, and D. Plank,

"Collections of functions for perfect hashing," *SIAM J. Comput.*, vol. 15, pp. 604-618, Feb. 1986.

[15] R. J. Cichelli, "Minimal perfect functions made simple," *Commun. ACM*, vol. 23, pp. 17-19, Jan. 1980.

[16] G. V. Cormack, R. N. S. Horspool, and M. Kaiserswerth," Practical perfect hashing," *Comput. J.*, vol. 28, pp. 54-58, Jan. 1985.

[17] S. C. Johnson, "YACC—Yet another compiler-compiler," Bell Lab., NJ, Comput. Sci. Tech. Rep. 32, pp. 1-34, 1975.

[18] G. Jaeschke, "Reciprocal hashing: A method for generating minimal perfect hashing functions," *Commun. ACM*, vol. 24, pp. 829-833, Dec. 1981.

[19] W. D. Jonge, A. S. Tanenbaum, and R. P. Reit, "Two access methods using compact binary trees," *IEEE Trans. Software Eng.*, vol. SE-13, pp. 799-810, July 1987.

[20] R. Fagin, J. Nievergelt, N. Pippenger, and H. R. Strong, "Extensible hashing—A fast access method for dynamic files," *ACM Trans. Database Syst.*, vol. 4, pp. 315-344, Sept. 1979.

[21] E. Fredkin, "Trie memory," *Commun. ACM*, vol. 3, pp. 490-500, Sept. 1960.

[22] M. L. Fredman, J. Komlos, and E. Szemeredi, "String a sparse table with $O(1)$ worst case access time," *J. ACM*, vol. 31, no. 3, pp. 538-544, Mar. 1984.

[23] D. E. Knuth, *The Art of Computer Programming*, vol. I, *Fundamental Algorithms*, vol. III, *Sorting and Searching*. Reading, MA: Addison-Wesley, 1973, pp. 295-304, 481-505.

[24] M. E. Lesk, "Lex—A lexical analyzer generator," Bell Lab. NJ, Comput. Sci. Tech. Rep. 39, pp. 1-13, Oct. 1975.

[25] K. Maly, "Compressed tries," *Commun. ACM*, vol. 19, no. 7, pp. 409-415, July 1976.

[26] J. L. Peterson, *Computer Programs for Spelling Correction* (Lecture Notes in Computer Science). New York: Springer-Verlag, 1980.

[27] B. A. Sheil, "Median split trees: A fast lookup techniques for frequency occurring keys," *Commun. ACM*, vol. 21, pp. 947-959, Nov. 1978.

[28] R. Sprugnoli, "Perfect hashing functions: A single probe retrieving method for static sets," *Commun. ACM*, vol. 20, pp. 841-850, Nov. 1977.

[29] R. E. Tarjan and A. C. Yao, "Storing a sparse table," *Commun. ACM*, vol. 22, pp. 606-611, Nov. 1979.

[30] T. A. Standish, *Data Structure Techniques*. Reading *MA: Addison-Wesley, 1980.*

Jun-ichi Aoe (M'87) received the B.E. and M.E. degrees in electronic engineering from the University of Tokushima, Tokushima, Japan, in 1974 and 1976, respectively, and the Ph.D. degree in communication engineering from the University of Osaka, Japan, in 1980.

Since 1976 he has been with the University of Tokushima. He is currently an Associate Professor in Information Science and Systems Engineering. He is the author of about 35 scientific papers.

His research interests include software engineering and natural language processing.

Dr. Aoe is a member of the Association for Computing Machinery, the American Association for Artificial Intelligence, the Association for Computational Linguistics, the Institute of Electronics, Information, and Communication Engineers of Japan, the Japan Society for Software Science and Technology, the Information Processing Society of Japan, and the Japanese Society for Artificial Intelligence.

Multikey Searching by Binary Search Trees

Multidimensional Binary Search Trees in Database Applications

JON L. BENTLEY, MEMBER, IEEE

Abstract—The multidimensional binary search tree (abbreviated k-d tree) is a data structure for storing multikey records. This structure has been used to solve a number of "geometric" problems in statistics and data analysis. The purposes of this paper are to cast k-d trees in a database framework, to collect the results on k-d trees that have appeared since the structure was introduced, and to show how the basic data structure can be modified to facilitate implementation in large (and very large) databases.

Index Terms—Best match query, binary trees, data structures, k-d trees, multikey searching, partial match query, range query.

I. INTRODUCTION

IT IS NO secret that the designer of a database system faces many difficult problems and is armed with only a few tools for solving them. Among those problems are reliability, protection, integrity, implementation, and choice of query languages. In this paper we will examine a solution to yet another problem that the database designer must face (while keeping the above problems in mind): the design of a database system that facilitates rapid search time in response to a number of different kinds of queries. We will confine our attention to databases of "fixed length records without pointers"; specifically we assume that we must organize a *file* of N *records*, each of which contains k *keys*. Much previous research has been done on problems cast in this framework; the interested reader is referred to Lin, Lee, and Du [1976], Rivest [1976], and Wiederhold [1977] for discussions of many different approaches.

In this paper we will examine a particular data structure, the *multidimensional binary search tree*, for its suitability as a tool in database implementation. The multidimensional binary search tree (abbreviated *k-d tree* when the records contain k keys) was introduced by Bentley [1975]. The k-d tree is a natural generalization of the well-known binary search tree to handle the case of a single record having multiple keys. It is a particularly interesting structure from the viewpoint of database design because it is easy to implement and allows a number of different kinds of queries to be answered quite efficiently. The original exposition of k-d trees was cast in geometric terms, and since that time the k-d tree has been used

Manuscript received September 14, 1978; revised March 13, 1979. The research in this paper was supported in part by the Office of Naval Research under Contract N00014-76-C-0370.

The author is with the Departments of Computer Science and Mathematics, Carnegie-Mellon University, Pittsburgh, PA 15213.

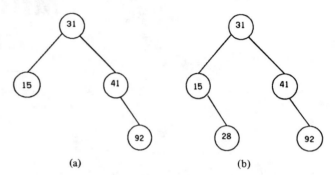

(a)   (b)

Fig. 1. Two abstract binary search trees.

to solve a number of problems in "geometric" databases arising in data analysis and statistics. The purposes of this paper are to cast k-d trees in a database framework, to collect the results on k-d trees that have appeared since the structure was introduced, and to show how the basic data structure can be modified to facilitate implementation in large (and very large) databases.

Since k-d trees are a natural generalization of the standard binary search trees we will review that well-known data structure in Section II. In Section III we develop the k-dimensional binary search tree (k-d tree). We describe how different types of searches can be performed in Section IV and discuss the maintenance of k-d trees in Section V. Section VI faces the problems of implementing k-d trees on different storage media, and a concrete example is then investigated in Section VII. Directions for further work and conclusions are offered in Sections VIII and IX.

II. ONE-DIMENSIONAL BINARY SEARCH TREES

In this section we will briefly review binary search trees; a more thorough exposition of this data structure can be found in Knuth [1973, section 6.2]. Fig. 1(a) is an illustration of a binary search tree representing the numerically-valued keys 31, 41, 15, and 92 (which were inserted in that order). In Fig. 1(b) the additional key 28 has been inserted. The defining property of a binary search tree is that for any node x the key values in the left subtree of x are all less than the key value of x and likewise the key values in the right son are greater than x's. To search to see if a particular value y is currently stored in a tree one starts at the root and compares y to the value of the key stored at the root, which we can call z. If y equals z then we have found it, if y is less than z then our search continues in the left son, and if y is greater than

Reprinted from *IEEE Transactions on Software Engineering*, Vol. SE-5, No. 4, July 1979, pages 333-340.

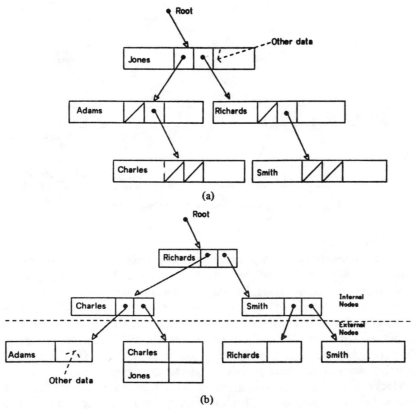

Fig. 2. Binary search tree implementations. (a) Homogeneous.
(b) Nonhomogeneous.

z then we continue in the right son. This process continues down the tree until the desired element is located. To insert an element we can apply the searching process until it "falls out" of the tree and then change the last "null pointer" observed to point to the new element.

The abstract binary search tree can be implemented on a computer in many different ways. The most popular representation of a node in a tree is what we will call the *homogeneous*. In this representation a node consists of a KEY field (which holds the single key defining the record), LEFT and RIGHT son pointers, and additional fields which hold the rest of the data associated with the record. Note that in this approach a node in the tree serves two distinct purposes: representation of a record and direction of a search. These two functions are separated in a *nonhomogeneous*[1] binary search tree, in which there are two kinds of nodes: internal and external. An internal node contains a KEY field and LEFT and RIGHT son pointers, but no data; all records are held in external nodes which represent sets of records (or perhaps individual records). In nonhomogeneous trees it is important to make the convention that if a search key is equal to the value of an internal node, then the search continues in the right subtree. Homogeneous trees are typically used when the elements of the tree are inserted successively, and nonhomo-

geneous trees are usually employed when the elements are to be built once-for-all into a perfectly balanced tree. Fig. 2 depicts a set of records stored in the two kinds of trees. A situation in which the nonhomogeneous tree is superior to the homogeneous tree occurs when the records are to be stored on a secondary storage device. In that case the nonhomogeneous tree offers the advantage that entire records do not have to be read into main memory to make a branching decision when only the key is required; we will cover this point in detail in Section VI.

In the above discussion we have alluded to a number of algorithms for performing operations on binary search trees. These operations are usually described only implicitly; we will name them explicitly to facilitate comparison with the analogous operations on k-d trees to be discussed later. Algorithm SEARCH tells if a record containing a given key is stored in the tree; Knuth [1973, section 6.2.2] shows that this algorithm takes $O(\lg N)$ expected time if N elements are currently stored in the tree. Algorithm INSERT inserts a new node into a (homogeneous) tree. Its average running time is also logarithmic; if one builds a tree of N elements by using INSERT N times the expected cost of that procedure is $O(N \lg N)$. An alternative approach is to build a perfectly balanced tree (for every node, the number of right descendants equals the number of left descendants) by algorithm BUILD; this can be accomplished in $O(N \lg N)$ worst case time. Note that while a homogeneous tree may be balanced by BUILD, it is usually the case that a nonhomogeneous tree is built by this algorithm.

[1] The distinction between homogeneous and nonhomogeneous trees is usually made but not named in discussions of binary trees. These terms will be used consistently throughout this paper.

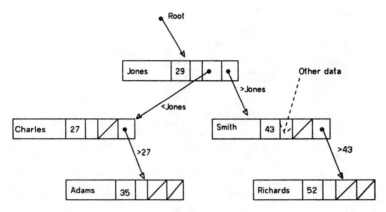

Fig. 3. A homogeneous 2-d tree: K_1 is name and K_2 is age.

Before we generalize this "one-dimensional" binary search tree to become "multidimensional" (that is, deal with several keys per record instead of just one), it is important that we stop for a moment and examine the "philosophy" of binary search trees. These structures perform three tasks at once. Firstly, they *store* the records of a given set. Secondly, they impose a *partition* on the data space (that is, they divide the line into segments). Thirdly, binary search trees provide a *directory* that allows us to locate rapidly the position of a new point in the partition by making a logarithmic number of comparisons. In the next section we will see how these essential features of binary search trees can be captured by a structure that allows a single record to be retrieved by many different search keys.

III. MULTIDIMENSIONAL BINARY SEARCH TREES

The binary search trees of Section II can be used to organize a file of data in which all records contain just one key field and other data fields. If there are many key fields in each record, however, binary search trees are inappropriate because they use only one of the key fields to organize the tree.[2] We will now see how standard binary search trees can be generalized to make use of all the key fields in a file F of N records of k keys each. A standard binary search tree "discriminates" during an insertion (that is, tells the insertion to proceed right or left) on the basis of one key field. In a multidimensional binary search tree (k-d tree) this discrimination is done on different keys. Specifically, assume that each record in the file has k keys, $K_1, K_2, \cdots, K_k$. On the first level of the tree we choose to go right or left when inserting a new record by comparing the first key (K_1) of the new record with the first key of the record stored at the root of the k-d tree (assume a homogeneous representation). At the second level of the tree we use the second key as the discriminator, and so on to the k-th level. Finally at the (k + 1)-st level of the tree we "wrap around" and use the first key as the discriminator again. We illustrate this concept in Fig. 3. Records in that tree each contain two keys: name (K_1) and age (K_2). Note how every record in the left subtree of the root has a name field less than the root's, and likewise every record in the right subtree has a greater name field. On the second level right subtrees have greater age values.

We can now give a more formal definition of k-d trees. A homogeneous k-d tree is a binary tree in which each record contains k keys, some data fields (possibly), right and left son pointers, and a discriminator which is an integer between 1 and k, inclusive. In the most straightforward version of k-d trees all nodes on level i have the same discriminator, namely (i mod k) + 1. The defining property of k-d trees is that for any node x which is a j-discriminator, all nodes in the left subtree of x have K_j values less than x's K_j value, and likewise all nodes in the right subtree have greater K_j value. To insert a new record into a k-d tree we start at the root and search down the tree for its position by comparing at each node visited one of the new record's keys with one of the keys of that node, namely the one specified by the discriminator. Bentley [1975] has shown that if a set of N random[3] records are inserted into a k-d tree then it will require approximately 1.386 lg N comparisons to insert the N-th record, on the average; the expected cost of performing all N insertions is O(N lg N).

As there are many implementations of one-dimensional binary search trees, so there are many implementations of k-d trees. The k-d trees that we have described above correspond to the homogeneous binary search trees; it is also possible to define nonhomogeneous k-d trees. Internal nodes in such k-d trees contain only a discriminator (an integer between 1 and k), one key value (chosen by the discriminator), and left and right son pointers. All records in nonhomogeneous k-d trees are stored in external nodes or "buckets." (This version of

[2]We say that a field is a key field if a query can refer to it. For example, a set of records might each contain employee number, department number, and salary fields; if queries can refer only to department number and salary then those two fields are keys while employee number is data.

[3]Random is defined here as all $(N!)^k$ permutations of the values of the keys being equally likely. In statistical terms this is saying that in any record, the values of the keys are chosen independently.

k-d trees was originally proposed by Friedman, Bentley, and Finkel [1977]; a similar implementation was later suggested by Willard [1978].) A file of N records can be built into a perfectly-balanced nonhomogeneous k-d tree in $O(kN \lg N)$ time; an algorithm for accomplishing this is given in Bentley [1975] and will be discussed in Section V. We will see that nonhomogeneous trees speed up many types of searches because records in the tree do not have to be examined "on the way down" in a search; only records in well-chosen buckets must be inspected in their entirety. We will also see that nonhomogeneous trees offer substantial advantages in implementations on secondary storage devices.

Another variation among k-d trees is the choice of discriminators; this is appropriate for both homogeneous and non-homogeneous trees. We originally described a "cyclic" method for choosing discriminators—we cycle in turn through all k keys. For many kinds of searches one might do better by choosing as discriminator (say) a key in which the data values are particularly well "spread," or by choosing a key which is often specified in queries. Such approaches are examined by Bentley and Burkhard [1976], Friedman, Bentley, and Finkel [1977], and Zolnowsky [1978].

IV. SEARCHING IN k-d TREES

In the last section we defined k-d trees and mentioned two algorithms for constructing them: by repeated insertion and a "once-for-all" algorithm that produces a perfectly balanced tree. In this section we will examine a number of different algorithms for searching k-d trees, each appropriate for answering a certain kind of query. We will discuss four particular types of searches in detail, and then briefly mention other types of searching possible in k-d trees.

A. Exact Match Queries

The simplest type of query in a file of k-key records is the exact match query: is a specific record (defined by the k keys) in the file? An algorithm for answering such queries is described by Bentley [1975]. The search proceeds down the tree, going right or left by comparing the desired record's key to the discriminator in the node, just as in the insertion algorithm. In the homogeneous version of k-d trees we will either find the record in a node on the way down or "fall out" of the tree if the record is not present. In the nonhomogeneous version we will be directed to a bucket and can then examine the records in that bucket to see if any are the desired. The number of comparisons to accomplish an exact match search is $O(\lg N)$ in the worst case if the tree is perfectly balanced; it is also $O(\lg N)$ on the average for randomly built trees.

B. Partial Match Queries

A more complicated type of query in a multikey file is a "partial match query with t keys specified." An example of such a query might occur in a personnel file: report all employees with length-of-service = 5 and classification = manager, ignoring all other keys in the records. In general we specify values for t of the k keys and ask for all records that have those t values, independent of the other k minus t values. Bentley [1975] describes an algorithm for searching a k-d tree

to answer such queries, which we will now sketch. We start the search by visiting the root of the k-d tree. When we visit a node of the k-d tree that discriminates by j-value we check to see if the value of the j-th key is specified in the query; if it is, then we need only visit one of the node's sons (which son is determined by comparing the desired K_j with that node's K_j value). If K_j is not one of the t keys specified, then we must recursively search both sons. Bentley [1975] shows that if t of k keys are specified then the time to do a partial match search in a file of N records is approximately $tN^{1-t/k}$.[4] As an example, if four of six keys are specified in a partial match search of one million records, then only approximately 400 records will be examined during the partial match search.

C. Range Queries

In a range query we specify a range of values for each of the k keys, and all records that have every value in the proper ranges are then reported as the answer. For example, we might be interested in querying a student database to find all students with grade point average between 3.0 and 3.5, parent's income between $12 000 and $20 000, and age between 19 and 21. This problem arises in many applications; Bentley and Friedman [1978b] mention some of those applications and survey the different data structures currently used for solving the problem.

It is easy to answer a range query in a k-d tree; Bentley [1975] describes an algorithm for range searching similar to the partial-match searching algorithm. As we visit a node that is a j-discriminator we compare the j-value of that node to the j-range of the query. If the range is entirely below the value then the search continues on the left son, if it is entirely above then the search visits the right son, otherwise both sons are recursively searched. Lee and Wong [1977] have analyzed the worst case performance of that algorithm and have established that the time required to perform a range search is never more than $O(N^{1-1/k} + F)$, where F is the number of points found in the range. Although it is nice to know that things can never get *really* bad (at least for small k), the average case of searching is much better. Bentley and Stanat [1975] reported results for a data structure very similar to k-d trees that imply that the expected time for range searching in k-d trees is $O(\lg N + F)$; that this is indeed the case, on the average, was confirmed by the analysis of Silva-Filho [1978a]. It is difficult to analyze the exact performance of range searching because it is so dependent on the "shape" of the particular query, but empirical evidence strongly suggests that k-d trees are very efficient.

D. Best Match Queries

In some database applications we would like to query the database and find that it contains exactly what we are looking for; a builder might hope to find that he has in his warehouse exactly the kind of steel beams he needs for the current project. But often the database will not contain the exact item,

---

[4]For t < k. If t = k then this is an exact match search and $O(\lg N)$ time is required.

and the user will then have to settle for a similar item. The most similar item to the desired is usually called the "best match" or the "nearest neighbor" to the desired. In information retrieval systems we hope for a book that discusses all ten topics in our list, but we must settle for one (say) that mentions only eight. Friedman, Bentley, and Finkel [1977] showed how k-d trees can be used to answer such best match queries (where "best" can be defined by many different kinds of "distance functions"). Their algorithm depends on choosing the discriminators in a sophisticated fashion. They showed that the expected amount of work to find the M best matches to a given record is proportional to lg N + M in any fixed dimension. Their algorithm was implemented in Fortran for applications in geometric databases and empirical tests showed that their algorithm is orders of magnitude faster than the previous algorithms, for practical problem sizes. Since that time Zolnowsky [1978] has analyzed the worst case of nearest neighbor searching in k-d trees and has shown that although any particular search can be rather expensive, if a search for the nearest neighbor of every point in some fixed set is performed then the cost of searching will average to at most $O((\lg N)^k)$.

E. Other Queries

The four types of queries we have already investigated are the most commonly discussed queries in fixed-format database applications. Other query types do arise, however, and k-d trees can often be used to answer them. Bentley [1975] gives a procedure that allows k-d trees to answer "intersection" queries, which call for all records satisfying properties that can be tested on a record-by-record basis. The best match algorithm of Section IV-D finds the best match to a particular record; that can be modified to find the best match to a more general description (such as a range, for example). An interesting modification to the basic idea of k-d trees was made by Eastman [1977], who developed a binary tree data structure appropriate for nearest neighbor searching in document retrieval systems.

V. MAINTAINING k-d TREES

In Section III we defined the k-d tree and in Section IV we described different algorithms for searching k-d trees; in this section we will investigate the problems of maintaining k-d trees. Specifically we will discuss the problems of *building* a set of records into a k-d tree, *inserting* a new element into an existing tree, and *deleting* an existing element from a tree. We will discuss these problems in the two cases of homogeneous and nonhomogeneous trees.

We have already seen the insertion algorithm for homogeneous trees in Section III. We mentioned that a perfectly balanced tree can be built in $O(kN \lg N)$ time; an algorithm to do so is given by Bentley [1975], which we will now sketch for the case of cyclic homogeneous trees. The first step of the algorithm finds the median K_1 value of the entire set (that element greater than one half of the K_1 values and less than the other half). We then let the record corresponding to that element be the root of the entire tree and put the N/2 elements with lesser K_1 value in the left subtree and the other

N/2 elements in the right subtree. At the next level we find for each of those two subfiles of N/2 points their K_2 medians, and use those two records as the roots of the two subtrees. This process continues, finding the medians at each level and partitioning around them. If a linear-time algorithm is used to find medians, then this can be accomplished in $O(kN \lg N)$ time. Deletion of a node in a homogeneous k-d tree seems to be a fairly difficult problem. Bentley [1975] gives an algorithm that can delete a node in $O(N^{1-1/k})$ worst case time. Fortunately, the average running time of that deletion algorithm is much less: $O(\lg N)$.

The problems of maintaining a nonhomogeneous k-d tree (compared to a homogeneous) seem to be much easier on the average but more difficult when considering the worst case. Recall that there are two types of nodes in a nonhomogeneous k-d tree: internal nodes that contain only discriminators and pointers, and external nodes (or buckets) that contain sets of records. Friedman, Bentley, and Finkel [1975] report that in best match searching the optimal number of records per bucket is about a dozen; this will probably be a reasonable number for many applications. The algorithm that we sketched above for building a homogeneous tree can be applied almost immediately to build a nonhomogeneous tree; its worst case running time is also $O(kN \lg N)$. A good average-case strategy for insertion and deletion in a nonhomogeneous k-d tree is merely to insert the record into or delete the record from the bucket in which it resides; both of these operations can be accomplished in logarithmic time. If the insertions and deletions are scattered almost equally throughout the file then this method will produce very good behavior. If the resulting tree ever becomes too unbalanced for a particular application, then the optimization algorithm could be run again to produce a new optimal tree. (This is especially appealing if there are periods of inactivity in the database, such as at night in a banking system.) Another benefit of nonhomogeneous trees is that if "multiple writers" are used to perform insertions and deletions then they will have to "lock" only the bucket containing the current record (and no nodes higher in the tree).

VI. IMPLEMENTING k-d TREES

Our discussion of k-d trees so far in this paper has assumed that the cost of going from a node to its son is constant for all nodes, but this is not true in all implementations of k-d trees. In this section we will investigate the problems of implementing k-d trees on various storage devices.

If k-d trees are to be implemented in the main memory of a computer then either the homogeneous or nonhomogeneous versions will serve well; the nonhomogeneous version is usually the method of choice, however. In a high-level programming language the nodes in the tree can be implemented as records, and links to sons are then pointers to records. In a fairly low-level programming language (such as Fortran) the nodes of the tree (both internal and external) are usually implemented by sets of arrays representing the various fields of the nodes. There are many general techniques for trees that can be applied to this domain that result in clean and efficient code. For instance, if the tree is known to be totally balanced (as is often the case in a homogeneous tree), then a heap structure

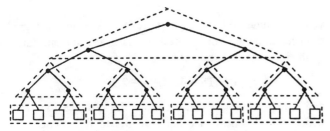

Fig. 4. Disk pages denoted by dashed lines.

can be used to implement the binary tree (we will return to this structure shortly).

Another technique that enhances k-d trees is the use of a *permutation vector*. We define a vector PERM [1..n], where n is the number of records in the tree. When the tree is built, the vector PERM originally contains pointers to all the records in the tree. We associate with the root of the tree the *permutation range* [1..n]; this implies that pointers to all descendants of the root can be found between positions 1 and n of PERM. If we partition at the root around the m-th record in a certain key, then we likewise partition the vector PERM such that all records in PERM [1..m−1] have lesser value in that key, and likewise that all records in PERM [m+1..n] have greater values. The permutation ranges associated with the left son and right son of the root will then be [1..m−1] and [m+1..n], respectively. The resulting permutation vector proves valuable in two contexts. Firstly, it gives a graceful way of keeping track of the records when BUILDing the tree. The second application of the permutation vector is in searching the tree. In range searching (and many other searches) we can often determine that all descendants of a particular node lie in the desired range and are therefore to be retrieved; without the permutation vector we would need to traverse that subtree to find the relevant records. With the permutation vector, however, we can just iterate through the appropriate range of PERM, and find pointers there to all the desired records.

If k-d trees are to be implemented on a secondary storage device such as disk then one would probably use nonhomogeneous trees.[5] As an example, assume that we have a file F of ten million records, each of five keys. If we allocate ten records in each bucket then there will be one million buckets in the system; this implies that the height of the "internal" part of the tree is twenty, since $\log_2 1000000 = 20$. Because there are too many internal nodes in the tree to store in the main memory, we must store both internal and external nodes on the disk. We will accomplish this by grouping together on the same disk pages internal nodes that are "close" in the tree (see Knuth [1973, section 6.2.4] for the application of this technique to one-dimensional trees). This process is illustrated in Fig. 4. If the discriminators are of reasonable length then compression techniques can be used to store an internal node in (say) ten bytes of storage; this implies that we can store one thousand internal nodes (or ten levels of the tree) on a ten-thousand-byte disk page. Thus there is a distance of only two

[5] For a description of an implementation of homogeneous trees on disk storage see Williams *et al.* [1975].

pages between the root of the tree and any external node, so if the page containing the root is kept in main memory at all times, any record can be accessed in only two page transfers from disk.

There are a few minor observations that can significantly improve the performance of k-d trees implemented on secondary storage devices. We saw above how it is crucial for the internal nodes to require as little space as possible. One means of achieving this space reduction is through key compression. Instead of storing the entire discriminating key in a node, we need only store enough of its first bits to allow us to later test whether to go right or left. For example, if the discriminator in a name field is "Jefferson" it might be sufficient to store only "Jef." Likewise, lower in the tree it is probably not necessary to store some of the leading bits of a discriminator. Another device that can be used to save space on the pages holding internal nodes is the "implicit" binary tree scheme which obviates the need for pointers in defining a binary tree (this is often called a heap). The root of the tree is stored in position 1 of a vector and the left and right sons of node i are found in locations 2i and 2i + 1, respectively. It might be that finding the exact median in building a k-d tree is very expensive. If this is so, then an approximation to the exact median would probably serve just as well as the exact discriminator. Weide [1978] has given an algorithm that finds approximate medians of large data sets very efficiently; his algorithm should probably be used in such an application. During a search in a k-d tree implemented on secondary storage only a relatively few pages will be kept in main memory at a time; a "least recently used" page replacement algorithm should probably be used to decide which old page to release when reading in a new page.

The above scheme appears very promising for many different applications of k-d trees on secondary storage devices. Though our analysis of the scheme is only for exact match searching, it should also work very well for all of the other search algorithms described in Section IV. Note the important role that nonhomogeneous k-d trees play in this secondary storage scheme: because the internal nodes are very small compared to the size of the entire records, many of them can reside on one disk page, drastically reducing the required number of disk accesses. A scheme similar to this has been investigated in detail by Silva-Filho [1978b]. He uses the k-d tree only as an *index*, and stores the records in their entirety in a separate data file.

VII. A CONCRETE EXAMPLE

In this section we will investigate the application of k-d trees in a student-record database to see how the issues discussed abstractly in previous sections would apply in a concrete example. Many other examples of k-d trees are available to the interested reader. Williams *et al.* [1975] describe a PL/I implementation of a database system containing the records of five thousand alumni of the University of North Carolina. Their system supported queries on four key fields (year of birth, year of graduation, geographical code, and alumnus name) and was implemented as a homogeneous tree

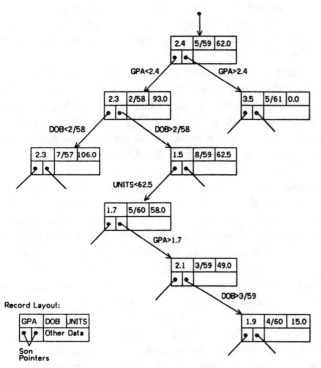

Record Layout:

GPA	DOB	UNITS
Other Data		

Son Pointers

Fig. 5. Part of the k-d tree for the student database.

on disk storage. Bentley [1975] discusses (unimplemented) applications of k-d trees in a geographic information retrieval system and in automatic speech recognition systems. Gotlieb and Gotlieb [1978] describe an (unimplemented) k-d tree approach to answering queries in a database of automobiles. Examples of k-d tree implementations in geometric databases can be found in Bentley and Friedman [1978a] (for constructing minimum spanning trees), Lauther [1978] (for performing design rule verification for integrated circuits), and Woodford [1977].

Suppose that we are to organize a database of student records. In this file, there is a record for every student containing three keys: date of birth (DOB), grade point average (GPA), and number of units completed (UNITS). Additionally, there will be other student data in each record that we will not mention here. We will organize this data in a homogeneous k-d tree in which the discriminators are chosen cyclically in the pattern GPA, DOB, UNITS. A portion of such a k-d tree is shown in Fig. 5.

The different queries supported by k-d trees might arise in many contexts in this student database. An exact match query (asking if a student existed with given GPA, DOB, and UNITS) would probably not occur. A partial match query, on the other hand, would be just the thing to help prepare the "Dean's List" by asking for all students with GPA = 4.0. If we wished to prepare an honor roll of all students in their junior year we might ask for a range search with ranges

$$3.5 \leqslant GPA \leqslant 4.0,$$
$$60 \leqslant UNITS \leqslant 90, \text{ and}$$
$$-\infty \leqslant DOB \leqslant \infty.$$

If a psychologist wanted to perform an experiment with a 25-

year old student at the sophomore level with medium grades, then he could ask for the best match in the student database to the hypothetical student with

$$DOB = 6/54, \ UNITS = 45, \ GPA = 2.2,$$

and the psychologist could choose the distance function by which the closeness of other students to this model will be judged.

A k-d tree implementing this student database in internal memory could be structured as either a homogeneous or non-homogeneous tree. The homogeneous tree might be the method of choice if the database were particularly active with insertions and deletions, but in most applications the non-homogeneous tree would be preferred. If the data fields of the records are not small enough to allow all of the records to fit into the primary memory of the computer, then two approaches can be taken to solving this problem. We could put all of the records on secondary storage device (such as disk) under the paging scheme discussed in Section VI, and then use an appropriate page replacement algorithm. A second approach would keep the records themselves in internal memory to serve as an *index* to the complete file, which resides as a direct-access file on disk.

VIII. FURTHER WORK

Although much research has been done on k-d trees since they were introduced in 1975, there are still many further areas that need work. On the practical side it is important that k-d trees be implemented in real database systems to see how the theory relates to practice. Another fascinating problem that needs investigation is methods for choosing discriminator values. Naive k-d trees chose discriminators cyclically, and the k-d trees of Friedman, Bentley, and Finkel [1977] chose as the discriminating key that key with the largest spread in its subspace of the key space. For many database applications, however, it is important to choose as discriminator a key which is used often in queries. Some heuristics proposed by Bentley and Burkhard [1976] for "partial match tries" might be useful in the context of k-d trees.

Perhaps the most outstanding open theoretical problem on k-d trees is that of maintaining dynamic k-d trees. One approach to this problem is to count for each node in the tree the number of left and right sons. If the ratio of sons' weights for any node ever becomes too unbalanced (defined as a parameter of the tree), then the entire subtree rooted at that node is rebuilt. This scheme guarantees that the length of the longest path in the tree is logarithmic, and the total cost of inserting n nodes is at most $O(n (\lg n)^2)$. For one-dimensional binary search trees there are a number of more sophisticated balancing schemes that allow insertions and deletions in logarithmic worst case time while ensuring that the tree never becomes unbalanced. It is not known whether or not there exist appropriate "balancing acts" for k-d trees; this problem appears to be very difficult. An alternative approach to the problem of dynamic k-d trees is to use a multiway tree such as those discussed in Knuth [1973, section 6.2.4]. Another strategy is to maintain a forest of static k-d trees as a dynamic structure; this approach has been investigated by Bentley [1979] and Willard [1978].

IX. Conclusions

In this paper we have investigated multidimensional binary search trees from the viewpoint of the database designer. The structure was defined in Section III, and in Section IV we saw that it supports a number of different kinds of queries. This is an especially important feature for database applications; it is essential that different query types be handled and it is most unattractive to have to store different data structures representing the same file. In Section V we saw a number of different maintenance algorithms for k-d trees. The maintenance algorithms for nonhomogeneous k-d trees are particularly simple to code and are very efficient on the average. In Section VI we investigated the implementation of k-d trees and saw that they can indeed be implemented very efficiently. This implies that k-d trees can be used effectively in large and very large databases. A concrete example was investigated in Section VII, and some areas for further research were then described in Section VIII.

This paper represents one of the first attempts to apply k-d trees to the problems that database designers must face. Although we have only scratched the surface of the application of this data structure in this problem domain, it appears that multidimensional binary search trees will be an important addition to the tool bag of the practicing database designer.

References

Bentley, J. L. [1975], "Multidimensional binary search trees used for associative searching," *Commun. Ass. Comput. Mach.*, vol. 19, pp. 509–517, Sept. 1975.

Bentley, J. L. [1979], "Decomposable searching problems," *Inform. Process. Lett.*, to be published.

Bentley, J. L. and W. A. Burkhard [1976], "Heuristics for partial match retrieval data base design," *Inform. Process. Lett.*, vol. 4, pp. 132–135, Feb. 1976.

Bentley, J. L. and J. H. Friedman [1978a], "Fast algorithms for constructing minimal spanning trees in coordinate spaces," *IEEE Trans. Comput.*, vol. C-27, pp. 97–105, Feb. 1978.

Bentley, J. L. and J. H. Friedman [1978b], "Algorithms and data structures for range queries," in *Proc. Computer Science and Statistics: 11th Ann. Symp. on the Interface*, Mar. 1978, pp. 297–307.

Bentley, J. L. and D. F. Stanat [1975], "Analysis of range searches in quad trees," *Inform. Process. Lett.*, vol. 3, pp. 170–173, July 1975.

Eastman, C. M. [1977], "A tree algorithm for nearest neighbor search in document retrieval systems," unpublished Ph.D. dissertation, Univ. of North Carolina, Chapel Hill, NC, 111 pp.

Friedman, J. J., J. L. Bentley, and R. A. Finkel [1977], "An algorithm for finding best matches in logarithmic expected time," *ACM Trans. Mathematical Software*, vol. 3, pp. 209–226, Sept. 1977.

Gotlieb, C. C. and L. R. Gotlieb [1978], *Data Types and Structures*. Englewood Cliffs, NJ: Prentice-Hall, pp. 357–363.

Knuth, D. E. [1973], *The Art of Computer Programming, Vol. 3: Sorting and Searching*. Reading, MA: Addison-Wesley.

Lauther, U. [1978], "4-dimensional binary search trees as a means to speed up associative searches in design rule verification of integrated circuits," *J. Design Automation and Fault-Tolerant Computing*, vol. 2, pp. 241–247, July 1978.

Lee, D. T. and C. K. Wong [1977], "Worst-case analysis for region and partial region searches in multidimensional binary search trees and balanced quad trees," *Acta Informatica*, vol. 9, pp. 23–29.

Lin, W. C., R. C. T. Lee, and H. C. Du [1976], "Towards a unifying theory for multi-key file systems," National Tsing-Hua University, Taiwan, Republic of China, Rep., 67 pp.

Rivest, R. L. [1976], "Partial match retrieval algorithms," *SIAM J. Comput*, vol. 5, pp. 19–50, Mar. 1976.

Silva-Filho, Y. V. [1978a], "Average case analysis of region search in balanced k-d trees," University of Kent, Canterbury, Rep., 16 pp, Nov. 1978.

Silva-Filho, Y. V. [1978b], "Multidimensional search trees as indices of files," University of Kent, Canterbury, Rep., 6 pp, Dec. 1978.

Weide, B. W. [1978], "Space-efficient on-line selection algorithms," in *Proc. Computer Science and Statistics: 11th Annu. Symp. on the Interface*, Mar. 1978, pp. 308–311.

Wiederhold, G. [1977], *Database Design*. New York: McGraw-Hill, chs. 3 and 4.

Willard, D. E. [1978], "Balanced forests of k-d* trees as a dynamic data structure," Harvard Univ., informative abstract, 29 pp, 1978.

Williams, Jr., E. H., A. Vaughn, B. McLaughlin, and M. Buchanan [1975], "PABST program logic manual," Univ. of North Carolina, Chapel Hill, NC, unpublished class project.

Woodford, B. [1977], "An investigation of some new tree structures," M.Sc. project, McMaster Univ., Hamilton, Ont., viii + 36 pp, Aug. 1977.

Zolnowsky, J. E. [1978], "Topics in computational geometry," Ph.D. dissertation, Stanford Univ., Stanford, CA; also Stanford Comput. Sci. Rep. STAN-CS-78-659 and Stanford Linear Accelerator Center Rep. SLAC-206, 53 pp.

Jon L. Bentley (M'79) was born in Long Beach, CA, on February 20, 1953. He received the B.S. degree in mathematical sciences from Stanford University, Stanford, CA, in 1974 and the M.S. and Ph.D. degrees in computer science from the University of North Carolina, Chapel Hill, in 1976.

He worked as a Research Intern at the Xerox Palo Alto Research Center from 1973 to 1974. During the summer of 1975 he was a Visiting Scholar at the Stanford Linear Accelerator Center. In 1977 he joined the faculty of Carnegie-Mellon University, Pittsburgh, PA, as an Assistant Professor of Computer Science and Mathematics. His current research interests include the design and analysis of computer algorithms (especially for geometrical and statistical problems) and the mathematical foundations of computation.

Dr. Bentley is a member of the Association for Computing Machinery and Sigma Xi. He was awarded the second prize in the 1974 ACM Student Paper Competition, and from 1975 to 1976 was a National Science Foundation Graduate Fellow.

Multikey Searching by
Extensible Hashing

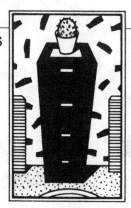

Multikey, Extensible Hashing for Relational Databases

Keith L. Kelley and **Marek Rusinkiewicz**, University of Houston

Today's databases rely on high-level data models to shield the user from the file structure. This addressing scheme offers a viable alternative to indexed sequential files.

An important feature of modern database systems is the data independence that lets users access information without regard for how the data is organized and accessed in secondary storage. However, the underlying file organization can have a major impact on the system's performance and its ability to efficiently support a high-level data model.

This article presents the design and implementation of a multikey, extensible hashing file addressing scheme and its application as an access method for a relational database.

This file organization was developed for Request, a testbed relational database-management system[1] running on a Digital Equipment Corp. VAX/VMS system. Our preliminary evaluation indicates that for many queries the performance of multikey, extensible hashing is no worse than that of indexed sequential files — and in

some cases it is clearly superior. This suggests that, for some queries, multikey, extensible hashing files are an attractive alternative to ISAM-like (indexed, sequential-access method) files.

In our implementation of multikey, extensible hashing, we specified four design objectives:

1. Support sequential, full-key, and partial-key retrieval.

2. Provide concurrent access to the file for read, insert, update, and delete operations.

3. Support the concept of a primary key (a subset of all the keys defined for a record).

4. Optionally enforce the uniqueness of the primary key with the access method.

Hashing schemes

Database systems frequently use direct-access files to provide fast access to records based on the value of a key attribute. Hashing addressing schemes use key-to-address

Kelley is now with IBM's Systems Integration Division.

Reprinted from *IEEE Software*, July 1988, pages 77-85. Copyright © 1988 by The Institute of Electrical and Electronics Engineers, Inc. All rights reserved.

Radix search trees

The idea to use radix search trees to implement extensible hashing files was proposed by Fagin and his colleagues.[1] A radix search tree is a tree in which searches are carried out a character at a time. Each node contains an entry for each element of the alphabet. This entry can either be nil (indicating that no key with the given prefix exists in the tree) or can point either to another node or to a bucket containing records (the keys of which begin with the characters encountered on the tree path).

Consider a radix search tree with the alphabet {0,1,2,3}. Figure A shows how, with the appropriate hash function, the strings 001, 112, 113, 12, and 3 could be stored. The problem with such a tree is that it grows randomly and tends to waste space when the alphabet is large because space is reserved for many keys that may not be in the tree.

If the keys of a radix search tree were uniformly distributed, it would be balanced. Uniform key distribution can be achieved by hashing the keys, which will yield a balanced radix search tree and better use the storage. A hashed radix search tree equivalent to the tree in Figure A is shown in Figure B1.

Because radix search trees are naturally extensible, using a hashed radix search tree as the index for a file lets the hash file grow and shrink. To minimize the length of the search path, some number of trees (say, 2^d) could be stored instead of storing the index to a file as a single radix search tree, as Figure B2 illustrates.

Each tree would reference all buckets containing records having keys with the first d bits equal to the value assigned to that tree. The

height of the radix search tree would then be less than the length of the binary string required to reference the buckets. If l were the longest radix search tree path, the tallest tree would have height l-d.

In extensible hashing the binary radix search tree is compressed into one level by setting d equal to l. This results in a collection of 2^d one-level trees, whose addresses are stored in an array called the file directory. The depth of the directory is known as d. Some buckets can be identified with an address of length less than d, say d'. In this case, shown in Figure B3, there are $2^{(d-d')}$ directory entries pointing to that bucket.

Reference

1. R. Fagin et al., "Extendible Hashing: A Fast Access Method for Dynamic Files," *ACM Trans. Database Systems*, Sept. 1979, pp. 315-344.

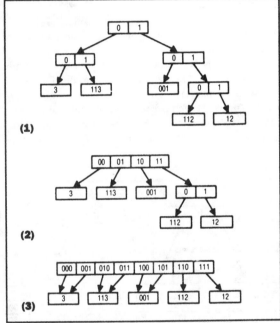

Figure B. (1) A hashed radix search tree equivalent to the tree in Figure A. **(2)** To minimize the length of the search path, some records could be stored as a single radix search tree. **(3)** A compressed hashed radix search tree.

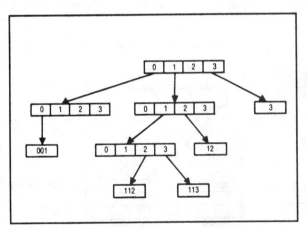

Figure A. A radix search tree with the alphabet {0,1,2,3}.

---

transformations to calculate a record's address. Collisions, which occur when hashing assigns identical addresses to distinct keys, are handled by a collision-resolution mechanism that usually chains to an overflow area or rehashes the keys.

If there are no collisions, access time is constant — it does not depend on the file size. When there are frequent collisions (when the number of records in the file has grown significantly, for example) constant access time is no longer guaranteed. Therefore, hash files must be reorganized periodically to maintain acceptable per-

formance. For these reasons, traditional hash files are considered to be applicable only to nonvolatile files whose sizes can be estimated reliably.

Dynamic hasing file organizations were introduced to let the file size grow and shrink without requiring costly reorganizations. Extensible hashing,[2] dynamic hashing,[3] virtual hashing,[4] and linear hashing[5] resolve collisions and improve storage use by adjusting the address space and hash function.

Directories. Extensible hashing re-

moves the addressing activities from the data proper by using a relatively small directory structure. This directory structure is based on the concept of a radix tree and is used to locate data buckets, each of which may contain one or more records. The process of locating data buckets with a radix tree is presented in the box above.

When a new record is inserted into a full data bucket, the access method allocates a new data bucket and adjusts the addressing mechanism. The records are then redistributed among the two data buckets, called brothers, based on the adjusted addressing mechanism.

This process is illustrated in Figure 1. The directory is a list of 2^d pointers to data buckets, d being the depth of the directory. The first d bits of the hash key are used to determine the position of the data-bucket address in the directory. In Figure 1a, bucket 1 has become full, so it splits. If necessary, d is incremented by 1 and the directory size increases. Figure 1b shows the split of bucket 1 into buckets 1 and 3 and the increase in the directory size. Figure 1c shows further splits and another increase in the directory size.

Multiple keys. A major problem with schemes based on hash addressing (both static and dynamic) is that records are located according to the value of a single key attribute. But a file may have several attributes that can be used to retrieve records, so a dynamic hashing method that uses multiple keys can provide fast answers to exact-match queries and improve partial-match query performance.

Huang[6] introduced such a scheme based on extensible hashing. Lloyd and Ramamohanarao[7] have proposed a multi-key generalization that can be applied to all dynamic hashing schemes by confining the multikey properties to the address key construction. In our approach we use the multikey scheme to implement an implicit multidimensional array scheme.

Multikey, extensible hashing

The main objective of our design was to preserve the natural extensibility of radix trees and take advantage of the uniform key distribution of hashing schemes.

In multikey, extensible hashing each attribute of the record key is hashed separately. As an example, let n be the number of attributes that constitute a record key.

Let $k_1, k_2, ..., k_n$ be a record key's attributes and $h_1, h_2, ..., h_n$ be hash functions. The pseudokeys of $(k_1, k_2, ..., k_n)$ are $(k_1', k_2', ..., k_n')$ where $k_i' = h_i(k_i)$.

Depth vectors. Because each attribute is hashed separately, the file directory is managed conceptually as an n-dimensional array.[6] Each dimension (attribute key) has a depth associated with it. Each depth is stored in a depth vector $(d_1, d_2, ..., d_n)$ where d_i is the depth of the pseudokey k_i'.

Therefore, the directory size is $2^{(d_1 + d_2 + ... + d_n)}$. The hash key of a record is computed by hashing each attribute (k_i) of the key separately and combining the leading d_i bits of each pseudokey to locate the directory entry.

Within each data bucket, a local depth vector $(d_1', d_2', ..., d_n')$ maintains the local depth of each dimension. The depth in this local depth vector must be less than or

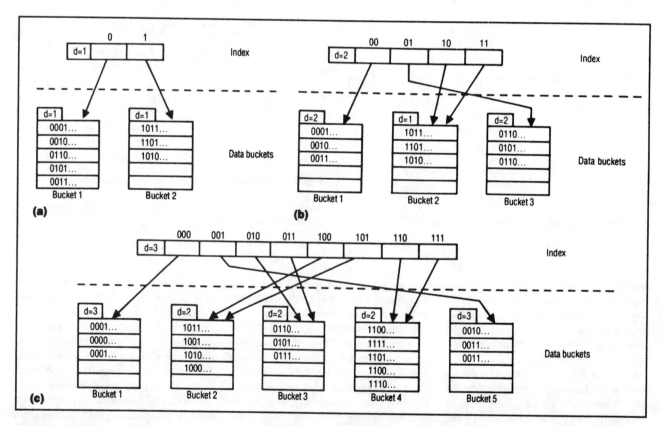

Figure 1. Splitting an extensible hashing file. The directory is a list of 2^d pointers to data buckets, d being the depth of the directory. **(a)** Bucket 1 is full, so it splits. **(b)** Bucket 1 has split into buckets 1 and 3 and directory size is incremented by 1. **(c)** The buckets split again and the directory size increases.

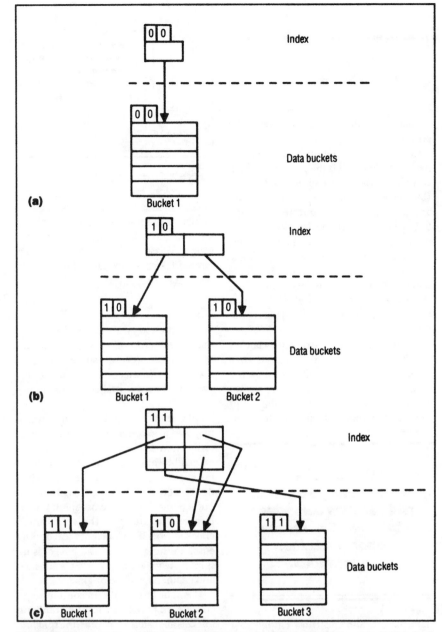

Figure 2. Depth vectors. **(a)** In the initial file organization, the depth is set to (0,0) in both the directory and local depth vector. **(b)** When the data bucket fills, it splits along dimension 1. **(c)** The next split occurs along dimension 2, doubling the directory size.

equal to the corresponding depth in the directory depth vector. When a bucket splits along the ith dimension, the ith component of the local depth vector is incremented by 1 in both of the resulting buckets. The number of directory entries pointing to a bucket can be computed as

$$2**[(d_1-d_1')+(d_2-d_2')+...+(d_n-d_n')]$$

where $(d_1', d_2', ..., d_n')$ is that bucket's local depth vector.

To further illustrate this concept, we use a two-dimensional file organization. Figure 2a shows the initial file organization. Here the depth is set to (0,0) in both the directory and local depth vector.

This organization is sufficient until the data bucket becomes full and must be split. Because the local depth vector is equal to the directory depth vector, the directory size must be doubled. The split will occur along dimension 1. After the bucket is split, the file organization may look like Figure 2b. The next split might occur along dimension 2, doubling the directory size again. In this case bucket 1 would be split and the file would be organized as in Figure 2c.

File shrinkage. Like single-key dynamic schemes, multikey, extensible hashing must allow file shrinkage. When a bucket is found to be less than half full, its brother bucket is checked to determine if the two can be merged. The problem is to determine which adjacent bucket is the brother bucket. In our implemenation, we chose to store the history of the bucket splits and allow merges only in reverse order of the splits — similar to the buddy system used in memory management.

Partial matches. Partial-match queries are answered by accessing the buckets corresponding to the specified key attributes. If only one key attribute, k_i, were not specified, then 2^{d_i} directory entries must be inspected. For example, consider a two-dimensional file with directory depths $d_1 = 3$ and $d_2 = 2$. If a query specifies only key attribute 1, four directory entries must be searched, since $2^{d_2} = 4$. The number of buckets searched may be less than the number of directory entries searched because a bucket may have multiple directory entries pointing to it. The cost of answering partial-match queries can be minimized by allocating more bits in the search string to the key elements that will be used most often.

Directory splits. To determine the order in which the directory splits will occur, the attribute's relative importance, or weight, can be specified at file creation. The splits will then occur in order of the attribute's relative importance.

The order of directory splits can be specified by a choice vector, $(c_1, c_2, ..., c_n)$, where each element of the vector (c_i) is the dimension chosen during split i. For example, the choice vector (1,2,1,3,2,1) means that, in a three-dimensional file, the splits will occur along the first, second, first, third, second, and first dimensions.

This means that, instead of maintaining the directory as a three-dimensional array with directory depths (3,2,1), it is maintained as a one-dimensional array with depth 6. To form the hash key of this record, the pseudokeys are interlaced according to the choice vector. For example, if the pseudokeys of the three attributes are 0100..., 1001..., and 0111..., the hash key would be formed as shown in Figure 3.

When several attributes define a record's hash key, some may have a limited range (the number of records in the file is

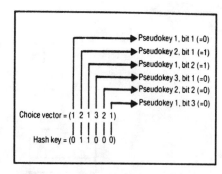

greater than the number of unique values for that attribute). In this case, splitting the directory dimension beyond its usable depth, u, would not let a bucket be split because the leading $u+1$ bits of all of the hash keys in the bucket have equal value.

Assuming a good hash function, the usable depth of attribute, is equal to floor [$\log_2$ card (attribute$_i$)] (floor being the largest integer less than or equal to x). For example, consider a key attribute with cardinality of 100. The usable depth of this dimension is floor [$\log_2 100$] = 6. The cardinalities of the domains of a multikey file's attributes can be specified at file creation and checked before a dimension split occurs.

Implementation

We chose to implement our scheme with a multikey, dynamic-hashing generalization that uses a choice vector.[7] With choice vectors, the directory may be stored as a one-dimensional table, and the directory and local depth vectors are replaced with a single depth value. This limits the multikey property to the construction of the hash key, so our scheme can use the same algorithms as single-key, extensible hashing to split and merge data buckets. Record operations (read, write, and update) need include only hash-key construction. The design and implementation for this structure is simpler than that for a structure that maintains the directory as a multidimensional array.

Our scheme does not maintain a choice vector at the file level. Instead, we maintain a choice-bit vector for each key attribute that denotes positions of that key attribute in the choice-vector file. For example, if the file-level choice vector is 11211212, the choice-bit vectors would be 11011010 and 00100101 for key attributes 1 and 2, respectively.

File operations. We combined the directory structure and the data component to speed up the create, open, and close operations. An added benefit of embedding the directory is that the access method more closely resembles the native access methods of the implementation environment. While this complicates system coding, we consider the performance and similarity to other access methods to be critical.

In our implementation, a file has three parts. The first part is the prologue, which contains all the information about the file (bucket size, record size, key definitions, and so on). The prologue requires one 512-byte block and is the first block of every multikey, extensible hashing file. The second part is the directory bucket (or buckets). The size of the directory bucket is specified when the file is created and is the same size as the data bucket. The data bucket (or buckets) is the third part of the file.

The prologue and one directory bucket are allocated when the file is created. Data buckets are appended to the end of the file as required. When a new directory bucket is needed, the data records contained in the first data bucket are moved to a new

---

We combined the directory structure and the data component to speed the create, open, and close operations.

---

data bucket, and the (now empty) first data bucket is redefined as a directory bucket. The directory does not shrink — the file must be reorganized to compress the directory.

Record organization. Our implementation supports only fixed-length records. The value of each record's hash key is computed and stored in its header. This value defines the hash key sequence and the ordering of the records in each bucket.

This scheme supports a more efficient bucket split because it does not require that key values be hashed during a split: The first record that contains a 1 in the differentiating bit position (local depth + 1) of its hash key begins the block of records moved to the new bucket.

During retrieval a simple match of the search hash key and the record hash key eliminates some records without comparing selection keys. If the hash keys do not match, the selection keys cannot possibly match, so the record can be ignored. If they do match, selection keys must be compared with the (unhashed) record keys.

Figure 3. To determine the order in which the directory splits occur, the attribute's relative importance, can be specified at file creation. To form the hash key, pseudokeys are interlaced according to this weight. This is how the hash key would be formed if the pseudokeys of the three attributes are 0100..., 1001..., and 0111....

Split limit. Dynamic hashing schemes may lead to excessive local collisions, especially when duplicate keys are allowed. In extensible hashing schemes, this introduces extra directory splits, each of which doubles the directory size. To control this, our scheme limits directory splits: When a bucket is to be split, the split limit is checked first. If the current local depth is equal to the split limit, the bucket is not split. Instead, another bucket is allocated and chained from the original bucket.

The split limit is the maximum depth considered reasonable for the number of buckets allocated. Of course, the split limit must be less than the maximum depth supported by the access method. In our implementation, the split limit is set to the $4*$floor ($\log_2 b$), where b is the number of buckets in use.

The split limit is designed to eliminate useless directory splits that occur in the rare instance when a bucket contains records that all have the same hash key. In these cases, splitting would not redistribute records.

Access operations

Access operations are performed according to the current position in the file. We cannot use relative record numbers to identify a record because its position can change — even in the time between its identification and its retrieval. Thus, our implementation uses cursors to fix positions: Each process that references a file

```
Let:
    D_i = depth of file i
    B_i = number of buckets in file i
    b_i = number of buffers for file i
    m_i = number of bits in the join key of file i
    k_i = known bits in file i

Compute:
    j = min (m_1, m_2)
    u = D_2 - (j + k_2)
    s = max (u - floor (log_2 b_2), 0)

Set known values in each file.
Loop 1: for i = 0 to 2^j - 1;
    Set join bits in file 1 to i;
    Set join bits in file 2 to i; {can be omitted}
    Loop 2: for r = 0 to 2^s - 1
        set high unknown bits in file 2 to r;
        while not end of file 1;
            read record from file 1;
            if record satisfies nonkey selection criteria
            then
                extract join value from record;
                set join value in file 2;
                while not end of file 2;
                    read record from file 2;
                    if record satisfies nonkey criteria
                    then
                        create join record
                    else
                        ignore record
                end; {file 2 loop}
            else
                ignore record;
        end {file 1 loop}
    end {Loop 2}
end {Loop 1}
```

Figure 4. The join algorithm for two multikey, extensible hashing files.

has two cursors: the current cursor and the next cursor.

A cursor has two parts: the record hash key and a sequence number. The sequence number is the relative order of the record in the set of records that have the same hash key. The cursors are set as a result of the find and read operations.

Before any access operation can occur, the cursor position in the file must be established. When a file is opened, the current cursor is undefined; the next cursor is the first record in hash-key order. If key retrieval is being performed, the current cursor is initially undefined and the next cursor is the first record that satisfies all the selection criteria. Once a record is changed — through a modify or delete operation — the current cursor is marked as undefined and is inaccessible for any later operation.

Concurrency control

The essential role of concurrency control is to let multiple processes read and update a file while preserving the file's integrity. The principal goal of our implementation is to provide maximum concurrency and minimum interprocess interference, with minimum processing overhead.

Our implementation provides concurrency control with a combination of intent locking and predicate locking. Intent locking controls concurrent access to the physical components of the file: the prologue, directory, and data buckets. Locking objects of different granularities, which are arranged in hierarchical sequence, are lock and unlocked using different modes. We use the operating system's local-buffer caching to resolve conflicts at the data-bucket level. Although each process is allocated a private buffer, its contents are refreshed when it is established that a concurrent update has been made to the physical bucket by another process. This prevents the "lost update" and "inconsistent read" phenomena.

A simplified predicate-locking mechanism determines if concurrent requests for data conflict. The predicate locking proposed by Eswaran[8] is an elegant and powerful synchronization mechanism. However, its main drawback is the complexity of determining if two locks expressed by general predicates are in conflict. For multikey, extensible hashing files, the locking predicates are expressed by the query's choice vector. Thus, simple operations involving hash keys and choice vectors determine if two queries may access a common set of records. Two requests conflict if either request seeks exclusive access to a set of records that is common to both requests.

Relational operations

One important goal of our implementation was to apply multikey, extensible hashing to relational database-management systems. The two most frequently executed relational operations are selection and equi-join.

Selection. Most access methods, with the possible exception of inverted-file organizations, support access based on a single key. Inverted-file organizations do allow specification of multiple keys for retrieval — but at a higher execution cost, because more lists must be intersected. Multikey, extensible hashing lets you specify any subset of keys for retrieval without this drawback. In fact, if more keys are specified in a query, the execution cost is *lower*.

To retrieve all records specified in a partial-match query, all buckets that may contain relevant records must be searched. To do this, the missing portions of the hash string value must be filled in: All possible values must be generated for them. As each key is specified and hashed, the choice-bit vector for that key is merged into a known bit vector.

For example, if two specified keys have choice-bit vectors 10001000 and 01100110, the known bit vector is 11101110. Two positions — the fourth and the eighth — are not known and must be filled in. In this case, four fill values are generated (00000000, 00000001, 00010000, and 00010001) and merged with the hash-bit vector to retrieve all the required records.

If no keys are specified, the known bit vector is 00000000 and all values for the hash key from 00000000 to 11111111 must be generated. We use this approach in sequential retrieval.

The cost of selection can be approximated as follows: If d equals the depth of the file, b equals the number of buckets in the file, and k = known bits in the selection condition, then the average cost for selection is

$$\frac{b * 2^{(d-k)}}{2^d} = b * 2^{-k}$$

For example, if the file contains 200 blocks, the depth of the directory is 8, and the number of known bits (specified by the selection criteria) is 6, then not more than 2^{-6} blocks of the file, or 4 blocks $(200 * 2^{-6})$ would have to be searched.

Equi-join. Multikey, extensible hashing is especially suited to performing equi-join operations on two tables when the join field is a key attribute in both tables. The hash key ordering can be used to join two tables pseudosequentially, based on the hash key values, assuming the same hash function is used for the join field in each table. Records with similar hash keys reside in the same bucket in a file. Therefore, you can view the equi-join operation as a series of bucket joins where all records in a subset of buckets in the first file will be joined with records contained in a (hopefully small) subset of buckets in the second file.

When joining two multikey, extensible hashing files, the leading j bits of the join field attribute in each file are set to an equal value. This lets the join operation be carried out as a series of partial file joins where a subset of buckets from file 1 are joined with a subset of buckets from file 2. Both sets of buckets contain all the records with the same leading j bits, so 2^j partial file joins are performed.

Figure 4 shows the join algorithm. Loop 1 generates the value that selects from

each file the subset of buckets that will participate in the join. If the size of the subset selected for file 2 (to be used in the inner loop) exceeds the available number of buffer buckets, the subset must be subdivided further.

The join operation then proceeds by limiting the buckets to be retrieved from file 2 and scanning the subset of file 1 buckets. This process, accomplished by loop 2, is repeated for each subdivision of the subset of buckets in file 2. The number of subdivisions (and therefore repetitions) is computed as 2 to the power of (depth of file 2 directory minus the number of bits involved in the join minus the number of additional selection bits in file 2 minus

---

Our method is especially suited to perform equi-join operations on two tables when the join field is a key attribute in both tables.

---

floor ($\log_2$ (buffers for file 2))).

Assume that two multikey, extensible hashing files with the parameters given in Table 1 are to be joined. The expected number of bucket accesses required for the join algorithm is 3,248 and 331 for files 1 and 2, respectively, significantly less than

if the usual nested-loop method were used. We can improve the algorithm's performance further by increasing the number of available buffers for file 2 to 32. The algorithm then becomes linear and the expected number of bucket accesses for file 1 decreases to 812. The expected number of accesses for file 2 remains 331.

Experimental evaluation

Multikey, extensible hashing is particularly appropriate as an underlying access method for a relational database-management system. Partial-match queries and table joins, the most frequent operations in a relational environment, are performed very efficiently for multikey, extensible hashing files.

Loading. To compare the performance of multikey, extensible hashing with native RMS indexed sequential files, we defined

Table 1.
Parameters for two multikey, extensible hashing files to be joined.

Parameters	File 1	File 2
Depth	10	10
Buckets	600	600
Specified bits	3	5
Join bits	3	3
Buffers	10	10

Table 2.
Description of files used for evaluation.

File	Field	Type	Card	Description
Supplier	Supno	char(5)	1000	supplier number
	Name	char(14)	1000	supplier name
	City	char(20)	23	supplier city
	Rating	char(1)	11	supplier rating
Parts	Partno	char(4)	1000	part number
	Weight	integer	1000	part weight
	Color	char(12)	20	part color
	Group	char(2)	41	part grouping
Stock	Supno	char(5)	29	supplier number
	Partno	char(4)	37	part number
	Qty	integer	1000	stock quantity

Table 3.
Loading times for different file organizations.

File	Access method	Elapsed time (min.:sec.)	CPU time (sec.)	I/O	Disk blocks
Supplier	Seq.	0:01.75	00.76	36	79
	Ind.	3:58.53	32.98	9353	186
	EH	1:03.64	11.82	2907	129
Parts	Seq.	0:01.58	00.80	34	43
	Ind.	4:21.10	32.80	9472	144
	EH	1:39.79	12.83	2972	73
Stock	Seq.	0:01.37	00.57	33	28
	Ind.	0:43.48	10.10	1435	105
	EH	0:51.43	10.27	2397	46

Seq.=sequential access; Ind.= Indexed, sequential access; EH= Extensible, hashing file access

three tables. We loaded the same 1,000 records using the two access methods for each table. Table 2 shows the names of attributes, their type, numbers of unique values, and description of each field.

The Supplier table has three key fields in both file organizations: Supno is the primary key, City and Rating are secondary keys. The Parts table also has three key fields: Partno is the primary key, Color and Group are secondary keys. The Name field in the Supplier table and the Weight field in the Parts table are nonkey data fields. For both tables, the weight of the primary key is two times that of each secondary key. Supno and Partno constitute the primary key for the Stock table.

Table 3 shows the elapsed time, CPU

Table 4.
Comparison of query execution using different file organizations.

Query	Records retrieved	Access method	Elapsed time (sec.)	CPU time (sec.)	I/O
1	1000	IS	09.23	04.98	207
		EH	07.10	04.75	232
2	1	IS	00.65	00.07	42
		EH	00.66	00.12	48
3	53	IS	02.43	00.59	97
		EH	01.60	00.53	81
4	5	IS	01.52	00.54	91
		EH	01.31	00.21	68
5	1	IS	03.03	02.15	89
		EH	04.00	02.03	114
6	1	IS	02.18	00.56	91
		EH	01.65	00.44	87
7	1000	IS	58.12	20.69	878
		EH	41.83	26.04	628
8	352	IS	46.41	18.21	808
		EH	24.20	08.24	186
9	54	IS	38.15	16.86	778
		EH	07.69	05.04	151

IS = indexed, sequential files; EH = extensible hasing files

time, and number of disk I/O operations, plus the number of disk blocks, required to store each file. Statistics for the corresponding sequential files are shown as a reference. The table shows that it is fairly expensive to load secondary keys in an indexed-sequential organization: The two secondary keys quadruple the elapsed time, triple the CPU time, and increase the I/O by six times. In the case of Supplier and Parts, the costs were significantly higher in indexed sequential than in multikey, extensible hashing. In all cases, indexed-sequential files took more space to store the data than extensible hashing.

Response time. To compare response times in a relational environment, we executed nine queries. We used an equal amount of memory (3,072 bytes) for data buffering. Table 4 gives the results of the comparison.

Queries 1 through 6 select records from the Supplier table. Query 1 selects all records in the table. Here performance of the two methods is roughly the same. Query 2 retrieves a record based on the primary key value. In this case, the indexed-sequential organization is better. The retrieved record is located directly. Under the multikey, extensible hashing scheme, all buckets that could possibly contain the primary key value must be scanned.

Query 3 specified a secondary key attribute. We can expect better performance from multikey, extensible hashing because the records containing the key value tend to be clustered in a few buckets. Under the indexed-sequential organization, no record clustering based on secondary key values occurs.

Query 4 retrieves records based on the values of two key attributes. The indexed-sequential organization can only use one key attribute for retrieval. The multikey, extensible hashing organization can use both key attributes to select records. For this reason, performance is better under multikey, extensible hashing.

Query 5 requires that all records in the table be scanned to satisfy the selection criteria. In this case, the indexed-sequential organization fared better.

Query 6 selects one record based on a secondary key attribute and a nonkey attribute. Because of the clustering effect of extensible hashing, the number of bucket accesses required is slightly less than that necessary under indexed-sequential organization.

Queries 7 through 9 join the Parts and Stock tables on the Partno key attribute. Query 7 performs a two-table join on the key attributes, with no selection. In this query the multikey, extensible hashing access method performed better than the indexed-sequential method. In query 8, we specified an additional key attribute in the Parts file during the table join. Multikey extensible hashing was able to take advantage of the additional key attribute while the indexed-sequential access method could not. In query 9, we specified the remaining key attribute in the Parts table. In this case, we specified all bits of the hash key during the scan of the Parts table, further reducing the number of buckets that must be scanned under the extensible hashing organization. The indexed-sequential organization could not take advantage of this additional key attribute.

We must solve several problems before this access method is practical for relational databases:

• Because key attributes are hashed, queries involving selection criteria that use comparisons other than equality cannot use the multikey, extensible hashing

access method. In a query with selection conditions of the form field_value > constant, performance gains of the indexed-sequential organization would correspond to the number of records that could be eliminated by using the index — the multikey, extensible hashing organization yields no performance gain in this case.

• Because all key attributes are used to create the hash key, they must be specified at file creation and cannot be modified. It is more difficult to implement a feature that allows dynamic addition and deletion of (secondary) indexes, which are common to most relational systems. The file must be reorganized to add or drop keys.

• Because the hash key of a record is derived using not only the primary key but also other attributes, a record with a given primary key may reside in one of several data buckets. To determine if a record with a given primary key already exists in the file, all possible buckets in which the primary key can occur must be searched. For this reason enforcement of primary-key uniqueness is fairly expensive.

• Finally, we have to solve many problems related to low-level optimization of relational algebra operations. In particular, we are investigating how to efficiently implement binary relational operations, such as joins, involving relations implemented using different file organizations. ❖

Keith L. Kelley works in the advanced software-engineering technology department at IBM's Systems Integration Division in Houston, where he is involved in software reusability. His other research interests include Ada programming environments and database-management systems.

Kelley received a BS in computer science from the University of Southwestern Louisiana and an MS in computer science from the University of Houston. He is a member of the Computer Society and ACM.

References

1. B. Czejdo, and M. Rusinkiewicz, "Request: A Testbed Relational Database-Management System for Instructional and Research Purposes," *Proc. Nat'l Computer Conf.*, CS Press, Los Alamitos, Calif., 1984, pp. 531-536.

2. R. Fagin et al., "Extendible Hashing: A Fast Access Method for Dynamic Files," *ACM Trans. Database Systems*, Sept. 1979, pp. 315-344.

3. P.-A. Larson, "Dynamic Hashing," *Bit*, 1978, pp. 185-201.

4. W. Litwin, "Virtual Hashing: A Dynamically Changing Hashing," *Proc. Int'l Conf. Very Large Databases*, CS Press, Los Alamitos,

Calif., 1978, pp. 517-523.

5. W. Litwin, "Linear Hashing: A New Tool for File and Table Addressing," *Proc. Int'l Conf. Very Large Databases*, CS Press, Los Alamitos, Calif., 1980, pp. 212-223.

6. S. Huang, "Multidimensional Extendible Hashing for Partial-Match Queries," *Int'l J. Computer and Information Science*, April 1985, pp. 73-82.

7. J.W. Lloyd and K. Ramamohanarao, "Partial Match Retrieval for Dynamic Files," *Bit*, 1982, pp. 150-168.

8. K. Eswaran et al., "The Notions of Consistency and Predicate Locks in a Database System," *Comm. ACM*, Nov. 1976, pp. 624-633.

Marek E. Rusinkiewicz is an associate professor of computer science at the University of Houston. His research interests include databases, knowledge bases, query languages, distributed systems, and concurrency-control techniques.

Rusinkiewicz received an MS in computer science from the Moscow Institute of Electrical Engineering and a PhD in informatics from the Polish Academy of Sciences.

Address questions about this article to Kelley at IBM Systems Integration Division, 3700 Bay Area Blvd., Houston, TX 77058.

B^+-Trees and Overflow Handling

Performance of B$^+$-Trees with Partial Expansions

RICARDO A. BAEZA-YATES AND PER-ÅKE LARSON

Abstract—A B$^+$-tree with partial expansions is based on the idea of gradually increasing the size of an overflowing bucket, instead of immediately splitting it. When the bucket reaches some maximum size, it is split in the normal way. In this paper we mathematically analyze the behavior of the new file structure under random insertions, focusing on the expected storage utilization and the expected cost of insertions. The model can be used for studying both the asymptotic and dynamic behavior. The accuracy of the model is confirmed by simulation. Disk space management is more difficult than for standard B$^+$-trees. We investigate two simple space management schemes specifically designed for handling buckets of two different sizes. It is found that an overall storage utilization of 81 percent can be achieved in practice.

Index Terms—Analysis of algorithms, B-trees, file structures, overflow techniques, partial expansions.

I. Introduction

THE B$^+$-tree is one of the most widely used file organizations. In a B$^+$-tree all data records are stored at the lowest level (the *bucket level*), and the upper levels merely serve as an index to the data buckets [5]. All buckets are of the same size. File growth is handled by bucket splitting, that is, when a bucket overflows, an additional bucket is allocated and half of the records from the overflowing bucket are moved to the new bucket. The same type of splitting is applied to index nodes.

Frederickson [7] and Lomet [9] independently proposed the use of *elastic buckets*. The idea is simply to increase the size of an overflowing bucket instead of splitting it. Each expansion step is called a *partial expansion* and a bucket is expanded until it reaches some predetermined maximum size. When a bucket of maximum size overflows, it is split into two buckets (of minimum size) in the same way as for a standard B$^+$-tree. This process of a bucket gradually growing from its minimum size until it splits, is called a *full expansion*. A full expansion increases the number of buckets by one. The idea of partial expansions has previously been applied to linear hashing [8].

Manuscript received October 23, 1987; revised January 19, 1988. This work was supported by the Natural Sciences and Engineering Research Council of Canada under Grant A-2406, by the Institute for Computer Research of the University of Waterloo, and by the University of Chile.

The authors are with the Data Structuring Group, Department of Computer Science, University of Waterloo, Waterloo, Ont., Canada N2L 3G1.

IEEE Log Number 8930119.

Let r be the number of expansion steps required to grow a bucket from its minimum size up to and including the final split. For simplicity, we assume that records are of fixed length and measure the bucket size (capacity) in number of records. Let the r different bucket sizes be s_0, $s_1, \cdots, s_{r-1}$, where $s_0 < s_1 \cdots < s_{r-1}$. We call this the bucket *growth sequence*. In principle, any strictly increasing sequence is a valid growth sequence, provided that $2s_0 > s_{r-1}$. However, due to hardware and software limitations, the following growth sequence seems most practical [9]. Let a *page* be the smallest unit of transfer between disk and main memory, and a *page block* some fixed number of consecutive pages. Assume that the capacity of a page block is b records. For simplicity, we assume that b is *integer*, that is, we assume that buckets can be completely filled. Then choose the growth sequence $rb, (r + 1)b, \cdots, (2r - 1)b$. In other words, the minimum bucket size is rb records and each partial expansion increases the bucket size by one page block, up to the maximum bucket size of $(2r - 1)b$. Throughout this paper it is assumed that a bucket occupies some number of contiguous page blocks. Fig. 1 shows the structure of the two lowest levels of the file.

Example: For page blocks of size 5 and 3 partial expansions, the growth sequence is 15, 20, 25. When inserting the 26th record into a bucket, it splits into two buckets of size 15, each one containing 13 records. The minimum storage utilization for the various bucket sizes is $13/15 = 0.866 \cdots$, $16/20 = 0.8$, $21/25 = 0.84$.

In this paper we analyze the expected performance of B$^+$-trees with elastic buckets. The analysis is based on a model for standard B$^+$-trees developed by Nakamura and Mizoguchi [10]. The model is an example of *fringe analysis*, which is a technique first introduced by Yao [11] in 1978 and formalized by Eisenbarth *et al.* [6]. In our case, the fringe consists of only the bucket level and the index part of the file is ignored. Frederickson [7] derived the asymptotic storage utilization for an arbitrary growth sequence and obtained the optimal growth sequence. Lomet [9] developed an approximate model which enabled him to compute the asymptotic storage utilization and bucket distribution for large buckets. Our model applies to any bucket size and can be used to study both dynamic and asymptotic behavior.

The rest of the paper is organized as follows. The basic model is developed in Section II, along with formulas for

Reprinted from *IEEE Transactions on Knowledge and Data Engineering*, Vol. 1, No. 2, June 1989, pages 248-257. Copyright © 1989 by The Institute of Electrical and Electronics Engineers, Inc. All rights reserved.

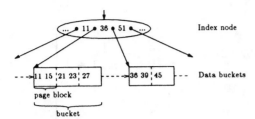

Fig. 1. Illustration of the structure of index nodes and data buckets.

computing the performance measures considered. Section II also contains some numerical results illustrating the convergence to the steady state. In Section III an asymptotic model is derived and some numerical results are given. In Section IV we study the problem of disk space management for the proposed scheme.

II. BASIC MODEL

Consider a file that contains n records. The n records divide the key space into $n + 1$ intervals. We assume that the keys of the n records are a random sample from some underlying key distribution. Similarly, the key of a new record to be inserted is assumed to be drawn at random from the key distribution. Under this assumption, the new key is equally likely to hit any one of the $n + 1$ intervals.

A bucket that contains j records "owns" j key intervals. For example, the data bucket on the right in Fig. 1 "owns" the intervals $(36, 39)$, $(39, 45)$, and $(45, 51)$. (The first or last bucket has one interval more, but for large n the effect of this is insignificant, and hence ignored in the subsequent analysis.) An interval that belongs to a bucket that contains j records will be called a j-interval. Let $p_j(n)$ denote the probability that an interval is a j-interval. Note that the total number of j-intervals is $(n + 1)p_j(n)$.

As explained in the previous section, we assume that there are buckets of r different sizes, rb, $(r + 1)b$, $\cdots$, $(2R - 1)b$. Let m denote the maximum number of records per bucket, that is, $m = (2r - 1)b$. The minimum number of records per bucket is then $\lfloor (m + 1)/2 \rfloor$. The amount of space allocated to a bucket is uniquely determined by the number of records it contains. A bucket of size $s_0 = rb$ contains from $\lfloor (m + 1)/2 \rfloor$

to rb records and a bucket of size $s_i = (r + i)b$, $i > 0$, contains from $(r + i - 1)b + 1$ to $(r + i)b$ records.

Assume, for the moment, that m is odd. The probability of a random insertion hitting a j-interval is $p_j(n)$. When a record hits a j-interval, the number of records in the corresponding bucket increases to $j + 1$, provided that $j < m$. If the bucket is full ($j = m$), it splits into two buckets, each one containing $(m + 1)/2$ records. However, we are more interested in the effect on the number of different j-intervals. For $j < m$, an insertion into a j-interval decreases the number of j-intervals by j and increases the number of $(j + 1)$-intervals by $j + 1$. For $j = m$, the number of m-intervals decreases by m and the number of $((m + 1)/2)$-intervals increases by $m + 1$. This gives us the following set of recurrence relations:

$$(n + 1)p_j(n)$$
$$= np_j(n - 1) - jp_j(n - 1) + (m + 1)p_m(n - 1),$$
$$\text{for } j = (m + 1)/2,$$
$$(n + 1)p_j(n)$$
$$= np_j(n - 1) - jp_j(n - 1) + jp_{j-1}(n - 1),$$
$$\text{for } (m + 1)/2 + 1 \le j \le m$$

which can be rewritten in the form

$$p_j(n) = p_j(n - 1) + \frac{1}{n + 1}\left[-(j + 1)p_j(n - 1)\right.$$
$$\left. + (m + 1)p_m(n - 1)\right]$$
$$\text{for } j = (m + 1)/2$$
$$p_j(n) = p_j(n - 1) + \frac{1}{n + 1}\left[-(j + 1)p_j(n - 1)\right.$$
$$\left. + jp_{j-1}(n - 1)\right]$$
$$\text{for } (m + 1)/2 + 1 \le j \le m.$$

Following [6], we write the recurrence in matrix form

$$\vec{p}(n) = \left(I + \frac{1}{n + 1}T\right)\vec{p}(n - 1) \qquad (1)$$

where I is the identity matrix, T is called the transition matrix, and $\vec{p}(n)$ is the probability vector $p_{\lfloor (m+1)/2 \rfloor}(n)$, $p_{\lfloor (m+1)/2 \rfloor + 1}(n)$, $\cdots$, $p_m(n)$. When m is odd, the transition matrix is

$$T = \begin{bmatrix} -((m + 1)/2 + 1) & 0 & \cdot & \cdot & \cdot & 0 & m + 1 \\ (m + 1)/2 + 1 & -((m + 1)/2 + 2) & 0 & \cdot & \cdot & \cdot & 0 \\ 0 & (m + 1)/2 + 2 & -((m + 1)/2 + 3) & 0 & \cdot & \cdot & \cdot \\ \cdot & 0 & \cdot & \cdot & \cdot & \cdot & \cdot \\ \cdot & \cdot & \cdot & \cdot & \cdot & \cdot & \cdot \\ \cdot & \cdot & \cdot & 0 & m - 1 & -m & 0 \\ 0 & \cdot & \cdot & \cdot & 0 & m & -(m + 1) \end{bmatrix}$$

115

The analysis for even m is similar. The resulting transition matrix is

$$T = \begin{bmatrix} -(m/2+1) & 0 & \cdot & \cdot & \cdot & 0 & m/2 \\ m/2+1 & -(m/2+2) & 0 & \cdot & \cdot & 0 & m/2+1 \\ 0 & m/2+2 & -(m/2+3) & 0 & \cdot & \cdot & 0 \\ \cdot & 0 & \cdot & \cdot & \cdot & \cdot & \cdot \\ \cdot & \cdot & \cdot & \cdot & \cdot & \cdot & \cdot \\ \cdot & \cdot & \cdot & 0 & m-1 & -m & 0 \\ 0 & \cdot & \cdot & \cdot & 0 & m & -(m+1) \end{bmatrix}$$

Given an initial state, we can use (1) to compute the effect of a sequence of random insertions. From $\vec{p}(n)$ we can then compute not only the storage utilization but several other performance measures. The expected number of buckets which contain j records [6] is

$$A_j(n) = \frac{p_j(n)(n+1)}{j}.$$

For the subsequent analysis it is convenient to express the amount of space used as *buckets per record*, that is, the total number of buckets divided by the number of records in the file. The expected number of buckets of size $s_i = (r+i)b$ per record is

$$Nb_i = \sum_j \frac{A_j(n)}{n+1}$$

where j ranges from $\lfloor (m+1)/2 \rfloor$ to rb for $i = 0$ (the minimum bucket size), and from $(r+i-1)b+1$ to $(r+i)b$ for $i = 1, 2, \cdots, r-1$. The expected total number of buckets per record is

$$NB = \sum_{i=0}^{r-1} Nb_i.$$

The expected fraction of records residing in buckets of size s_i is

$$Nr_i = \sum_j \frac{jA_j(n)}{n+1} = \sum_j p_j(n)$$

where j ranges over the same values as in the definition of Nb_i.

The expected storage utilization in buckets of size s_i is

$$u_i = E\left(\frac{\text{number of records in buckets of size } s_i}{\text{space used by buckets of size } s_i}\right)$$

that is, the expected value of the quotient of two random variables. We estimate this by

$$u_i = \frac{Nr_i}{s_i Nb_i}.$$

For finite n this is not entirely correct because, in general, $E(x/y) \neq E(x)/E(y)$. However, it can be shown that the above estimate is asymptotically correct. The details of showing this are somewhat involved, but in essence it

follows directly from the law of large numbers. In the same way, we estimate the expected fraction of buckets of size s_i as

$$f_i = \frac{Nb_i}{NB}$$

which is also an asymptotically correct estimate. The amount of space actually in use is n, the number of records in the file, and the expected total amount of space allocated is

$$S = (n+1) \sum_{i=0}^{r-1} (r+1)bNb_i.$$

The expected storage utilization is defined as

$$U = E\left(\frac{n}{\text{total space}}\right)$$

which we estimate by

$$U = \frac{n}{E(\text{total space})} = \frac{n}{S}.$$

This is also in an asymptotically correct estimate. For finite n we can find upper and lower bounds on U by using the Kantorovich inequality [4, p. 314]

$$1 \leq E(x)E(1/x) \leq 1 + \frac{(x_{max} - x_{min})^2}{4x_{min}x_{max}}$$

with $x_{min} = n$ and $x_{max} = n/U_{min}$, where U_{min} is the minimum possible storage utilization. This gives the bounds

$$\frac{n}{S} \leq U \leq \left(1 + \frac{(1 - U_{min})^2}{4U_{min}}\right)\frac{n}{S}.$$

The final performance measure to be considered is the cost of insertions. The total cost of an insertion depends on the height of the index, which in turn depends on how the index is organized. Following Lomet [9], we consider only accesses to the bucket level and the bottom level of the index. Note that we only count accesses, ignoring the fact that the transfer time depends on the bucket size. For disks the total access time is dominated by the seek time. The fanout of an index is typically sufficiently high that the amount of activity in the index above the bottom level is insignificant. It is also assumed that the bookkeeping necessary for allocating and freeing disk space is done entirely in main memory. Under these assumptions, insertion of a new record requires a minimum of two disk accesses (one read and one write). If the insertion causes a partial expansion, three accesses are needed: read the old bucket, write the expanded bucket, and update and write the affected index node. A split requires four accesses: read the old bucket, write two new buckets, and update and write the affected index node. Note that we assume that the index node affected is already in main memory as a result of traversing the index. The expected number of accesses for an insertion is then

$$\bar{I}_{acc} = 2 + Prob\left\{partial\ expansion\right\} + 2\ Prob\left\{split\right\}$$

$$= 2 + \sum_{i=0}^{r-2} p_{(r+i)b}(n) + 2p_{2(r-1)b}(n).$$

To obtain the "true" total cost of an insertion, the number of accesses required to traverse the index would have to be added.

Fig. 2(a) and (b) shows the development of the overall storage utilization for 1, 2, and 3 partial expansions. In Fig. 2(a) the smallest bucket size is 12 and in Fig. 2(b) it is 60. In the initial state, all buckets were of the smallest size and completely filled. Fig. 3 shows the expected cost of an insertion and Fig. 4(a) and (b) the expected fraction of buckets of different sizes. Table I shows the growth sequences for these cases.

It is apparent from Figs. 2–4 that initially filling the buckets completely is not a good strategy. As records are inserted the overall storage utilization drops very rapidly and then slowly converges with considerable oscillation. The oscillations increase with the page size. Partial expansions improve the storage utilization, as expected, and also reduce the oscillations. The variation in the storage utilization is accompanied by a similar variation in the expected insertion cost.

Fig. 4(a) and (b) reveals the cause of the varying insertion cost. When two partial expansions are used, all buckets of smallest size are quickly expanded. These larger buckets then slowly fill up and start splitting. This alternation between an excess of buckets of the smallest size and an excess of larger buckets eventually dies out, but very slowly. The pattern is similar for three partial expansions, with the difference that there is alternation between three different bucket sizes.

Figs. 5 and 6 show the development of the overall storage utilization starting from a different initial state. In Fig. 5 the file initially consisted of only smallest buckets, but these were filled to approximately the steady-state utilization. The variation decreases but it is still significant. Fig. 6 shows the development when starting with an empty file. It is rather surprising how long the oscillations persist even in this case.

What conclusions can we draw from these results? It is clearly not advisable to "overload" a B$^+$-tree, with or without elastic buckets, during initial loading. As new

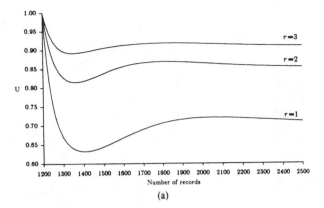

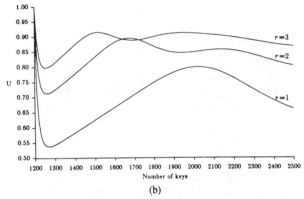

Fig. 2. (a) Expected storage utilization after initial loading for smallest bucket size 12. (b) Expected storage utilization after initial loading for smallest bucket size 60.

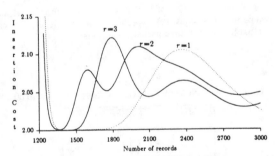

Fig. 3. Insertion cost after initial loading for smallest bucket size 60.

records are inserted, the overall storage utilization will drop fairly rapidly and oscillate around the steady-state level quite long. How long the oscillations persist (measured in number of records inserted) depends on the initial distribution and the initial file size. Oscillations cause increased activity in allocating and freeing disk space. As we will see in the next section, this affects the overall storage utilization.

We have performed rather extensive simulation experiments to test the accuracy of the model. Fig. 7 shows the results from two series of simulation experiments. The solid lines show the 95 percent confidence interval for the average storage utilization as obtained from 100 simulated file loadings. The dotted line shows the theoretical values. The results are in excellent agreement. Other experiments gave similar results. In particular, theoretical results obtained by using the approximate formulas for u_i,

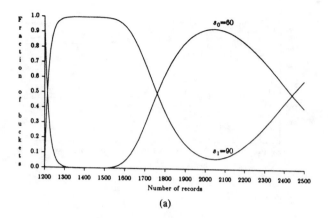

(a)

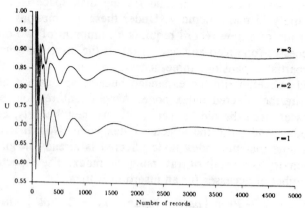

Fig. 6. Expected storage utilization starting from an empty file (smallest bucket size 60).

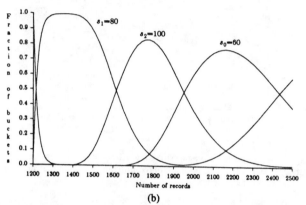

(b)

Fig. 4. (a) Expected fraction of buckets of each size after initial loading for two partial expansions. (b) Expected fraction of buckets of each size after initial loading for three partial expansions.

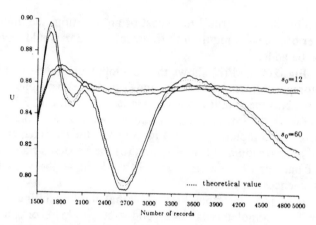

Fig. 7. 95 percent confidence interval for the average storage utilization for smallest bucket sizes 12 and 60.

TABLE I
GROWTH SEQUENCE FOR SMALLEST BUCKET SIZE 12 AND 60

Smallest bucket size	r	b	Growth sequence		
12	1	12	12		
	2	6	12	18	
	3	4	12	16	20
60	1	60	60		
	2	30	60	90	
	3	20	60	80	100

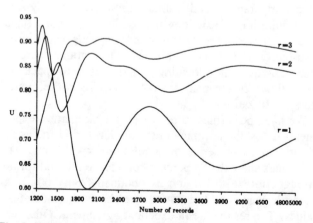

Fig. 5. Expected storage utilization after initial loading to steady utilization using only buckets of smallest size (smallest bucket size 60).

f_i, and U seem not to differ significantly from the experimental results. One other observation from the experiments is worth mentioning. If we want an initial load of 100 percent, it is better to use two different bucket sizes. For example, in the case of partial expansions, use the same number of buckets of each size.

III. ASYMPTOTIC ANALYSIS

When $n \to \infty$, recurrence (1) converges to the solution of the following linear system of equations [6, p. 135] (with an error term of order n^{λ_2} with $\mathrm{Re}(\lambda_2) < 0$):

$$T\vec{p}(\infty) = 0, \qquad \sum_j p_j(\infty) = 1.$$

Let $p_j = p_j(\infty)$ denote the steady-state probabilities. The system is easily solved because of the simple structure of T. When m is odd, the solution is

$$p_j = \frac{1}{(j+1)(H_{(m+1)} - H_{(m+1)/2})},$$

for $j = (m+1)/2, \cdots, m$

118

where $H_m = \sum_{i=1}^{m} 1/i$. When m is even, the solution is

$$p_j = \frac{1}{(j+1)(H_m - H_{m/2})},$$

$$\text{for } j = m/2 + 1, \cdots, m$$

$$p_{m/2} = \frac{m}{(m+2)(m+1)(H_m - H_{m/2})}.$$

The following formulas are valid for all m, unless explicitly separated for m odd and m even. They are obtained from the corresponding formulas in the previous section by using the steady-state probabilities. Define

$$\alpha(m) = \begin{cases} \left(H_{(m+1)} - H_{(m+1)/2}\right)^{-1} & m \text{ odd} \\ \left(H_m - H_{m/2}\right)^{-1} & m \text{ even.} \end{cases}$$

The expected number of buckets of size $s_i = (r+i)b$ per record is

$$Nb_i = \sum_j \frac{\alpha(m)}{j(j+1)}$$

$$= \begin{cases} \dfrac{(b+1)\alpha(m)}{(rb+1)(m+1)} \\ \qquad i = 0 \\ \dfrac{b\alpha(m)}{((r+i)b+1)((r+i-1)b+1)} \\ \qquad i = 1, 2, \cdots, r-1 \end{cases}$$

and the total expected number of buckets per record is

$$NB = \frac{\alpha(m)}{(2r-1)b+1} = \frac{\alpha(m)}{m+1}.$$

Hence, the expected fraction of buckets of size $s_i = (r+i)b$ is

$$f_i = \frac{Nb_i}{NB} = \begin{cases} \dfrac{b+1}{rb+1} \\ \qquad i = 0 \\ \dfrac{b(m+1)}{((r+i)b+1)((r+i-1)b+1)} \\ \qquad i = 1, 2, \cdots, r-1. \end{cases}$$

The expected fraction of records residing in buckets of size $s_i = (r+i)b$ is

$$Nr_i = \begin{cases} \alpha(m)(H_{rb+1} - H_{(m+1)/2}) \\ \qquad i = 0, m \text{ odd} \\ \alpha(m)\left(H_{rb+1} - H_{m/2} - \dfrac{1}{m+1}\right) \\ \qquad i = 0, m \text{ even} \\ \alpha(m)(H_{(r+i)b+1} - H_{(r+i-1)b+1}) \\ \qquad i = 1, 2, \cdots, r-1 \end{cases}$$

and the expected storage utilization in buckets of size $s_i = (r+i)b$ is

$$u_i = \begin{cases} \dfrac{(rb+1)(m+1)}{rb(b+1)}(H_{rb+1} - H_{(m+1)/2}) \\ \qquad i = 0, m \text{ odd} \\ \dfrac{(rb+1)(m+1)}{rb(b+1)}\left(H_{rb+1} - H_{m/2} - \dfrac{1}{m+1}\right) \\ \qquad i = 0, m \text{ even} \\ \dfrac{((r+i)b+1)((r+i-1)b+1)}{b^2(r+i)} \\ \qquad \times (H_{(r+i)b+1} - H_{(r+i-1)b+1}) \\ \qquad i = 1, 2, \cdots, r-1. \end{cases}$$

For large n, the expected storage utilization ($U_{\min} = r/(r+1)$, in the first partial expansion) is bounded by

$$\frac{\alpha(m)^{-1}}{F(2r, r, 1/b)} \le U \le \left(1 + \frac{1}{4r(r+1)}\right)\frac{\alpha(m)^{-1}}{F(2r, r, 1/b)}$$

and asymptotically, it is equal to the lower bound. The function $F(m, n, x)$ is defined as

$$F(m, n, x) = \sum_{i=n}^{m-1} \frac{1}{i+x} \qquad m > n$$

for integers n and m. If x is also an integer, then $F(m, n, x) = H_{m+x-1} - H_{n+x-1}$.

The probability that an insertion causes a split equals p_m, that is,

$$Prob\{split\} = \frac{\alpha(m)}{m+1}.$$

The probability that an insertion causes a bucket to expand from size s_{j-1} to s_j equals p_{j-1}, that is,

$$Prob\{j\text{th } partial\ expansion\}$$

$$= \frac{1}{(r+j-1)b+1}\alpha(m)$$

and hence the probability that an insertion triggers a partial expansion is

$$Prob\{partial\ expansion\} = F(2r-1, r, 1/b)\frac{\alpha(m)}{b}$$

Therefore, the expected number of accesses for an insertion is

$$\bar{I}_{acc} = 2 + \frac{\alpha(m)}{b}\left(F(2r, r+1, 1/b)\right.$$

$$\left. + \frac{1}{2r-1+1/b}\right).$$

The expected number of page blocks per record is

$$\overline{P} = \sum_{i=0}^{r-1} (r+i)Nb_i = \frac{\alpha(m)}{b} F(2r, r, 1/b).$$

When $b \to \infty$, we get the following formulas:

$$f_i = \begin{cases} \dfrac{1}{r} & i = 0 \\[2mm] \dfrac{2r-1}{(r+i)(r+i-1)} & i > 0 \end{cases}$$

$$u_i = \begin{cases} (2r-1)\bigl(\ln(r) - \ln(r-1/2)\bigr) & i = 0 \\[2mm] (r+i-1)\bigl(\ln(r+i) - \ln(r+i-1)\bigr) & i > 0 \end{cases}$$

$$U = \frac{\ln 2}{H_{2r-1} - H_{r-1}}.$$

Table II and Fig. 8 show the asymptotic storage utilization for different page block sizes and number of partial expansions. The storage utilization decreases when the size of page blocks is increased. Fig. 8 shows more clearly the effect of increasing the number of partial expansions. The additional gain in storage utilization decreases rapidly, and in practice it hardly seems worthwhile to go beyond three partial expansions.

Fig. 9 plots the expected cost of an insertion as a function of the page block size. Increasing the page block size dramatically reduces the cost of insertions because the overhead of bucket expansions and splits is distributed over more records. The figure also seems to indicate that increasing the number of partial expansions reduces the cost. This should be taken with a grain of salt, however, because buckets are not of the same size. If page blocks are of size 5, for example, then buckets are of size 5 when using one partial expansion but of size 10 and 15 when using two partial expansions. The reduced insertion cost is largely due to the larger bucket size.

Table III lists the asymptotic storage utilization for one to eight partial expansions and $b \to \infty$. Also, we include the asymptotic storage utilization of the optimal growth sequence (noninteger sizes) derived by Frederickson [7] ($U = \ln 2/(r(2^{1/r} - 1))$). They agree with the results obtained by Lomet [9]. Table IV shows the expected fraction of buckets of different size and the corresponding storage utilization for each bucket size for the case $b \to \infty$.

The accuracy of the asymptotic model was also tested by simulation. Table V summarizes the results from two simulation experiments and compares them to the corresponding theoretical results. Each experiment consisted of 100 file loadings. The number of partial expansions was two in both experiments. For a smallest bucket size of 12, all the theoretical results are within the 95 percent confidence interval. For a smallest bucket size of 60, and 150 000 records, the theoretical values are slightly out-side the 95 percent confidence interval. However, for 120 000 records they were all within the confidence interval. This indicates that there are small, but noticeable, oscillations even for a file containing over 150 000 records.

TABLE II
ASYMPTOTIC STORAGE UTILIZATION FOR 1, 2, 3, AND 4 PARTIAL EXPANSIONS

b	Partial expansions (r)			
	1	2	3	4
2	.75	.8993	.9360	.9523
4	.7292	.8685	.9118	.9335
8	.7138	.8509	.8987	.9233
12	.7076	.8447	.8942	.9198
20	.7022	.8397	.8905	.9169
40	.6978	.8358	.8877	.9148
60	.6963	.8344	.8868	.9140
∞	.6931	.8318	.8849	.9126

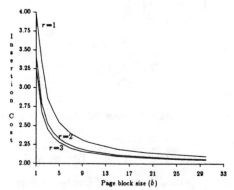

Fig. 8. Asymptotic storage utilization for different page block sizes as a function of the number of partial expansions (smallest bucket size rb).

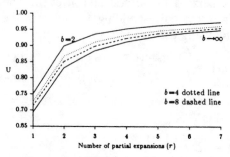

Fig. 9. $\bar{I}_{acc}$ as a function of the page block size for 1, 2, and 3 partial expansions (smallest bucket size $= rb$).

TABLE III
ASYMPTOTIC STORAGE UTILIZATION FOR $b \to \infty$

r	1	2	3	4	5	6	7	8
Utilization	.6931	.8318	.8849	.9126	.9296	.9411	.9493	.9556
Optimal	.6931	.8367	.8880	.9159	.9323	.9433	.9513	.9573

TABLE IV
EXPECTED FRACTION OF THE TOTAL NUMBER OF BUCKETS AND THE EXPECTED STORAGE UTILIZATION FOR EACH BUCKET SIZE WHEN $b \to \infty$

r	f_0	f_1	f_2	f_3	f_4	f_5	u_0	u_1	u_2	u_3	u_4	u_5
1	1						0.69					
2	0.50	0.50					0.86	0.81				
3	0.33	0.42	0.25				0.91	0.86	0.89			
4	0.25	0.35	0.23	0.17			0.93	0.89	0.91	0.92		
5	0.20	0.30	0.21	0.16	0.13		0.94	0.91	0.92	0.93	0.94	
6	0.17	0.26	0.20	0.15	0.12	0.10	0.95	0.92	0.93	0.94	0.95	0.95

Measure	Smallest bucket size 12		Smallest bucket size 60	
	Simulation (20000 records)	Theoretical	Simulation (150000 records)	Theoretical
U	0.85678 ± 0.00043	0.85696	0.83762 ± 0.00051	0.83706
u_0	0.87820 ± 0.00062	0.87783	0.86582 ± 0.00059	0.86645
u_1	0.84019 ± 0.00064	0.84073	0.81752 ± 0.00082	0.81681
NB	0.079004 ± 0.000085	0.079010	0.016027 ± 0.000020	0.01598
f_0	0.5377 ± 0.0026	0.5385	0.5168 ± 0.0032	0.5082
f_1	0.4623 ± 0.0026	0.4615	0.4832 ± 0.0020	0.4918

IV. DISK SPACE MANAGEMENT

With two partial expansions the minimum storage utilization is 67 percent and the expected value 83 percent (for large buckets). This is slightly higher than the expected value of 81 percent predicted for B*-trees [2]. In a B*-tree we attempt to move records to an adjacent bucket instead of immediately splitting an overflowing bucket. When this is not possible, two buckets are expanded into three. B*-trees also provide a minimum storage utilization of 67 percent. Using partial expansions appears to be a better solution than B*-trees because is not necessary to read and write adjacent buckets. It is easier to implement and the insertion costs are lower. However, this conclusion may be premature. Disk space management is more difficult because we have to handle buckets of different sizes. We have investigated two simple space management schemes specifically designed for handling buckets of two different sizes. Results from simulation experiments are reported in this section.

The first method divides the total file space into chunks of five page blocks. The second method divides it into chunks of six page blocks. When more space is needed for the file, an additional chunk is requested from the operating system. A chunk stores either one, two, or three buckets. Denoting the relative bucket sizes by 2 and 3, the following classification of the states of a chunk is sufficient for our purpose:

Size 5: empty, 2 + 0, 0 + 2, 3 + 0, 0 + 3,

2 + 0 + 2, full

Size 6: empty, 2 + 0, 0 + 2 + 0, 0 + 2, 3 + 0,

0 + 3, 2 + 2 + 0, 2 + 0 + 2, 0 + 2 + 2,

2 + 3, 3 + 2, full.

The notation 2 + 0 means that a bucket of size 2 occupies the two leftmost page blocks and the rest are free. 2 + 0 + 2 means that there is free space in the middle of the chunk. An in-core table is used for keeping track of the state of each chunk of the file. We must be able to distinguish between the states listed above. Hence, the first scheme requires 3-bit entries and the second scheme 4-bit entries. From this table we can find out not only whether a chunk has room for a new bucket, but also the exact size and location of the free space within the chunk. We can therefore write out a new bucket directly without first having to read in the chunk. Even for a large file, the bit table is small enough to be kept in main memory.

Space may now be wasted because of internal and external fragmentation. Internal fragmentation refers to the space wasted within buckets. External fragmentation refers to the space wasted because chunks are not completely filled. The results in the previous sections took into account only internal fragmentation. We are now interested in the storage utilization taking into account also the space wasted by external fragmentation. To distinguish between the two, we will refer to them as *internal storage utilization* and *total storage utilization*, respectively.

The scheme with chunks of size 5 allocates space as follows. When space is needed for a bucket of size 2, a chunk already containing a bucket of size 2 is used only if there are no chunks containing a bucket of size 3. That is, we try to avoid wasting 1/5 of a chunk. When space is needed for a bucket of size 3, we first try to place it in an existing chunk. When there is not sufficient space in any existing chunk, a new chunk is requested.

We can find an upper bound on the average total storage utilization for the first scheme in the steady state as follows. In the best case, most of the buckets will be completely filled. However, in the steady state there is an excess of buckets of size 2. The highest storage utilization is achieved if the excess buckets are stored in chunks in state 2 + 0 + 2. In each such chunk 1/5 of the space is wasted. Hence, an upper bound for the average total utilization is given by

$$U_t \leq \left(\tfrac{2}{5}u_0 + \tfrac{3}{5}u_1\right)\left(1 - (f_0 - f_1)\right) + \tfrac{4}{5}u_0(f_0 - f_1)$$
$$= \tfrac{4}{5}u_0 f_0 + \tfrac{6}{5}u_1 f_1.$$

The scheme with chunks of size 6 searches for chunks with free space in a certain order. The order used was

Size 2: 0 + 2 + 0; 2 + 2 + 0 or 2 + 0 + 2 or

0 + 2 + 2; 2 + 0 + 0 or 0 + 0 + 2;

0 + 3 or 3 + 0

Size 3: 0 + 3 or 3 + 0; 0 + 0 + 2 or 2 + 0 + 0.

That is, when space is needed for a bucket of size 2, we first try to find a chunk in state 0 + 2 + 0. If no such chunks exist, we try to find a chunk in one of the states 2 + 2 + 0, 2 + 0 + 2, or 0 + 2 + 2, and so on. In this case, the theoretical upper bound is equal to the internal storage utilization. In the best case all buckets of size 2 will be in 2 + 2 + 2 chunks and all buckets of size 3 in 3 + 3 chunks.

Fig. 10 shows the development of the average total storage utilization for the two schemes for smallest bucket size 60. The two solid lines represent averages from 100 simulated file loadings. The dotted line represents the theoretically expected storage utilization for a standard B+-tree with bucket size 60. Initially, the file consisted of completely filled smallest buckets. This initial state was deliberately chosen to see how the schemes perform when

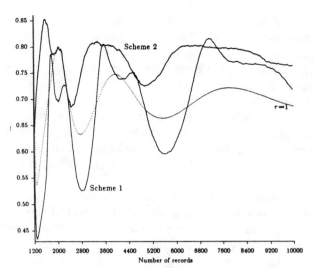

Fig. 10. Average external storage utilization for smallest bucket size 60.

TABLE VI
EXTERNAL STORAGE UTILIZATION FOR LARGE FILES (95 PERCENT CONFIDENCE INTERVAL)

Smallest bucket size	Lower bound [3]	Simulation (100 runs)		Upper bound	
		Scheme 1	Scheme 2	Scheme 1	Scheme 2
12 (20000 records)	0.7970	0.8377 ± 0.0011	0.82800 ± 0.00071	0.84377	0.85696
60 (150000 records)	0.7776	0.8232 ± 0.0014	0.81020 ± 0.00056	0.83431	0.83706

there is heavy expansion and splitting activity, and when there is a significant excess of buckets of one type.

It is apparent from Fig. 10 that the second scheme performs significantly better than the first scheme when the bucket distribution is highly skewed. The performance of the first scheme is simply too erratic and unreliable. The lowest storage utilization for the first scheme occurs when most of the buckets are of size 3. Many chunks will then contain just one bucket of size 3 because there are not enough buckets of size 2 to fill the "holes." For the second scheme, the lowest storage utilization occurs when there has been an excess of buckets of size 3 and they start splitting. When there is an excess of buckets of size 3, there will be many buckets in state 3 + 3. When these buckets start splitting, a significant fraction of buckets in state 2 + 3 (or 3 + 2) will be created, wasting 1/6 of a chunk. This is further exacerbated by the low internal storage utilization in the newly created buckets of size 2.

Table VI shows simulation results and theoretical lower and upper bounds for large files and two different smallest bucket sizes. The lower bounds are from [3]. Note that the upper bound cannot be achieved without relocation of buckets. In the steady state there is still expansion and splitting activity going on. When a bucket is expanded or split, a "hole" may be created which then will persist for some time until it is eventually filled. At any given point in time, a few such "holes" may exist. To fill a "hole" immediately would require relocation of some existing bucket.

As seen from Table V, the first scheme gives a higher total storage utilization in the steady state. However, the difference is small (less than 1 percentage point) and the second scheme is more reliable during transient phases. Scheme two also handles clustered or ordered insertions better than scheme one. The total storage utilization is over 80 percent, which is more than 10 percentage points higher than the storage utilization of a standard B⁺-tree. The results are close to the upper bound which indicates that there is little to be gained by bucket relocation.

We also simulated two variants of the basic schemes presented above. The first one was a variant of the scheme with chunks of size 5 which never stored two buckets of size 2 in the same chunk. The idea is to avoid wasting 1/5 of a chunk. Both its steady-state storage utilization and its performance during transient phases were worse than for the basic scheme. The second variant was a simplified version of the scheme using chunks of size 6. This version did not attempt to use the chunks in any particular order. The first chunk with enough free space to store the new bucket was used. Its performance was slightly worse than the basic scheme, but only marginally so.

V. CONCLUSION

The following points summarize the main results.
• Compared to standard B^+-trees [10], the storage utilization of B^+-trees with partial expansions is higher. Using buckets of two different sizes we can increase the storage utilization by more than 10 percentage points.
• During dynamic phases the storage utilization varies less than in standard B^+-trees, but takes longer to stabilize. This variation increases with the bucket size.
• The asymptotic storage utilization depends on the bucket size. It is slightly higher for small buckets.
• The expected insertion cost does not differ significantly from the insertion cost for standard B^+-trees.
• Among the space management schemes investigated, the basic scheme using chunks of size 6 performs best. Its dynamic behavior is fairly stable and asymptotically the storage utilization is reduced by as little as 2–3 percentage points due to external fragmentation.
• Based on the storage utilization alone, it is hardly worthwhile to go beyond four partial expansions. Taking into account other factors as well, it seems that two partial expansions is the best choice in practice—an overall storage utilization of approximately 81 percent or more can be achieved, the dynamic behavior is relatively good, and storage management is easy.
• Compared to B*-trees, a B^+-tree with two partial expansions is easier to implement, the storage utilization is about the same, but insertion costs are significantly lower [2]. Compared to other known overflow handling techniques, this method appears to have the lowest insertion cost.

REFERENCES

[1] M. Abramowitz and I. Stegun, *Handbook of Mathematical Functions*. New York: Dover, 1972.
[2] R. Baeza-Yates, "The expected behavior of B⁺-trees," *Acta Inform.*, vol. 26, pp. 439–471, 1989.

[3] ——, "A dynamic storage allocation algorithm and its application to B$^+$-trees," in *Proc. XIII Latin Amer. Conf. Inform. Sci. (EXPODATA 87)*, vol. 2, Bogota, Colombia, 1987, pp. 1122–1132.

[4] A. Clausing, "Kantorovich-type inequalities," *Amer. Math. Monthly*, vol. 89, no. 5, pp. 314–330, 1982.

[5] D. Comer, "The ubiquitous B-tree," *Comput. Surveys*, vol. 11, no. 2, pp. 121–137, 1979.

[6] B. Eisenbarth, N. Ziviani, G. Gonnet, K. Mehlhorn, and D. Wood, "The theory of fringe analysis and its application to 2-3 trees and B-trees," *Inform. Contr.*, vol. 55, nos. 1–3, pp. 125–174, 1982.

[7] G. Frederickson, "Improving storage utilization in balanced trees," in *Proc. 17th Allerton Conf. Commun., Contr. Comput.*, Monticello, IL, 1979, pp. 255–264.

[8] P-Å. Larson, "Linear hashing with partial expansions," in *Proc. 6th Int. Conf. Very Large Data Bases*, Montreal, Canada, 1980, pp. 224–232.

[9] D. Lomet, "Partial expansions for file organizations with an index," *ACM Trans. Database Syst.*, vol. 12, no. 1, pp. 65–84, 1987.

[10] T. Nakamura and T. Mizoguchi, "An analysis of storage utilization factor in block split data structuring scheme," in *Proc. 4th Int. Conf. Very Large Data Bases*, Berlin, 1978, pp. 489–495.

[11] A. Yao, "On random 2-3 trees," *Acta Inform.*, vol. 9, pp. 159–170, 1978.

Ricardo A. Baeza-Yates received the B.S. and M.S. degrees in computer science in 1983 and 1985, respectively, the B.E. and M.E. degrees in electrical engineering in 1982 and 1986, respectively, all from the University of Chile, Santiago, Chile, and the Ph.D. degree in computer science from the University of Waterloo, Waterloo, Ont., Canada, in 1989.

He currently holds a postdoctoral fellowship and is working with the New Oxford English Dictionary Project at Waterloo. His research interests include design and analysis of algorithms, data structures, and large textual databases.

Dr. Baeza-Yates is a student member of the Association for Computing Machinery, the IEEE Computer Society, and the American Mathematical Society.

Per-Åke (Paul) Larson received the Ph.D. degree in business administration and operations research from Åbo Swedish University, Finland, in 1976.

He was Assistant Professor of Computer Science at Åbo Swedish University, Finland, from 1974 to 1981. In 1981 he joined the University of Waterloo, Waterloo, Ont., Canada, where he is currently Professor of Computer Science. His research interests include database systems, file structures, and design and analysis of algorithms. He is the author of many scientific publications.

Dr. Larson is a member of the Association for Computing Machinery and the IEEE Computer Society.

BIBLIOGRAPHY

1. Primary References

[1] A.V. Aho, J.E. Hopcroft and J.D. Ullman, *Data Structures and Algorithms*, Addison-Wesley, Reading Mass., chs.4, 5 and 11, 1983.

[2] P. Berlioox and P. Bizard, *Algorithms 2: Data Structures and Search Algorithms*, John Wiley & Sons Limited, 1990.

[3] C. Faloutos, "Access methods for text," *Comput. Surveys*, 7, 3, pp.49-74, Mar. 1985.

[4] G.H. Gonnet, *Handbook of Algorithms and Data Structures*, Addison-Wesley, Reading Mass., ch.3, 1984.

[5] D. E. Knuth, *The Art of Computer Programming*, Addison-Wesley, Reading Mass., vol.III, *Sorting and Searching*, 1973, pp.389-550.

[6] K. Mehlhorn, *Data Structure and Algorithms 1: Sorting and Searching*, Springer-Verlag, Berlin, 1984.

[7] C.E. Price, "Table lookup techniques," *Comput. Surveys*, 3, 2, pp.49-65, June 1971.

[8] R. Sedgewick, *Algorithms*, Addison-Wesley, Reading Mass., pp.193-387, 1988.

[9] D.G. Severange, "Identifier search mechanisms: Survey and generalized model," *Comput. Surveys*, 6, 9, pp.175-194, Sept. 1974.

[10] T.A. Standish, *Data Structure Techniques*, Addison-Wesley, Reading Mass., pp.131-181, 1980.

2. Hashing
[Surveys]
[11] R. Devillers and G. Louchard, "Hashing techniques, a global approach, " *BIT*, 19, 3, pp.302-311, 1979.

[12] T.G. Lewis and C.R. Cook, "Hashing for dynamic and static internal tables," *IEEE Comput.*, pp.45-56, Oct. 1988.

[13] W.D. Maurer and T.G. Lewis, "Hash table methods," *Comput. Surveys*, 1, 1, pp.5-19, Mar. 1975.

[14] D.G. Severange and R. Duhne, "A practitioner's guide to addressing algorithms," *C.ACM*, 19, 6, pp.314-326, June 1976.

[15] J.D. Ullman, "A note on the efficiency of hashing functions," *J.ACM*, 19, 3, pp.569-575, July 1972.

[Hashing Functions]
[16] L.J. Carter and M.L. Wegman, "Universal classes of hash functions," *J.CSS*, 18, 2, pp.143-154, Apr. 1979.

[17] A.K. Garg and C.C. Gotlieb, "Order-preserving key transformation," *ACM Trans. Database Syst.*, 11, 2, pp.213-234, June 1986.

[18] G.D. Knott, "Hashing functions," *Comput. J.*, 18, 3, pp.265-278, Aug. 1975.

[19] V.Y. Lum, P.S.T. Yuen, and M. Dood, "Key-to-address transformation techniques; A fundamental performance study on large existing formatted files," *C.ACM*, 14, 4, pp.228-239, Apr. 1971.

[20] V.Y. Lum and P.S.T. Yuen, "Additional results in key-to-address transform techniques: A fundamental performance study on large existing formatted files," *C.ACM*, 15, 11, pp.996-997, Nov.1972.

[21] V.Y. Lum, "General performance analysis of key-to-address transformation methods using an abstract file concept," *C.ACM*, 16, 4, pp.603-612, Apr. 1973.

[22] P.K. Pearson, "Fast hashing of variable-length text strings, " *C.ACM*, 33, 6, pp.677-680, June 1990.

[23] D.V. Sarwate, "A note on universal classes of hash functions," *Inf. Proc. Lett.*, 10, 1, pp.41-45. Feb. 1980.

[Open Addressing]
[24] A.F. Ackerman,"Quadratic search for hash tables of size p^n", *C.ACM*, 17, 3, p.164, Mar. 1974.

[25] M. Ajtai., J. Komlos and E. Szemeredi, "There us no fast single hashing algorithm," *Inf. Proc. Lett.*, 7, 6, pp.270-273, Oct. 1978.

[26] O. Amble and D.E. Knuth,"Ordered hash tables," *Comput. J.*, 17, pp.135-142, 1974.

[27] S.K. Bandyopadhyay, "Comment on weighted increment linear search for scatter tables, " *C.ACM*, 20, 4, pp.262-263, Apr. 1977.

[28] V. Batagelj, "The quadratic hash method when the table size is not a prime number, " *C.ACM*, 18, 4, pp.216-217, Apr. 1975.

[29] J.R. Bell and C.H. Kaman, "The linear quotient hash code, " *C.ACM*, 13, 11, pp.675-677, Nov. 1970.

[30] J.R. Bell, "The quadratic quotient method: A hash code eliminating secondary clustering, " *C.ACM*, 13, 2, pp107-109, Feb. 1970.

[31] I.F. Blake and A.G. Konheim, "Big buckets are (are not) better!," *J.ACM*, 24, 4, pp.591-606, Oct. 1977.

[32] B. Bllobas, A.Z. Broder and I. Simon, "The cost distribution of clustering in ramdom probing," *J.ACM*, 37, 2, pp.224-237, 1990.

[33] R. P. Brent, "Reducing the retrieval time of scatter storage techniques, " *C.ACM*, 16, 2, pp.105-109, Feb. 1973

[34] W.A. Burkhard, "Full table quadratic quotient searching," *Comput. J.*, 18, 1, pp.161-163, Feb. 1975.

[35] P. Clapson, "Improving the access time for random access files," *C.ACM*, 20, 3, pp.127-135, Mar. 1977.

[36] J.G. Cleary, "Compact hash tables using bidirectional linear probing," *IEEE Trans. Comput.*, C-33, 9, pp.828-834, Sept. 1984.

[37] A. Ecker, "The period of search for the quadratic and related hash methods," *Comput. J.*, 17, 4, pp.340-343, Nov. 1974.

[38] J.A. Feldman and J.R. Low, "Comment on Brent's scatter storage algorithm," *C.ACM*, 16, 11, pp.703, Nov. 1973.

[39] G.H. Gonnet and J.I. Munro, "Efficient ordering of hash tables," *SIAM J. on Comput.*, 8, 3, pp.463-478, Aug. 1979.

[40] G.H. Gonnet, "Open addressing hashing with unequal probability keys, " *J.CSS*, 21, 3, pp.354-367, Dec. 1980.

[41] G.H. Gonnet, "Expected length of the longest probe sequence in hashing," *J.ACM*, 28, 2, pp.289-304, Apr. 1981.

[42] L.J. Guibas and E. Szemeredi, "The analysis of double hashing," *J.CSS*, 16, 2, pp.226-274, Apr. 1978.

[43] L.J. Guibas," The analysis of hashing techniques that exhibit k-ary clustering," *J.ACM*, 25, 4, pp.544-555, Oct. 1978.

[44] L.R. Johnson,"An indirect chaining method for addressing on secondary keys," *C.ACM*, 4, 5, pp.218-222, May 1981.

[45] A.G. Konheim and B. Weiss, "An occupancy discipline and applications, "*SIAM J. Appl. Math.*, 14, pp.1266-1274, 1966.

[46] G.D. Knott, "Linear open addressing the Peterson's theorem rehashed," *BIT*, 28, 2, pp.364-371, 1988.

[47] P.A. Larson, "Expected worst-case performance of hash files," *Comput. J.*, 25, 3, pp.347-352, Aug. 1977.

[48] P.A. Larson, "Frequency loading and linear probing," *BIT*, 19, 2, pp.223-228, 1979.

[49] P.A. Larson, "Analysis of repeated hashing," *BIT*, 20, 1, pp.25-32, 1980.

[50] P.A. Larson, "Analysis of uniform hashing," *J.ACM*, 30, 4, pp.805-819, Oct. 1983.

[51] F. Luccio, "Weighted increment linear search for scatter tables," *C.ACM*, 15, 12, pp.1045-1047, Dec. 1972.

[52] G.E. Lyon, "Hashing with linear probing and frequency ordering, " *J. Res. Nat Bureau of Standards*, 83, 5, pp.445-447, Sep. 1978.

[53] G.E. Lyon, "Packed scatter tables," *C.ACM*, 21, 10, pp.857-865, Oct. 1978.

[54] G.E. Lyon, "Batch scheduling from short lists," *Inf. Proc. Lett.*, 8, 2, pp.57-59, Feb. 1979.

[55] J.A.T. Maddison, "Fast lookup in hash tables with direct rehashing," *Comput. J.*, 23, 2, pp.188-189, Feb. 1980.

[56] E.G. Mallach, "Scatter storage techniques: a unifying viewpoint and a method for reducing retrieval times," *Comput. J.*, 20, 2, pp.137-140, May 1977.

[57] W.D. Maurer, "An improved hash code for scatter storage," *C.ACM*, 11, 1, pp.35-38, Jan. 1968.

[58] H. Mendelson and U. Yechiali, "A new approach to the analysis of linear probing schemes," *J.ACM*, 27, 2, pp.474-483, July 1980.

[59] R. Morris, "Scatter Storage Techniques," *C.ACM*, 11, 1, pp.38-44, Jan. 1968.

[60] L. Pagli, "Self-adjusting hash tables," Inf. Proc. Lett., 21, 1, pp.23-25, 1985.

[61] P.V. Poblete and J.I. Munro, "Last-come-first-served hashing," *J. Algorithms*, 10, 2, pp.228-248, 1989.

[62] P. Quittner, S. Csoka, S.Halasz, D. Kotsis and K. Varnai, "Comparison of synonym handling and bucket organization methods," *C.ACM*, 24, 9, pp.579-583, Sep. 1981.

[63] C.E. Radke, "The use of the quadratic residue research," *C.ACM*, 13, 2, pp.103-105, Feb. 1970.

[64] R.L. Rivest, "Optimal Arrangement of keys in a hash table," *J.ACM*, 25, 2, pp.200-209, Apr. 1978.

[65] W.B. Samson and R.H. Davis, "Search times using hash tables for records with nonunique keys," *Comput. J.*, 21, 3, pp.210-214, Aug. 1978.

[66] W.B. Samson, "Hash table collision handling on storage devices with latency," *Comput. J.*, 24, 2, pp.130-131, May 1981.

[67] N. Santoro, "Full table search by polynomial functions," *Inf. Proc. Lett.*, 5, 3, pp.72-74, Aug. 1976.

[68] G. Schay and W.G. Spruth, "Analysis of a file addressing method," *C.ACM*, 5, 8, pp.459-462, Aug. 1962.

[69] A.C. Yao, "Uniform hashing is optimal," *J.ACM*, 32, 2, pp.687-693, July 1985.

[Chaining]

[70] J. Banerjee and V, Ramaraman, "A dual link data structure for ramdom file organization, " *Inf. Proc. Lett.*, 4, 3, pp.64-69, Dec. 1975.

[71] C. Bays, "The reallocation of hash-tables," *C.ACM*, 16, 1, pp.11-14, Jan. 1973.

[72] C. Bays, "A note on when to chain overflow items within a direct-access table," *C.ACM*, 16, 1, pp.46-47, Jan. 1973.

[73] C. Bays, "Some techniques for structuring chained hash tables," *Comput. J.*, 16, 2, pp.126-131, May 1973.

[74] D.G. Bobrow, "A note on hash linking," *C.ACM*, 18, 7, pp.413-415, July 1975.

[75] A. Bolour, "Optimal retrieval algorithms for small region queries," *SIAM J. Comput.*, 10, 4, pp.721-741, Nov. 1981.

[76] W.C.Chen and J.S. Vitter, "Analysis of early-insertion standard coalesced hashing," *SIAM J. Comput.*, 12, 4, pp.667-676, Nov. 1983.

[77] W.C. Chen and J.S. Vitter,"Analysis of new variants of coalesced hashing," *ACM Trans. Database Syst.*, 9, 4, pp.616-645, Dec. 1984.

[78] C. Halatsis and G. Philokipru, "Pseudo chaining in hash tables," *C.ACM*, 21, 7, pp.554-557, July 1978.[including open addressing approach]

[79] L.R. Johnson, "An indirect chaining method for addressing on secondary keys," *C.ACM*, 4,5, pp.218-222, May 1961.

[80] G.D. Knott, "Directed chaining with coalesced lists," *J. Algorithms*, 5, 1, pp.7-21, Mar. 1984.

[81] G.D. Knott and P. de La Torre, "Hash table collision resolution with direct chaining," *J. Algorithms*, 10, 1, pp.20-34, 1989.

[82] E. Lodi and F. Luccio, "Split sequence hash search," *Inf. Proc. Lett.*, 20, 3, 131-136, 1985.

[83] H. Mendelson and U. Yechiali, "Performance Measures for ordered lists in random-access files," *J.ACM*, 26, 4, pp.654-667, Oct. 1979.

[84] R.M. Norton and D.P. Yeager, "A probability model for overflow sufficiency in small hash tables," *C.ACM*, 28, 10, pp.1068-1075, Oct. 1985.

[85] B. Pittel and J.H. Yu, "On search times for early-insertion coalesced hashing," *SIAM J. Comput.*, 17, 3, pp.492-503, June 1988.

[86] J.S. Vitter, "A Shared-memory scheme for coalesced hashing," *Inf. Proc. Lett.*, 13, 2, pp.77-79, Nov. 1981.

[87] J.S. Vitter, "Deletion algorithms for hashing that preserve randomness," *J. Algorithms*, 3, pp.261-275, Sept. 1982.

[88] J.S. Vitter, "Implementation for coaleased hashing," *C.ACM*, 25, 12, pp.911-926, Dec. 1982.

[89] J.S. Vitter, "Analysis of the search performance of coalesced hashing," *J.ACM*, 30, 2, pp.231-258, Apr. 1983.

[90] J.S. Vitter and C.W. Chen, *Design and Analysis of Coaleased Hashing*, Oxford University Press, New York, 1987.

[91] F.A. Williams, "Handling identifiers as internal symbols in language processors," *C.ACM*, 2, 6, pp.21-24, June 1959.

[92] J. Wogulis, "Self-adjusting and split sequence hash tables," *Inf. Proc. Lett.*, 30, 4, pp.185-188, 1989. [Including open addressing techniques]

[Perfect and Minimal Perfect Hashing]

[93] M.R. Anderson and M.G. Anderson, "Comments on perfect hashing functions: A single probe retrieving method for static sets," *C.ACM*, 22, 1, p.104, 1979.

[94] R.C. Bell and B. Floyd,"A Monte Carlo study of Cichelli hash-function solvability," *C.ACM*, 26, 11, pp.924-925, Nov. 1983.

[95] F. Berman et al., "Collections of functions for perfect hashing," *SIAM J. Comput.*, 15, 2, pp.604-618, Feb. 1986.

[96] M.D. Brain and A.L. Thanp, "Near-perfect hashing of large word sets," *Software-Practice & Experience*, 19, 10, pp.967-978, Oct. 1989.

[97] N. Cercone, M. Krause and J. Boates, "Minimal and almost minimal perfect hash function search with application to natural language lexicon design," *Comput. Math. Appl.*, 9, 1, pp.215-231, 1983.

[98] N. Cercone, J. Boates and M. Krause, "An interactive system for finding perfect hash functions," *IEEE Software*, pp.39-53, Nov. 1985.

[99] C.C. Chang, "The study of an ordered minimal perfect hashing scheme," *C.ACM*, 27, 4, pp.384-387, Apr. 1984.

[100] C.C. Chang and R.C.T. Lee, "A letter-oriented minimal perfect hashing scheme," *Comput. J.*, 29, 3, pp.277-281, 1986.

[101] C.C. Chang and C.H. Chang, "An ordered minimal perfect hashing scheme with single parameter," *Inf. Proc. Lett.*, 27, 2, pp.79-83, 1988.

[102] R.J. Cichelli, "Minimal perfect hash functions made simple," *C.ACM*, 23, 1, pp.17-19, Jan. 1980.

[103] C.R. Cook and R. Oldehoeft, "A letter-oriented minimal perfect hashing function," *ACM SIGPlan Notices*, 17, 9, pp.18-27, Sept. 1982.

[104] G.V. Cormac, R.N.S. Horspool, and M. Kaiserwerth, "Practical perfect hashing," *Comput. J.*, 28, 1, pp.54-58, 1985.

[105] M.W. Du, T.M. Hsieh, K.F. Jea and D.W. Shieh, "The study of a new perfect hash scheme," *IEEE Trans. Softw. Eng.*, SE-9, 3, pp.305-313, May 1983.

[106] M.L. Fredman, J. Komlos, and E. Szemeredi, "Storing a sparse table with O(1) worst case access time," *J.ACM*, 31, 3, pp.538-544, Mar. 1984.

[107] M. Gori and G. Soda, "An algebraic approach to Cichelli's perfect hashing," *BIT*, 29, 1, pp.2-13, 1989.

[108] G. Haggard and K. Kaeplus, "Finding minimal perfect hash functions," *ACM SIGCSE Bull.*, 18, 1, pp.191-193, Feb. 1986.

[109] G. Jaeschke and G. Osterburg, "On Cichelli's minimal perfect hash functions method, " *C.ACM*, 23, 12, pp.728-729, Dec. 1980.

[110] G. Jaeschke, "Reciprocal hashing: A method for generating minimal perfect hashing functions," *C.ACM*, 24, 12, pp.829-833, Dec. 1981.

[111] M.V. Ramakrishna, and P. A. Larson, "File Organization Using Composite Prefect Hashing," *ACM Trans. Database Syst.*, 14, 2, pp.231-263, June1989.

[112] M.V. Ramakrishna, "Computing the probability of hash table/urn overflow," *Comm. Stat Theor. Methods*, 16, 11, pp.3343-3353, 1987.

[113] T. Sager, "A polynomial time generator for minimal perfect hash functions," *C. ACM*, 28, 5, pp.523-532, May 1985.

[114] R. Sebesta and M. Taylor, "Fast identification of Ada and Modula-2 reserved words," *J. Pascal, Ada, and Modula-2*, pp.36-39, Mar./Apr. 1986.

[115] R. Sprugnoli, "Perfect hashing functions: A single probe retrieving method for static sets," *C.ACM*, 20, 11, pp.841-850, Nov. 1977.

[116] W.P. Yang, M.W. Du, "A backtracking method for constructing perfect hash functions from a set of mapping functions," *BIT*, 25, 1, pp.148-164, 1985

[Other Problems]

[117] R.E. Barkley, "Point representation and hashing of an interval," *Inf. Proc. Lett.*, 30, 4, pp.201-203, 1989.

[118] F.J. Burkowski, "Hardware hashing scheme in the design of a multiterm string comparator," *IEEE Trans. Comput.*, C-31, 9, pp.825-834, Sept,. 1982.

[119] G.H. Gonnet and P.A. Larson, "External hashing with limitted internal storage," *J.ACM*, 35, 1, pp.161-184, Jan. 1988.

[120] T. Ida and E. Goto,"Analysis of parallel hashing algorithm with key deletion," *Journal of Information Processing*, 1, 1, pp.25-32, Jan. 1978.

[121] T. Ida and E. Goto,"Parallel hash algorithms for virtual key index tables," *Journal of Information Processing*, 1, 3, pp.130-137, Mar. 1978.

[122] R.J. Lipton, A.L. Rosenberg and A.C-C Yao, "External hashing schemes for collection of data structures," *J.ACM*, 27, 1, pp.81-95, Jan. 1980.

[123] C.H. Papadimitriou and P.A. Bernstein, "On the performance of balanced hashing functions when keys are not equiprobable," *ACM Trans. Prog. Lang. & Syst.*, 2,1, pp.77-89, Jan. 1980.

[124] N. Pippenger, "On the application of coding theory to hashing," *IBM J. Res. Development*, 23, 2, pp.225-226, Mar. 1979.

[125] M.V. Ramakrishna, "Analysis of random probing hashing," *Inf. Proc. Lett.*, 31, 2, pp.83-90, 1989.

[126] M. Tamminen, "On search by address computation," *BIT*, 25, 1, pp.135-147, 1985.

[127] A.A. Torn, "Hashing with overflow indexing, " *BIT*, 24, 3, pp.317-332, 1984.

3. Binary Search Trees

[Surveys]
[128] J. Nievergelt, "Binary search trees and file organization, " *Comput. Surveys*, 6, 3, pp.195-207. 1974.

[Optimal Binary Search Trees]
[129] B. Allen and J.I. Munro, "Self-organizing search tree, "*J.ACM*, 25, 4, pp.526-535, Oct. 1978.

[130] B. Allen,"On the costs of optimal and near-optimal binary search trees, "*Acta Inf.*, 18, 3, pp.255-263, 1982.

[131] A. Anderson and S. Carlsson, "Construction of a tree from its traversals in optimal time and space," *Inf. Proc. Lett.*, 32, 4, pp.183-186, 1990.

[132] B.W. Bent, D.D. Sleator and R.E. Tarjan, "Biased search trees," *SIAM J. Comput.*, 14, 3, pp.545-568, Aug. 1985.

[133] D.M. Choy and C.K. Wong, "Bounds for optimal $\alpha-\beta$ binary trees, " *BIT*, 17, 1, pp.1-15, 1977.

[134] D.M. Choy and C.K. Wong, "Optimal $\alpha-\beta$ trees with capacity constraint, "*Acta Inf.*, 10, 3, pp.272-296, 1978.

[135] D. Comer, "A note on median split trees, "*ACM Trans. Prog. Lang. Syst.*, 2, 1, pp.129-133, Jan. 1980.

[136] M.R. Garey, "Optimal binary search trees with restricted maximal depth, " *SIAM J. Comput.*, 3, 2, pp.101-110, June 1974.

[137] M.R. Gasia and M.L. Wachs, "A new algorithm for minimum cost binary trees, " *SIAM J. Comput.*, 6, 4, pp.622-642, Dec 1977.

[138] A. Gill, "Hierarchical binary search, "*C.ACM*, 23, 5, pp.294-300, May 1980.

[139] C.C. Gotlieb and W.A. Walker, "A top-down algorithm for constructing nearly optimal lexicographical trees, " *in Graph Theory and Computing*, Academic Press, NY, 1972.

[140] J.H. Hester et al., "Faster construction optimal binary split trees, " *J. Algorithms*, 7, 3, pp.412-424, 1986.

[141] J.H. Hester and D.S. Hirschberg and L.L. Larmore, "Construction of optimal binary split trees in the presence of bounded access probabilities," *J. Algorithms*, 9, 2, pp.245-253, 1988.

[142] Y. Horibe and T.O.H. Nemetz, "On the max-entropy rule for a binary search tree, " *Acta Inf.* 12, 1, pp.63-72, 1979.

[143] W.H. Hosken, "Optimum partitions of tree addressing structures," *SIAM J. Comput.*, 4, 3, pp.341-347, Sep. 1975.

[144] T.C. Hu and A.C. Tucker, "Optimal computer search trees and variable-length alphabetical codes," *SIAM J. Appl. Math.*, 21, 4, pp.514-532, Dec. 1971.

[145] T.C. Hu and K.C. Tan, "Least upper bound on the cost of optimum binary search trees," *Acta Inf.*, 1, 4, pp.307-310, 1972.

[146] T.C. Hu, D.J. Kleitman and J.K. Tamaki, "Binary trees optimum under various criteria," *SIAM J. Appl. Math.*, 37, 2, pp.246-256, Oct. 1979.

[147] T.C. Hu, "A New proof of the T-C algorithm," *SIAM J. Appl. Math.*, 25, 1, pp.83-94, July 1973.

[148] I. Kalantari and G. Mcdonald, "A date structure and an algorithm for the nearest point problem, "*IEEE Trans. Softw. Eng.*, SE-9, 5, pp.631-634, Sept. 1983.

[149] A. Itai, "Optimal alphabetic trees," *SIAM J. Comput.*, 5, 1, pp.9-18, Mar. 1976.

[150] S. Kennedy, "A note on optimal doubly-chained trees," *C.ACM*, 15, 11, pp.997-998, Nov. 1972.

[151] J.F. Korsh, "Greedy binary search trees are nearly optimal," *Inf. Proc. Lett.*, 13, 1, pp.16-19, Oct. 1981.

[152] J.F. Korsh, "Growing nearly optimal binary search trees," *Inf. Proc. Lett.*, 14,3, pp.139-143, May 1982.

[153] W.A. Martin and D.N. Ness, "Optimizing binary trees grown with a sorting algorithm," *C.ACM*, 15, 2, pp.88-93, Feb. 1972.

[154] E.M. McCreight," Priority search trees," *SIAM J. Comput.*, 14, 2, pp.257-276, May 1985.

[155] K. Mehlhorn, "A best possible bound for the weighted path length of binary search trees," *SIAM J. Comput.*, 6, 2, pp.235-239, June 1977.

[156] K. Mehlhorn, "Nearly optimal binary search trees," *Acta Inf.*, 5, pp.287-295, 1975.

[157] L.L. Larmore, "Height restricted optimal binary trees," *SIAM J. Comput.*, 16, 6, pp.1115-1123, 1987.

[158] LL. Larmore, "A subquadratic algorithm for constructing approximately optimal binary search trees," *J. Algorithms*, 8, 4, pp.579-591, 1987.

[159] N. Sarnak and R.E. Tarjan, "Planar point location using persistent search trees, "*C.ACM*, 29, 7, 99.669-679, July 1986.

[160] B.A. Sheil,"Median split trees:A fast lookup techniques for frequency occurring keys," *C.ACM*, 21, 11, pp.947-959, Nov.1978.

[161] J.L. Szwarcfiter and L.B. Wilson, "Some properties of ternary trees," *Comput. J.*, 21, 1, pp.66-72, Feb. 1978.

[162] R.L. Wessner, "Optimal alphabetic search trees with restricted maximal height," *Inf. Proc. Lett.*, 4, 4, pp.90-94, Jan. 1976.

[163] A. Wikstrom, "Optimal search trees and length restricted codes," *BIT*, 19, 4, pp.518-524, 1979.

Balanced Binary Search Trees]

[164] G.M. Adel'son-Vel'skii and E.M.Landis, "An algorithm for the organization of information," *Dokl. Acad. Nauk SSSR Math.*, 146, 2, pp.263-266, 1962. English translation in Sov. Math, *Dokl.*, 3, pp.1259-1262.

[165] J.L. Baer and B. Schwab, "A comparison of tree-balancing algorithms, "*C.ACM*, 20, 5, pp.3322-330, May 1977.

[166] J.L. Baer, H.C. Du and R.E. Ladner, "Binary search in a multiprocessing environment," *IEEE Trans. Comput.*, C-32, 7, pp.667-677, July 1983.

[167] M.R. Brown, "A storage scheme for height-balanced trees, " *Inf. Proc. Lett.*, 7, 5, pp.231-232, Aug. 1978.

[168] M.R. Brown, Addendum to "A storage scheme for height-balanced trees, " *Inf. Proc. Lett.*, 8, 3, pp.154-156, Aug. 1978.

[169] M.R. Brown, "A partial analysis of random height-balanced trees, " *SIAM J. Comput.*, 8, 1, pp.33-41, Feb 1979.

[170] H.A. Burgdorff and S. Jajodia, "Alternative methods for the reconstruction of trees from their traversals," *BIT*, 27, 2, pp.134-140, 1987.

[171] L. Devroye, "A note on the expected height of binary search trees, " *J.ACM*, 33, 3, pp.489-498, July 1986.

[172] L. Devroye, "Branching processes in the analysis of the heights of trees, " *Acta. Inf.*, 24, 3, pp.277-298, 1987.

[173] C.S. Ellis,"Concurrent search and insertion in AVL Trees," *IEEE Trans. Comput.*, C-29, 9, pp.811-817, Sept. 1980.

[174] C.C. Foster, "A generalization of AVL trees," *C.ACM*, 16, 8, pp.513-517, Aug. 1973.

[175] G.H. Gonnet, H.J. Olivie and D. Wood, "Height-ratio-balanced trees, "*Comput. J.*, 26, 2, pp.106-108, May 1983.

[176] D.S. Hirschberg, "An insertion technique for one-sided height-balanced trees, " *C.ACM*, 19, 8, pp.471-473, Aug. 1976.

[177] S.S. Huang and C.K. Wong," Generalized binary split trees," *Acta Inf.*, 21, 1, pp.113-123, 1984.

[178] S.S. Huang and C.K. Wong," Average number of rotations and access cost in IR-trees," *BIT*, 24, 3, pp.387-390, 1984.

[179] P.L. Karlton, S.H. Fuller, R.E. Scroggs, and E.B. Kaehler, "Performance of height balanced trees, "*C.ACM*, 19, 1, pp.23-28, Jan. 1976.

[180] D.J. Kleitman and M.E. Saks, "Set orderings requiring costliest alphabetic binary trees," *SIAM J. Alg. Disc. Methods*, 2, 2, pp.142-146, June 1981.

[181] S.R. Kosaraju, "Insertions and deletions on one-sided height-balanced trees," *C.ACM*, 21, 3, pp.226-227, Mar. 1978.

[182] J. Leeuwen and M. Overmars, "Stratified balanced search trees, " *Acta Inf.*, 18, pp.345-359, 1983.

[183] C.C. Lee, D.T. Lee and C.K. Wong, "Generating binary trees of bounded height," *Acta Inf.*, 23, 5, pp.529-544, 1986.

[184] L. Li, "Ranking and unranking of AVL-trees," *SIAM J. Comput.*, 15, 4, pp.1025-1035, Nov. 1986.

[185] C. Lin, "O(1) space complexity deletion for AVL trees," *Inf. Proc. Let.*, 22, 3, pp.147-149, 1986.

[186] F. Luccio and L. Pagli, "On the height of height balanced trees, " *IEEE Trans. Comput.*, C-25, 1, pp.87-90, Jan. 1976.

[187] F. Luccio and L. Pagli, "Rebalancing height balanced trees," *IEEE Trans. Comput.*, C-27, 5, pp.386-396, May 1978.

[188] F. Luccio and L. Pagli, "Power trees," *C.ACM*, 21, 11, pp.941-947, Nov. 1978.

[189] F. Luccio and L. Pagli, "Comment on generalized AVL trees," *C.ACM*, 23, 7, pp.394-395, July 1980.

[190] F. Luccio and L. Pagli, "On the upper bound on the rotation distance of binary trees," *Inf. Proc. Lett.*, 31, 2, pp.57-60, 1989.

[191] E. Makinen, "On the rotation distance of binary trees," *Inf. Proc. Lett.*, 26, 5, pp.271-272, 1988.

[192] K. Mehlhorn, "A partial analysis of height-balanced trees under random insertions and deletions," *SIAM J. on Comput.*, 11, 4, pp.748-760, Nov. 1982.

[193] Th. Ottmann and D. Wood, "Deletion in one-sided height-balanced search trees," *Int. J. Comput. Math.*, 6, 4, pp.265-271, 1978.

[194] Th. Ottmann, H.W. Six and D. Wood, "One-sided k-height-balanced trees," *Computing*, 22, 4, pp.283-290, 1979.

[195] Th. Ottmann and D. Wood, "1-2 brother trees or AVL trees revised," *Comput. J.*, 23, 3, pp.248-255, Aug. 1980.

[196] J. Pallo, "On the rotation distance in the lattice of binary trees," *Inf. Proc. Lett.*, 25, 6, pp.369-373, 1987.

[197] W. Pugh, "Skip lists: A probabilistic alternative to balanced trees," *C.ACM*, 33, 6, pp.668-676, June 1990.

[198] K.J. Raiha and S.H. Zweben, "An optimal insertion algorithm for one-sided height-balanced binary search trees," *C.ACM*, 22, 9, pp.508-512, Sep. 1979.

[199] J.M. Robson, "The Height of binary search trees," *Australian Comput. J.*, 11, 4, pp.151-153, Nov. 1979.

[200] M. Snir, "Exact balancing is not always good,"*Inf. Proc. Lett.*, 22, 2, pp.97-102, 1986.

[201] Q.F. Stout and B.L. Warren," Tree rebalanceing in optimal time and space, "*C.ACM*, 29, 9, pp.902-908, Sept. 1986.

[202] K.C. Tan, "On Foster's information storage and retrieval using AVL trees," *C.ACM*, 15, 9, pp.843, Sep. 1972.

[203] K. Unterauer, "Dynamic weighted binary search trees," *Acta Inf.*, 11, 4 pp.341-362, 1979.

[204] V.K. Vaishnavi, "Weighted leaf AVL-trees," *SIAM J. Comput.*, 16, 3, pp.503-537, June 1987.

[205] A. Walker and D. Wood, "Locally balanced binary trees," *Comput. J.*, 19, 4, pp.322-325, Nov. 1976.

[206] W.E. Wright. "Binary search trees in secondary memory," *Acta Inf.*, 15, 1, pp.3-17, 1981.

[207] S.H. Zweben and M.A. McDonald, "An optimal method for deletions in one-sided height-balanced trees," *C.ACM*, 21, 6, pp.441-445, June 1978.

[Generating Binary Trees and Other Problems]

[208] S. Anily and R. Hassin," Ranking the best binary trees," *SIAM J. Comput.*, 18, 5, pp.882-892, Oct. 1989.

[209] B. Arazi, "A binary search with a parallel recovery of the bits," *SIAM J. Comput.*, 15, 3, pp.851-855, Aug. 1986.

[210] K. Brinck and N.Y. Foo, "Analysis of algorithms on threaded trees, "*Comput. J.*, 24, 2, pp.148-155, May 1981.

[211] K. Brinck, "On deletion in threaded binary trees," *J. Algorithms*, 7, 3, pp.395-411, 1986.

[212] G.G. Brown and B.O. Shubert, "On ramdom binary trees, " *Math, Oper. Res* 9, pp.43-65, 1984.

[213] W.H. Burge, "An analysis of binary search trees formed from sequences of nondistinct keys," *J.ACM*, 23, 3, pp.451-454, July 1976.

[214] W. Cunto and J.L. Gascon, "Improving time and space efficiency in generalized binary search trees, "*Acta Inf.*, 24, 5, pp.583-594, 1987.

[215] B. Dasarathy and C. Yang, "A transformation on ordered trees, "*Comput. J.*, 23, 2, pp.161-164, Feb. 1980.

[216] J. R. Driscoll and Y.E. Lien, "A selective traversal algorithm for binary search trees, "*C.ACM*, 21, 6, pp.445-447. June 1978.

[217] J.L. Eppinger, "An empirical study of insertion and deletion in binary search trees, "*C.ACM*, 26, 9, pp.663-669, Sep. 1983.

[218] U. Faigle et al., "Searching in trees, series-parallel and interval orders, " *SIAM J. Comput.*, 15, 4, pp.1075-1084, Nov. 1986.

[219] W.D. Gillett," On binary tree encodements, "*Acta Inf.*, 21, 2, pp.183-192, 1984.

[220] C. Gen-Huey, M.S. Yu and L.T. Liu, "Two algorithms for constructing a binary tree from its traversals," *Inf. Proc. Lett.*, 28, 6, pp.297-299, 1988.

[221] D. Gordon, "Eliminating the flag in threaded binary search trees," *Inf. Proc. Lett.*, 23, 4, pp.209-214, 1986.

[222] L.J. Guibas, "A principle of independence for binary tree searching, "*Acta Inf.*, 4, pp.293-298, 1975.

[223] A.T. Jonassen and D.E. Knuth, "A trivial algorithm whose analysis isn't," *J.CSS*, 16, 3, pp.301-322, June 1978.

[224] R. Kemp, "A note on the stack size of regularly distributed binary trees," *BIT*, 20, 2, pp.157-163, 1980.

[225] R. Kemp, "The average number of registers needed to evaluate a binary tree optimally," *Acta Inf.*, 11, 4, pp.363-372, 1979.

[226] D.G. Kirpatrick and M.M, Klawe," Alphabetic minimum trees, "*SIAM J. Comput.*, 14, 3, pp.514-526, Aug. 1985.

[227] G.D. Knott, "A numbering system for binary trees," *C.ACM*, 20, 2, pp.113-115, Feb. 1977.

[228] G.D. Knott, "Fixed-bucket binary storage trees," *J. Algorithms*, 3, 3, pp.276-287, Sep. 1982.

[229] D.E. Knuth, "Deletions that preserve randomness," *IEEE Trans. Softw. Eng.*, 3, pp.351-359, 1977.

[230] K.P. Lee, "A linear algorithm for copying binary trees using bounded workspace," *C.ACM*, 23, 3, pp.159-162, Mar. 1980.

[231] U Manber, "Concurrent maintenance of binary search trees," *IEEE Trans. Softw. Eng.*, SE-10, 6, pp.777-784, 1984.

[232] H.M. Mahmoud and B. Pittel, "Analysis of the space of search trees under the random insertion algorithm," *J. Algorithms*, 10, 1, pp.52-75, 1989.

[233] Th. Ottmann and D. Wood, "A comparison of iterative and defined classes of search trees," *Int. J. of Comp. and Inf. Sciences*, 11, 3, pp.155-178, June 1982.

[234] E.M. Palmer, M.A. Rahimi and R.W. Robinson, "Efficiency of a binary comparison storage technique," *J.ACM*, 21, 3, pp.376-384, July 1974.

[235] P.V. Poblete and J.I. Munro, "The analysis of a fringe heuristic for binary search trees," *J. Algorithms*, 6, pp.336-350, 1985.

[236] B. Pittel, "Asymptotical growth of a class of random trees," *Ann. Probab.*, 13, pp.414-427, 1985.

[237] A. Proskurowski, "On the generation of binary trees," *J.ACM*, 27, 1, pp.1-2, Jan. 1980.

[238] B.D. Roelants and F. Ruskey, "Generating t-ary trees in A-order," *Inf. Proc. Lett.*, 27, 4 pp.205-213, 1988.

[239] D. Rotem and Y.L.Varol, "Generation of binary trees from ballot sequences," *J.ACM*, 25, 3, pp.396-404, July 1978.

[240] F. Ruskey and T.C. Hu, "Generating binary trees lexicographically," *SIAM J. Comput.*, 6, 4, pp.745-758, Dec. 1977.

[241] F. Ruskey, "Generating t-ary trees lexicographically," *SIAM J. Comput.*, 6, 4, pp.745-758, Dec. 1977.

[242] F, Ruskey and A. Proskurowski, "Generating binary trees by transpositions," *J. Algorithms*, 11, 1, pp.68-84, 1990.

[243] D.D. Sleator and R.E. Tarjan," Self-adjusting binary search trees," *J.ACM*, 32, 3, pp.652-686, 1985.

[244] W. Slough and K. Efe, "Efficient algorithms for tree reconstruction," *BIT*, 29, 2, pp.361-363, 1989.

[245] M. Solomon and R.A. Finkel, "A note on enumerating binary trees," *J.ACM*, 27, 1, pp.3-5, Jan. 1980.

[246] C.J. Stephenson, "A method for constructing binary search trees by making insertions at the root," *Int. J. of Comp. and Inf. Scie.*, 9, 1, pp.15-29, Feb. 1980.

[247] R. Sprugnoli, "On the allocation of binary trees to secondary storage," *BIT*, 21, 3, pp.305-316, 1981.

[248] L.B. Wilson, "Sequence search trees: their analysis using recurrence relations," *BIT*, 16, 3, pp.332-337, 1976.

[249] T. Yuba and M. Hoshi, "Binary search networks : A new method for key searching," *Inf. Proc. Lett.*, 24, 1, pp.56-65, 1987.

[250] D. Zerling, "Generating binary trees using rotations," *J.ACM*, 32, 3, pp.694-701, July 1985.

4. Multiway Search Trees

[Surveys]

[251] D. Comer, "The ubiquitous B-Tree," *Comput. Surveys*, 11, 2, pp.121-137, 1979.

[B-Trees]

[252] D.S. Batory, "B^{+-}trees and indexed sequential files: A performance comparison, " *Proc. in ACM-SIGMOD*, pp.30-39, Apr. 1981.

[253] R.Bayer and E. McCreight, "Organization and maintenance of large ordered indexes,"*Acta Inf.*, 1, 3, pp.173-189, 1972.

[254] R. Bayer, "Symmetric binary B-trees: Data structure and maintenance algorithms," *Acta Inf.*, 1, 4, pp.290-306, 1972.

[255] R.Bayer and K.Unterauer, "Prefix B-trees," *ACM Trans. Database Syst.*, 2, 1, pp.11-26, Mar. 1977.

[256] R.A. Baeza-Yates, " Some average measures in m-ary search trees," *Inf. Proc. Lett.*, 25, 6, pp.375-381, 1987.

[257] R.A. Baeza-Yates, "The expected behaviour of B^{+}-tree," *Acta Inf.*, 26, 439-471, 1989.

[258] K. Culik, T. Ottmann, and D. Wood, "Dense multiway trees, "*ACM Trans. Database Syst.*, 6, 3, pp.486-512, Sep. 1981.

[259] J.R. Driscoll, L. Sheau-Dong and L.A. Franklin," Modeling B-trees insertion activity," *Inf. Proc. Lett.*, 26, 1, pp.5-18, 1987.

[260] L.R. Gotlieb, "Optimal multi-way search trees," *SIAM J. Comput.*, 10, 3, pp.422-433, Aug. 1981.

[261] U.I. Gupta, D.T. Lee and C.K. Wong, "Ranking and unranking of B-trees," *J. Algorithms*, 4, 1, pp.51-60, Mar. 1983.

[262] W.J. Hansen, "A cost model for the internal organization of B^{+}-tree nodes," *ACM Trans. Prog., Lang. & Syst.*, 3, 4, pp.508-532, Oct. 1981.

[263] S.S. Huang, "Height-balanced trees of order (β,γ,δ), "*ACM Trans. Database Syst.*, 10, 2, pp.261-284, June 1985.

[264] G. Held and M. Stonebraker, "B-trees re-examined," *C.ACM.* 21,2, pp.139-143, Feb. 1978.

[265] S. Huddleston and K. Mehlhorn, "Robust balancing in B-trees," *Lecture Notes in Comput. Scie.*, 104, pp.234-244, 1981.

[266] S. Huddleston and K. Mehlhorn, "A new data structure for representing sorted lists," *Acta Inf.*, 17, 2, pp.157-184, 1982.

[267] K. Kuspert,"Storage utilization in B-trees with a generalized overflow technique," *Acta Inf.*, 19, pp.33-55, 1983.[Including overflow techniques]

[268] Y.S. Kwong, "A new method for concurrency in B-trees, "*IEEE Trans. Softw. Eng.*, SE-8, 3, pp.211-222, May 1984.

[269] D.B. Lomet, "Simple bounded disorder file organization with good performance," *ACM Trans. Database Syst.*, 13, 4, pp.525-551,1988.

[270] H.M. Mahmoud," On the average internal path length of m-ary search trees," *Acta Inf.*, 23, 1, pp.111-117, 1986.

[271] K. Maly, "A note on virtual memory indexes," *C.ACM*, 21, 9, pp.786-787, Sep. 1978.

[272] E. McCreight, "Pagination of B*-trees with variable length records," *C.ACM*, 20, 9, pp.670-674, Sep. 1977.

[273] A.L. Rosenberg and L. Snyder, "Time- and space-optimality in B-trees, "*ACM Trans. Database Syst.*, 6, 1, pp.174-193, Mar. 1981.

[274] B. Samadi, "B-trees in a system with multiple views," *Inf. Proc. Lett.*, 5, 4, pp.107-112, Oct. 1976.

[275] L. Snyder, "On B-trees re-examined," *C.ACM*, 21, 7, pp.594, July 1978.

[276] J.L. Szwarcfier," Optimal multiway search trees for variable size keys, "*Acta Inf.*, 21, 1, 1984.

[277] M. Tamminen, "Analysis of N-trees," *Inf. Proc. Lett.*, 16, 3, pp.131-137, Apr. 1983.

[278] N. Ziviani and F.W. Tompa, "A look at symmetric binary B-trees," *Infor.*, 20, 2, pp.65-81, May 1982.

[2-3 Trees and Other Problems]

[279] S.W. Bent, D.D. Sleator, and R. E. Tarjan, "Biased search trees," *SIAM J. Comput.*, 4, pp.545-568, 1985.

[280] J. Bitner and S. Huang, "Key comparison optimal 2-3 trees with maximum storage utilization, " *SIAM J. Comput.*, 10, 3, pp.558-570, Aug. 1981.

[281] H.P. Kriegel, V.K. Vaishnavi, and D. Wood, "2-3 brother trees," *BIT* 18, pp.425-435, 1978.

[282] M.R. Brown and R.E. Tarjan, "Design and analysis of a data structure for representing sorted lists, "*SIAM J. Comput.*, 9, 3, pp.594-614, Aug. 1980.

[283] M.R. Brown, "Some observations on random 2-3 trees, "*Inf. Proc. Lett.*, 9, 2, pp.57-59, Aug. 1979.

[284] B. Eisenbarth et al.,"The theory of fringe analysis and its application to 2-3 trees and B-trees," *Inf. Control*, 55, nos1-3, pp,125-174, 1984.

[285] J. Feigenbaum and R. E. Tarjan,"Two new kinds of biased search trees," *Bell Syst. Tech. J.*, 62, pp.3139-3158, 1983.

[286] U.I. Gupta, D.T. Lee and C.K. Wong, "Ranking and unranking of 2-3 trees," *SIAM J. Comput.*, 11, 3, pp.582-590, Aug. 1982.

[287] U. Guntzer and M. Paul, "Jump interpolation search trees and symmetric binary numbers," *Inf. Proc. Lett.*, 26, 4, pp.193-204, 1987.

[288] K. Hwang and S.B. Yao, "Optimal batched searching of tree structured files in multiprocessor computer systems," *J.ACM*, 24, 3, pp.441-454, July 1977.

[289] S.R. Kosaraju, "Localized search in sorted lists," *Proc. SIGACT*, Milwaukee WI, 13, pp.62-69, May 1981.

[290] H.P. Kriegel and Y.S. Kwong, "Insertion-safeness in balanced trees," *Inf. Proc. Lett.*, 16, 5, pp.259-264, June 1983.

[291] H.P. Kriegel, V.K. Vaishnavi and D. Wood, "2-3 Brother trees," *BIT*, 18, 4, pp.425-435, 1978.

[292] D. Maier and S.C. Salveter, "Hysterical B-trees," *Inf. Proc. Lett.*, 12, 4, pp.199-202, Aug. 1981.

[293] H.A. Maurer, Th. Ottmann and H.W. Six, "Implementing dictionaries using binary trees of very small height," *Inf. Proc. Lett.*, 5, 1, pp.11-14, May 1976.

[294] K. Mehlhorn and A. Tsakalidis, "An amortized analysis of insertions into AVL-trees, " *SIAM J. Comput.*, 15, 1, pp.22-33, Feb. 1986.

[295] R. Miller, N. Pippenger, A.L. Rosenberg, and L. Snyder, "Optimal 2-3 trees, " *SIAM J. Comput.*, 8, 1, pp.42-59, 1979.

[296] H.L. Olivie, "On the relationship between son-trees and symmetric binary trees," *Inf. Proc. Lett.*, 10,1, pp.4-8, Feb. 1980.

[297] H.J. Olivie, "On a relationship between 2-3 brother trees and dense ternary trees," *Int. J. Comput. Math.*, A8, pp.233-245, 1980.

[298] H.J. Olivie, "On random son-trees," *Int. J. Comput. Math.*, 9, pp.287-303, 1981.

[299] Th. Ottmann, H.W. Six and D. Wood, "Right brother trees," *C.ACM*, 21, 9, pp.769-776, Sep. 1978.

[300] Th. Ottmann, H.W. Six and D. Wood, "On the correspondence between AVL trees and brother trees." *Computing* 23, 1, pp.43-54, 1979.

[301] Th. Ottmann and W. Stucky. "Higher order analysis of random 1-2 brother trees," *BIT*, 20,3, pp.302-314, 1980.

[302] Th. Ottmann, H.W. Six and D. Wood, "The implementation of insertion and deletion algorithms for 1-2 brother trees," *Computing*, 26, pp.369-378, 1981.

[303] A.L. Rosenberg and L. Snyder, "Minimal-comparison 2-3 trees," *SIAM J. Comput.*, 7, 4, pp.465-480, 1978.

[304] E.M. Reingold, "A note on 2-3 trees," *Fibonacci Quarterly*, 17, 2, pp.151-157, Apr. 1979.

[305] H.R. Strong, G. Markowsky and A.K. Chandra, "Search within a page," *J.ACM*, 26,3, pp.457-482, July 1979.

[306] R.E. Tarjan, "Updating a balanced search tree in O(1) rotations," *Inf. Proc. Lett.*, 16, 5, pp. 253-257, June 1983.

[307] A.K. Tsakalidis,"AVL-trees for localized search," *Lecture Notes is Comput. Scie. 172*, Springer-Verlag, Berlin 1984.

[308] V.K. Vaishnavi, H.P. Kriegel and D. Wood, "Height balanced 2-3 trees," *Computing*, 21, pp.195-211, 1979.

[309] A. Yao, "On random 2-3 trees," *Acta Inf.*, 9, 2, pp.159-170, 1978.

[Digital Search Trees]

[310] J.-I. Aoe, "An efficient digital search algorithm by using a double-array structure," *IEEE Trans. Softw. Eng.*, SE-15, 9, Sept. 1989.

[311] M. Al-Suwaiyel and E. Horowitz, "Algorithms for trie compaction, "*ACM Trans., Database Syst.*, 9, 2, pp.243-263, June 1984.

[312] W. Burkhard, "Hashing and trie algorithm for partial match retrieval," *A C M Trans. Database Syst.*, 11, 2, pp.175-187, June 1976.

[313] D. Cormer and R. Sethi, "Complexity of trie index construction, "*J.ACM*, 24, 3, pp.428-440, July 1977.

[314] D. Comer, "Heuristics for trie index minimization, "*ACM Trans., Database Syst.*, 4, 3, pp.383-395, Sept. 1979.

[315] D. Comer, "Analysis of a heuristic for full trie minimization, "*ACM Trans. Database Syst.*, 6, 3, pp.513-537, Sep. 1981.

[316] P. Flajolet and R. Sedgewick," Digital search trees revised," *SIAM J. Comput.*, 15, 3, pp.748-767, Aug. 1986.

[318] E. Fredkin, "Trie memory," *C.ACM*, 3, 9, pp.490-500, Sept. 1960.

[319] P. Flajolet, "On the performance evaluation of extendible hashing and trie searching," *Acta Inf.*, 20, 4, pp.345-369, 1983.

[320] W.D. Jonge, A.S. Tanenbaum and R.P. Riet, "Two access methods using compact binary trees," *IEEE Trans. Softw. Eng.*, SE-13, 7, July 1987.

[321] W. Litwin, "Trie hashing," *Proc. ACM SIGMOD Conf. Management of Data*, ACM, New York, pp.19-29, 1981.

[322] K. Malty, "Compressed tries," *C.ACM*, 19, 7, pp.409-415, July 1976.

[323] M. Miyakawa, T. Yuba, Y. Sugito and M. Hoshi, "Optimum sequence trees," *SIAM J. Comput.*, 6, 2, pp.201-234, June 1977.

[324] B.M. Nicklas and G. Schlageter, "Index structuring in inverted data bases by tries," *Computer J.*, 20,4, pp.321-324, Nov. 1977.

[325] J.A. Orenstein, "Multidimensional tries used for associative searching," *Inf. Proc. Lett.*, 14,4, pp.150-157, June 1982.

[326] J.L. Peterson, Computer Programs for Spelling Correction (*Lecture Notes in Computer Science*), New York:Stringer-Verlag, 1980.

[327] B. Pittel, "Paths in a random digital tree: Limiting distributions," *Adv. Appl. Probab.*, 18, pp.139-155, 1986.

[328] R. Ramesh, A.V.G. Babu and J.P. Kincad, "Variable-depth trie index optimization: Theory and experimental results, "*ACM Trans. Database Syst.*, 14, 1, pp.41-74, Mar. 1989.

[329] M. Regnier, "On the average Height of trees in digital search and dynamic hashing," *Inf. Proc. Lett.*, 13,2, pp.64-66, Nov. 1981.

[330] F. Ruskey, "Generating t-ary trees lexicographically," *SIAM J. Comput.*, 7,4, pp.424-439, Nov. 1978.

[331] E. Sussenguth, "Use of trie structures for processing files," *C.ACM*, 6, 5, May 1963.

[332] V.K. Vaishnavi, H.P. Kriegel and D. Wood, "Optimum multiway search trees," *Acta Inf.*, 14, 2, pp.119-133, 1980.

5. Dynamic Hashing
[Surveys]

[333] R.J. Enbody and H.C. Du, "Dynamic hashing schemes," Comput. Surveys, 20, 2, pp. 85-113, 1988.[Including overflow techniques]

[334] P.A. Larson, "Dynamic hash tables," *C.ACM*, 31, 4, pp.446-457, 1988.

[Extendible, Linear, Dynamic Hashing Techniques]

[335] E.G. Coffman and J. Eve, "File structures using hashing functions," *C.ACM*, 13, pp.427-436, 1970.

[336] M.Greniewski and W. Turski, "The external hashing with limited internal storage," *J.ACM*, 35, 1, pp.161-184, 1988.

[337] R. Fagin, J. Nievergelt, N. Pippenger and H.R. Storing, "Extendible hashing-A fast access method for dynamic files," *ACM Trans. Database Syst.*, 4, 3, pp.315-344, Sept.1979.

[338] V. Kumar, "Concurrent operations on extensible hashing and its performance," *C.ACM*, 33, 6, pp.681-694, June 1990.

[339] V. Kumar, "Concurrency control on extendible hashing," *Inf. Proc. Lett.*, 31, 1, pp.35-41, 1989.

[340] P.A. Larson, "Dynamic hashing," *BIT* 18, pp.184-201, 1978.

[341] P.A. Larson, "Linear hashing with partial expansions," *Proc. Sixth Conf. Very Large Databases*, CS Press, Los Alamitors, Calif., pp.24-232, 1980.

[342] P.A. Larson, "Performance analysis of linear hashing with partial expansions," *ACM Trans. Database Syst.*, 7, 4, pp.566-587, 1982.

[343] P.A. Larson, "Linear hashing with overflow-handling by linear probing," *ACM Trans. Database Syst.*, 10, 1, pp.75-89, Mar. 1985.

[344] P.A. Larson, "Linear hashing with separaters-A dynamic hashing scheme achieving one-access retrieval," *ACM Trans. Database Syst.*, 13, 13, pp.366-388, Sept.1988.

[345] W. Litwin, "Linear hashing:A new tool for file and table addressing," *Proc. Sixth Conf. Very Large Databases*, CS Press, Los Amatios, Calif., pp.212-223, 1980.

[346] D. Lomet, "Bounded index exponential hashing," *ACM Trans. Database Syst.*, 8, 1, pp.136-165, Mar. 1983.

[347] K. Mehlhorn, "Dynamic binary search tree," *SIAM J. Comput.*, 8, 2, pp.175-198, May 1979.

[348] H. Mendelson, "Analysis of extensible hashing," *IEEE Trans. Softw. Eng.*, SE-8, 6, pp.611-619, Nov. 1982.

[349] J. K. Mullin, " Tightly controlled linear hashing without separate overflow storage, "*BIT* 21, pp.390-400, 1981.

[350] M. Ouksel and P. Scheuermann, "Implicit data structures for linear hashing schemes," *Inf. Proc. Lett.*, 29, 4, 1988.

[351] K. Ramamohanarao, and J.W. Lloyd, "Dynamic hashing schemes, *Comput. J.* 25, 4, Nov. 1982.

[352] K. Ramamohanarao, and R. Sacks-Davis, "Recursive linear hashing, "*ACM Trans. Database Syst.*, 9, 3, pp.369-391, Sept. 1984.

[353] M. Scholl, "New file organization based on dynamic hashing," *ACM Trans. Database Syst.*, 6, 1, pp.194-211, Mar. 1981.

[354] M. Tamminen, "Extendible hashing with overflow," *Inf. Proc. Lett.*, 15, 5, pp.227-232, Dec. 1982.

[355] M. Tamminen, "Order preserving extendible hashing and bucket tries," *BIT*, 21, 4, pp.419-435, 1981.

[356] E. Veklerov, "Analysis of dynamic hashing with deferred splitting, " *ACM Trans. Database Syst.*, 10, 1, pp.90-96, Mar. 1985.[Including overflow techniques]

[357] B.P. Weems, "A study of page arrangements for extensible hashing," *Inf. Proc. Lett.*, 27, 5, pp.245-248, 1988.

[358] A.C. Yao, "A note on the analysis of extensible hashing," *Inf. Proc. Lett.*, 11, pp.84-86, 1980.

6. Multikey Searching
[Surveys]

[359] J.L. Bentley and J.H. Friedman, "Data structure for range searching," *Comput. Surveys*, 11, 4, pp.397-409, Dec. 1979.

[360] K.L. Kelley and M. Rusinkiewicz, "Multikey, extensible hashing for relational databases," *IEEE Software*, pp.77-85, July 1988.

[Multidimensional and Partial Match]

[361] A.V. Aho and J.D. Ullman, "Optimal partial-match retrieval when fields are

independently specified," *ACM Trans. Database Syst.*, 4, 2, pp.168-179, 1979.

[362] J.L. Bentley, "Multidimensional binary search trees used for associative searching, " *C.ACM*, 18, 9, pp.509-517, Sep. 1975.

[363] J.L. Bentley, "Multidimensional binary search trees in database applications," *IEEE Trans. Softw. Eng.*, SE-5, 4, pp.33-340, July 1979. [Selected in this volume]

[364] J.L. Bentley, "Multidimensional divide-and-conqur, "*C.ACM*, 23, 4, pp.214-229, Apr. 1980.

[365] J.L. Bentley and D.F. Stanat, "Analysis of range searching in quad trees, "*Inf. Proc. Lett.*, 3, 6, pp.170-173, July 1975.

[366] J.L. Bentley and H.A. Maurer, "A note on euclidean near neighbour searching in the plane, " *Inf. Proc. Lett.*, 8, 3, pp.133-136, Mar 1979.

[367] J.L. Bentley and H.A. Maurer, "Efficient worst-case data structures for range searching, " *Acta Inf.*, 13, 2, pp.155-168, 1980.

[368] A. Bolour, "Optimality properties of multiple-key hashing functions, "*J.ACM*, 26, 2, pp.196-210, Apr. 1979.

[369] W.A. Burkhard, "Partial-match hash coding: Benefits of redundancy," *ACM Trans. Database Syst.*, 4, 2, pp.228-239, June 1979.

[370] J.M. Chang and K.S. Fu, "Extended k-d tree database organization: A dynamic multiattribute clustering method, "*IEEE Trans. Softw. Eng.*, SE-7, 3, pp.284-290, May 1981.

[371] C.C. Chang, R.C.T. Lee and M.W. Du, "Symbolic gray codes as a perfect multiattribute hashing scheme for partial match queries, " *IEEE Trans. Softw. Eng.*, SE-8, 3, pp.235-249, May 1982.

[372] B. Chazelle, "A functional approach to data structure and its use in multidimensional searching," *SIAM J. Comput.*, 17, 3, pp.427-462, June 1988.

[373] D. Dobkin and R.J. Lipton, "Multidimensional searching problems, "*SIAM J. Comput.*, 5, 2, pp.181-186, June 1976.

[374] H.C. Du, "On the file design problem for partial match retrieval," *IEEE Trans. Softw. Eng.*, SE-11, 2, pp.213-222, Feb. 1985.

[375] M.E. Dyer, "On a multidimensional search technique and its application to the Euclidean one-centre problem," *SIAM J. Comput.*, 15, 3, pp.725-738, Aug. 1986.

[376] C.M. Eastman, "Optimal bucket size for nearest neighbour searching in k-d trees," *Inf. Proc. Lett.*, 12, 4, pp.165-167, Aug. 1981.

[377] C.M. Eastman and M. Zemankova, "Partially specified nearest neighbour searches using k-d trees," *Inf. Proc. Lett.*, 15, 2, pp.53-56, Sep. 1982.

[378] R.A. Finkel and J.L. Bentley, "Quad trees -a data structure for retrieval on composed keys," *Acta Inf.*, 4, 1, pp.1-9, 1974.

[379] P. Flajolet and C. Puech, "Partial match retrieval of multidimensional data," *J.ACM*, 33, 2, pp.371-407, 1986.

[380] J.H. Friedman, F. Baskett and L.J. Shustek, "An algorithm for finding nearest neighbors," *IEEE Trans. Comput.*, C-24, 10, pp.1000-1006, Oct. 1975.

[381] J.H. Friedman, J.L. Bentley and R.A. Finkel, "An algorithm for finding best matches in logarithmic expected time," *ACM Trans. Math. Softw.*, 3, 3, pp.209-226, Sept. 1977.

[382] O. Fries et al., "A log(log n) data structure for three-sided range queries," *Inf. Proc. Lett.*, 25, 4, pp.269-273, 1987.

[383] I. Gargantini,"An effective way to represent quadtrees," *C.ACM*, 25, 12, pp.905-910, Dec, 1982.

[384] H. Guting and H.P. Kriegel, "Multidimensional B-tree: an efficient dynamic file structure for exact match queries," *Informatik Fachberichte*, 33, pp.375-388, 1980.

[385] H. Guting and H.P. Kriegel, "Dynamic k-dimensional multiway search under time-varying access frequencies," *Lecture Notes in Computer Science*, 104, pp.135-145, 1981.

[386] S. Huang, "Multidimensional extendible hashing for partial-match queries,"*Intr. J. Comput. and Infor. Scie.*, pp.73-82, Apr. 1985.

[387] D.S. Hirschberg, "On the complexity of searching a set of vectors," *SIAM J. Comput.*, 9, 1, pp.126-129, Feb. 1980.

[388] M. Hoshi and T. Yuba, "A counter example to a monotonicity property of k-d trees," *Inf. Proc. Lett.*, 15, 4, pp.169-173, Oct. 1982.

[389] R.L. Kashyap, S.K.C. Subas and S.B. Yao,"Analysis of the multiple-attribute-tree database organization, "*IEEE Trans. Softw. Eng.*, SE-3, 6, pp.451-467, June 1977.

[390] S.R. Kosaraju, "On a multidimensional search problem," *Proc. SIGACT*, Atlanta GA, 11, pp.67-73, Apr. 1979.

[391] D. Lea, "Digital and Hilbelt k-d trees," *Inf. Proc. Lett.*, 27, 1, pp.35-41, 1988.

[392] D.T. Lee and C.K. Wong, "Worst-case analysis for region and partial region searches in multidimensional binary search trees and quad trees," *Acta Inf.*, 9, 1, pp.23-29, 1979.

[393] D.T. Lee and C.K. Wong, "Quintary trees: A file structure for multi-dimensional database systems," *ACM Trans. Database Syst.*, 5, 3, pp.339-353, Sep. 1980.

[394] R.C.T. Lee, Y.H. Chin and S.C. Chang, "Application of principal component analysis to multikey searching," *IEEE Trans. Softw. Eng.*, SE-2, 3, pp.185-193, Sep. 1976.

[395] W.C. Lin, R.C.T. Lee and H.C. Du, "Common properties of some multiattribute file systems," *IEEE Trans. Softw. Eng.*, SE-5, 2, Mar. pp.160-174, Mar. 1979.

[396] J.H. Liou and S. B. Yao, "Multi-dimensional clustering for data base organization," *Inf. Syst.*, 2, pp.187-198, 1977.

[397] V.Y. Lum, " Multi-attribute retrieval with combined indexes," *C.ACM*, 13, 11, pp.660-665, Nov. 1970.

[398] J.W. Lloyd and K. Ramamohanarao, "Partial-match retrieval for dynamic files," *BIT*, 22, 2, pp.150-168, 1982.

[399] J.W. Lloyd, "Optimal partial-match retrieval for dynamic files," *BIT*, 20, pp.406-413, 1980.

[400] O.L. Murphy and S.M. Selkow, "The efficiency of using k-d trees for finding nearest neighbors in discrete space," *Inf. Proc. Lett.*, 23, 4, pp.215-218, 1986.

[401] J. Nievergelt, H. Hinterberger and K.C. Sevcik, "The grid file: An adaptable, symmetric mutikey file structure," *A C M Trans. Database Syst.*, 9, 1, pp.38-71, 1984.

[402] M. Ouksel and P. Scheuermann, "Multidimensional B-trees: analysis of dynamic behavior," *BIT*, 21, 4, pp.401-418, 1981.

[403] M.H. Overmars and J. vanLeeuwen, "Dynamic multidimensional data structures based on quad- and k-d trees," *Acta Inf.*, 17, 3, pp.267-285, 1982.

[404] J.L. Pfaltz, W.J. Berman and E.M. Cagley, "Partial-match retrieval using indexed descriptor files," *C.ACM*, 2,3 9, pp.522-528, Sept. 1980.

[405] V.V. Raghavan and C.T. Yu, "A note on a multidimensional searching problem," *Inf. Proc. Lett.*, 6, 4, pp.133-135, Aug. 1977.

[406] K. Ramamohanarao and A,T, James, "Partial-match retrieval using hashing and descriptors," *ACM Trans. Database Syst.*, 8, 4, pp.552-576, 1983.

[407] K. Ramamohanarao and R. Sacks-Davis," Partial match retrieval using recursive linear hashing," BIT, 25, 3, pp.477-484, 1985.

[408] R.L. Rivesr, "Partial match retrieval algorithms," *SIAM J. Comput.*, 5, 1, pp.19-50, Mar. 1976.

[409] C.S. Roberts, "Partial-match retrieval via superimposed codes," *Proc. IEEE*, 67, 12, pp.1624-1642, Dec. 1979.

[410] J.B. Rothnie and T. Lozano, "Attribute based file organization in a paged memory environment," *C.ACM*, 17, 2, pp.63-69, Feb. 1974.

[411] H. Samet, "Deletion in two-dimensional quad trees," *C.ACM*, 23, 12, pp.703-710, Dec. 1980.

[412] H. Samet, "A quadtree medial axis transform," *C.ACM*, 26, 9, pp.680-693, Sep. 83.

[413] H. Samet, "The quadtree and related hierarchical data structures, " *Comput. Surveys*, 16, 2, pp.187-260, June 1984.

[414] H. Samet, "Data structures for quadtree approximation and compression," *C.ACM*, 28, 9, pp.973-993, Sep. 1986.

[415] J.B. Saxe, "On the number of range queries in k-space," *Discr. App. Math.*, 1, 3, pp.217-225, 1979.

[416] B. Shneiderman, "Reduced combined indexes for efficient multiple attribute retrieval," Inf. Syst., 2, pp.149-154, 1977.

[417] M. Shlomo, "On the complexity of designing optimal partial-match retrieval systems," ACM Trans. Database Syst., 8, 4, pp.543-551, Dec. 1983.

[418] Y.V. Silvia Filho, "Average case analysis of region search in balanced k-d trees," *Inf. Proc. Lett.*, 8, 5, pp.219-223, June 1979.

[419] Y.V. Silvia Filho, "Optimal choice of discriminators in a balanced k-d binary search tree," *Inf. Proc. Lett.*, 13, 2, pp.67-70, Nov. 1981.

[420] H. Tropf and H. Herzog, "Multidimensional range search in dynamically balanced trees," *Angewandte Informatik*, 2, pp.71-77, 1981.

[421] V.K. Vaishnavi, "Multidimensional height-balanced trees," *IEEE Trans. Comput.*, C-33, pp.334-343, 1984.

[422] V.K. Vaishnavi, "On the height of multidimensional height-balanced trees," *IEEE Trans. Comput.*, C-35, pp.773-780, 1986.

[423] V.K. Vaishnavi, "Multidimensional balanced binary trees, " *IEEE Trans. Comput.*, C-38, 7, pp.968-985, 1989.

[424] D.E. Willard, "Polygon retrieval," *SIAM J. Comput.*, 11, 1, pp.149-165, Feb. 1982.

[425] D.E. Willard, "Multidimensional search trees that provide new types of memory reductions," *J.ACM*, 34, 4, pp.846-858, Oct. 1987.

[426] C.T. Wu and W.A. Burkhard, "Associative searching in multiple storage units," *ACM Trans. Database Syst.*, 12, 1, pp.38-64, 1987.

[427] C. Yang, "Avoiding redundant record accesses in unsorted multilist file organizations," *Inf. Syst.*, 2, pp.155-158, 1977.

[428] C. Yang, "A class of hybrid list file organizations," *Inf. Syst.*, 3, pp.49-58, 1978.

[429] T.S. Yuen and D.H. Du, "Dynamic file structure for partial match retrieval based on overflow bucket sharing, " *Trans. IEEE Softw. Eng.*, SE-12, 8, pp.801-810, Aug. 1986.

[430] G. Yuga, "Finding near neighbors in k-dimensional space," *Inf. Proc. Lett.*, 3, 4, pp.113-114, Mar. 1975.

[431] N. Zvegintzov, "Partial-match retrieval in an index sequential directory," *Comput. J.*, 23, 1, pp.37-40, Feb. 1980.

7. Overflow Handling

[432] R.A. Baeza-Yates and P.A. Larson, "Performance of B$^+$-trees with partial expansions," *IEEE Trans. Knowledge and Data Eng.*, 1, 2, pp.248-257.

[433] D. Comer, "The difficulty of optimum index selection," *ACM Trans. Database Syst.*, 3, 4, pp.440-445, Dec. 1978.

[434] R.B. Cooper and M.K. Solomon, "The average time until bucket overflow," *ACM Trans. Database Syst.*, 9, 3, pp.392-408, Sept. 1984.

[435] B.K. Gairola and V. Rajaraman, "A distributed index sequential access method," *Inf. Proc. Lett.*, 5, 1, pp.1-5, May 1976.

[436] S. Ghosh and M. Senko, "File organization: On the selection of random access index pointers for sequential files," *J. ACM*, 16, 10, pp.569-579, Oct. 1969.

[437] D.G. Keehn and J.O. Jacy, "VSAM data set design parameters," *IBM Systems J.*, 13,3, pp.182-212, 1974.

[438] P.A. Larson and A. Kajla, "File organization -Implementation of a method guaranteeing retrieval in one access," *C.ACM*, 27, 7, pp.670-677, 1984.

[439] P.A. Larson, "Analysis of index-sequential files with overflow chaining, " *ACM Trans. Database Syst.*, 6, 5, pp.671-680, Dec. 1981.

[440] T. Leipala, "On optimal multilevel indexed sequential files," *Inf. Proc. Lett.*, 15, 5, pp.191-195, Dec. 1982.

[441] W. Litwin and D.B. Lomet, "A new method for fast data searches with keys," *IEEE Software*, pp.16-24, Mar. 1987.

[442] D. Lomet, "Partial expansions for file organizations with an index," *ACM Trans. Database Syst.*, 12, 1, pp.65-84, 1987.

[443] D.B. Lomet, "A simple bounded discover file organization with good performance," *ACM Trans. Database Syst.*, 13, 4, pp,525-551, 1988.

[444] K. Maruyama and S.E. Smith, "Analysis of design alternatives for virtual memory indexes," *C.ACM*, 20, 4, pp.245-254, Apr. 1977.

[445] J.K. Mullin, "An improved index sequential access method using hashed overflow," *C.ACM*, 15, 5, pp.301-307, May 1972.

[446] M. Schkolnick and P. Tiberio, "Estimating the cost of updates in a relational database," *ACM Trans. Database Syst.*, 10, 2, pp.163-179, 1985.

[447] B. Shneiderman, "A model for optimizing indexed file structures," *Int. J. Comput. and Inf. Scie.*, 3, 1, pp.93-103, Mar. 1974.

ABOUT THE AUTHOR

Dr. Jun-ichi Aoe is an associate professor at the Department of Information Science and Intelligent Systems at the University of Tokushima, Japan. He is the author of 35 scientific papers. His research interests include compiler optimization and verification; design and analysis of algorithms; and natural language processing.

He received the M.S. and B.E. degrees from the University of Tokushima, Japan, in 1974 and 1976, respectively, and the Ph.D. degree from the University of Osaka, Japan, in 1980.

He is the leader of various projects supported by Just Systems Corp. of Japan; the Japanese Ministry of Education; and the Japan Institute of Systems Research. He served as chairperson of a panel session on AI Techniques and Systems for the COMPSAC 88 conference.

He is a member of the IEEE Computer Society; the Association for Computing Machinery; the American Association for Artificial Intelligence; the Association for Computational Linguistics; the Institute of Electronics, Information, and Communication Engineers of Japan; the Japan Society for Software Science and Technology; the Information Processing Society of Japan; and the Japanese Society for Artificial Intelligence.

IEEE Computer Society

OTHER IEEE COMPUTER SOCIETY PRESS TITLES

For Further Information:

IEEE Computer Society, 10662 Los Vaqueros Circle, P.O. Box 3014,
Los Alamitos, CA 90720

IEEE Computer Society, 13, avenue de l'Aquilon, 2
B-1200 Brussels, BELGIUM

IEEE Computer Society, Ooshima Building, 2-19-1 Minami-Aoyama,
Minato-ku, Tokyo 107, JAPAN

Parallel Architectures for Database Systems
Edited by A.R. Hurson, L.L. Miller, and S.H. Pakzad
(ISBN 0-8186-8838-6); 478 pages

Programming Productivity: Issues for '80s
(Second Edition)
Edited by C. Jones
(ISBN 0-8186-0681-9); 472 pages

Recent Advances in Distributed Database Management
Edited by C. Mohan
(ISBN 0-8186-0571-5); 500 pages

Reduced Instruction Set Computers (RISC)
(Second Edition)
Edited by William Stallings
(ISBN 0-8186-8943-9); 448 pages

Reliable Distributed System Software
Edited by J.A. Stankovic
(ISBN 0-8186-0570-7); 400 pages

Robotics (Second Edition)
Edited by C.S.G. Lee, R.C. Gonzalez, and K.S. Fu
(ISBN 0-8186-0570-7); 630 pages

Software Design Techniques (Fourth Edition)
Edited by P. Freeman and A.I. Wasserman
(ISBN 0-8186-0514-6); 736 pages

Software Engineering Project Management
Edited by R. Thayer
(ISBN 0-8186-0751-3); 512 pages

Software Maintenance and Computers
Edited by D.H. Longstreet
(ISBN 0-8186-8898-X); 304 pages

Software Management (Third Edition)
Edited by D.J. Reifer
(ISBN 0-8186-0678-9); 526 pages

Software-Oriented Computer Architecture
Edited by E. Fernandez and T.J. Lang
(ISBN 0-8186-0708-4); 376 pages

Software Quality Assurance: A Practical Approach
Edited by T.S. Chow
(ISBN 0-8186-0569-3); 506 pages

Software Restructuring
Edited by R.S. Arnold
(ISBN 0-8186-0680-0); 376 pages

Software Reusability
Edited by Peter Freeman
(ISBN 0-8186-0750-5); 304 pages

Software Reuse—Emerging Technology
Edited by Will Tracz
(ISBN 0-8186-0846-3); 400 pages

Software Risk Management
Edited by B.W. Boehm
(ISBN 0-8186-8906-4); 508 pages

Standards, Guidelines and Examples: System and Software
Requirements Engineering
Edited by Merlin Dorfman and Richard H. Thayer
(ISBN 0-8186-8922-6); 626 pages

System and Software Requirements Engineering
Edited by Richard H. Thayer and Merlin Dorfman
(ISBN 0-8186-8921-8); 740 pages

Test Access Port and Boundary-Scan Architecture
Edited by C. M. Maunder and R. E. Tulloss
(ISBN 0-8186-9070-4); 400 pages

Test Generation for VLSI Chips
Edited by V.D. Agrawal and S.C. Seth
(ISBN 0-8186-8786-X); 416 pages

Visual Programming Environments: Paradigms and Systems
Edited by Ephraim Glinert
(ISBN 0-8186-8973-0); 680 pages

Visual Programming Environments: Applications and Issues
Edited by Ephraim Glinert
(ISBN 0-8186-8974-9); 704 pages

Visualization in Scientific Computing
Edited by G.M. Nielson, B. Shriver, and L. Rosenblum
(ISBN 0-8186-1979-1); 304 pages

VLSI Support Technologies: Computer-Aided Design
Edited by Rex Rice
(ISBN 0-8186-0386-1); 464 pages

VLSI Testing and Validation Techniques
Edited by H. Reghbati
(ISBN 0-8186-0668-1); 616 pages

Volume Visualization
Edited by Arie Kaufman
(ISBN 0-8186-9020-8); 494 pages

Reprint Collections

Dataflow and Reduction Architectures
Edited by S.S. Thakkar
(ISBN 0-8186-0759-9); 460 pages

Expert Systems: A Software Methodology for Modern Applications
Edited by Peter Raeth
(ISBN 0-8186-8904-8); 476 pages

Logic Design for Testability
Edited by C.C. Timoc
(ISBN 0-8186-0573-1); 324 pages

Milestones in Software Evolution
Edited by Paul W. Oman and Ted G. Lewis
(ISBN 0-8186-9033-X); 332 pages

Software (Third Edition)
Edited by M.V. Zelkowitz
(ISBN 0-8186-0789-0); 440 pages

Validation and Verification of Knowledge-Based Systems
Edited by Uma G. Gupta
(ISBN 0-8186-8995-1); 400 pages

VLSI Technologies and Computer Graphics
Edited by H. Fuchs
(ISBN 0-8186-0491-3); 490 pages

Artificial Neural Networks Technology Series

Artificial Neural Networks—Concept Learning
Edited by Joachim Diederich
(ISBN 0-8186-2015-3); 160 pages

Artificial Neural Networks—Electronic Implementation
Edited by Nelson Morgan
(ISBN 0-8186-2029-3); 144 pages

Artificial Neural Networks—Theoretical Concepts
Edited by V. Vemuri
(ISBN 0-8186-0855-2); 160 pages

Software Technology Series

Computer-Aided Software Engineering (CASE)
Edited by E.J. Chikofsky
(ISBN 0-8186-1917-1); 110 pages

Communications Technology Series

Multicast Communication in Distributed Systems
Edited by Mustaque Ahamad
(ISBN 0-8186-1970-8); 110 pages

Robotic Technology Series

Multirobot Systems
Edited by Rajiv Mehrotra and Murali R. Varanasi
(ISBN 0-8186-1977-5); 122 pages